This book is a gift to
Union College
in memory of
Hon. Samuel B. Pettengill
He was Director of the Coe
Foundation's Summer Refresher
Courses in American Studies
for high school teachers, in
which Union College
participated,

Helen M. Pettengill

Dec. 1979

*"Sam was first a thinker and second a philosopher. He was a towering, rugged man, a truly great man. He was born in Oregon, but his roots were in Vermont. Had he been less honest, he might have been President. But he was a man not interested in Sam Pettengill, but in his country."*

Rev. Norman Vincent Peale, 1974

# My Story

by

# Samuel B. Pettengill

*Edited By His Wife,
Helen M. Pettengill*

328.73
P499

Copyright © 1979 by Helen M. Pettengill
All rights reserved


Library of Congress Catalog Card No. 78-78208
ISBN 0-9602392-1-9


Printed in the United States of America
by Whitman Press, Inc., Lebanon, New Hampshire

## CONTENTS

|  |  |  |
|---|---|---|
|  | Foreword |  |
| I | My Mother and My Clagett Forebears | 1 |
| II | My Grandfather, Thomas Clagett | 21 |
| III | My Grandfather's Children | 31 |
| IV | My Uncle Will | 35 |
| V | My Mother | 49 |
| VI | Boyhood in Vermont | 56 |
| VII | My Father | 95 |
| VIII | The Pettengill Family | 105 |
| IX | My Barrett Ancestors | 118 |
| X | Another Ancestor, Roger Bates | 128 |
| XI | Capt. John Barrett of Grafton | 130 |
| XII | Preparatory School | 132 |
| XIII | College | 143 |
| XIV | Yale Law School | 160 |
| XV | Practicing Law | 169 |
| XVI | My Masonic Record | 182 |
| XVII | Professor | 187 |
| XVIII | Congress | 190 |
| XIX | My Break With Roosevelt | 204 |
| XX | A Most Important Decision | 220 |
| XXI | In the Enemy's Camp | 224 |
| XXII | My Books | 233 |
| XXIII | How Robin Lawn Became Our Home | 240 |
| XXIV | More Memories | 247 |
| XXV | The Man Himself | 282 |
|  | *Selections From the Many Speeches and Writings of Samuel B. Pettengill* | 287 |

# FOREWORD

Originally this story of his life by Samuel Barrett Pettengill was not meant for publication. He gave me the manuscript on our seventh wedding anniversary in 1956 with the following letter:

Dearest Love:

Every anniversary you give me something or do something that is as surprising as it is lovely.

I have been keeping something from you that I began in 1950 and have added to from time to time. It is still incomplete, but now that we are at home for always at Robin Lawn, I thought this would be a very good time to give you, with a heart filled with love, these scattered historical notes.

I hope this book will be a surprise!

It is not only a disconnected record of facts, but contains bits of whatever wisdom life has taught me. We will add to them as the years go by.

Everyone has moments when he wishes he had made a note of something now slipped from memory, even if nothing more than a funny story he wanted to tell others. This is especially true of both truth and fiction which has been passed on by word of mouth from those no longer living. Trying to remember what my elders said when I was a boy, I have so often wished that they or I had written down the events, wise sayings, tall tales, folklore and family history which I can no longer bring to mind.

Decades ago, when families lived in the same place for generations, the written record was not so necessary. For if the story came to you from someone who had since passed on, it was almost sure that some old neighborhood granny still living could resurrect the wanted information. Moreover in those days the search for family data, whether by lip or pen, was in a small circumference. You could easily put your hand on the family Bible that great-grandfather once owned, with its record of births, marriages and deaths. The words carved on gravestones were in easy distance.

But now families are on the move and widely scattered. Even the old family album has gone out of style and pictures and snapshots are strewn far and wide. The need for some member of the family to assemble and make a written record of facts and legends from the past which he or she still remembers, thus becomes more important to each generation in order to retain pride of ancestry and a feeling of having roots. As Edmund Burke said, "Society is a great and silent compact between the dead, the living and the unborn."

So, much later than I should, I began to set down in odd moments these fragments from the past. I know I'll enjoy reading them myself ten, twenty or thirty years hence (?) and hope you will be glad to keep these pages, not only for their information, but as proof of my love.

Your devoted husband,<br>Sam.

As stated in this letter he hoped to add more to the manuscript as the years of retirement went by, and did so to some extent, but he was sidetracked by other interests and finally by increasingly poor eyesight, so that many of his memories that should have been included remained untold by him. However he left voluminous files and from them and things he told me, I have added highlights of his very full life without which this book would be even more incomplete. It remains for historians to do the research necessary to produce a truly well rounded account of the life and times of this great American patriot.

With the exception of the final pages following the chapter entitled "Robin Lawn" this book is Sam's autobiography. I have not changed anything that he wrote, for he was a gifted writer with a style and simplicity all his own which no one could match, let alone improve upon.

As is obvious from his letter, Sam did not write his autobiography for publication, but after his death I found notes among his papers to the effect that he would like copies made and given to the Grafton Historical Society and the Vermont Historical Society. Therefore I have felt it permissible to give a wider audience the intimate story of a great man's life and the picture of an era now almost incomprehensible in the midst of today's complexities. Sam Pettengill was born in 1886 in a time and place where daily life was the same as it had been for decades before. Between that year and his death in 1974 the entire world changed more than it had in a thousand preceding years. Yet up until the first quarter of the Twentieth Century the majority of Americans continued to live in much the same life style. It was a hard life, but it fostered courage and strength of character and the moral fortitude which produced the men and women who built this nation.

This is the story of a man who grew up on a remote, rocky, hillside farm in Vermont, yet with no help except the character he had inherited from his forebears and his own indomitable spirit, he had a successful life and became nationally known and respected. It is my hope that he will be remembered always not only as a great American patriot, but also for his great character.

*Helen M. Pettengill*

# I

# MY MOTHER AND MY CLAGETT FOREBEARS

I was born. But I can't prove it because there is no official record of the fact. None was kept where and when I arrived. A newspaper did mention the fact that an "infant" had arrived. But infants come in two sexes.

Many years later, in order to get a passport, Uncle Sam demanded proof that I was a native born citizen. This was a puzzler. Fortunately a first cousin who lived in Idaho and was a few years older than I, made an affidavit that he had heard that I had actually been born in Portland, Oregon. Uncle Sam grumbled about that as proof but finally gave in and this is how I became a Vital Statistic.

Even so, for a long time I was not certain in what month I had arrived. My mother died when I was a little over four years old and Father brought me up thinking that I shared with Washington and Lincoln the honor of being born in February. Until I was married I thought that my birthday was on February 19th, because Father had said so, but after our marriage we had sent on to South Bend, where we were living and I had begun the practice of law, some trunks and boxes which had been stored in Oregon after my mother's death. In the collection was the baby book my mother had started for me, and in her own handwriting she gives the date as January 19, 1886, the time 5:45 A.M. and my weight as nine pounds. This was also the birthday of Gen. Robert. E. Lee, a fact of which I have always been proud, since he is one of my heroes.

I have no memory of my first years in Portland.

Mother died August 15, 1890, when I was four and a half years old. It is my understanding that she had cancer of the breast attributed to her foot slipping while she was climbing into a carriage, and knocking her against the iron rim of a wheel. Her brother, my Uncle Will Clagett, famous throughout the Northwest as the "silver tongued orator of the West" had a home in a little village in Idaho named Osburne, near Kellogg, where he was practicing law. This was situated in the Coeur d'Alene mountains in northern Idaho and my mother had gone to stay with his family hoping the change of climate would benefit her. But she died there, just past her forty-seventh birthday. I saw the house when I visited my first cousin Horace Clagett in 1928, when he was living in Kellogg. My mother is buried in Riverview Cemetery in Portland, Oregon. Her stepmother, Sarah Blanchard Clagett, is buried next to her in the same lot, as close in death as they were in life. The youngest of six children, one of whom died in infancy, my mother was only eight months old when her own mother died, and when her father remarried a year or so later, her stepmother fulfilled so beautifully the task of raising the five children, that my mother is said to have remarked of her "I have said a thousand times of my mother and to my mother, that she was faultless." When my mother's novel "Her Lovers" was published in 1877, she dedicated it "To my own dear stepmother, to whom I owe everything but my birth."

When I went out to Seattle in 1929 to attend the meeting of the American Bar Association, I went down to Portland to see my mother's grave. So far as I knew, no member of the family had visited it in over twenty-five years. I expected to find it overgrown with weeds with the gravestone needing care. I went out to the cemetery on a Sunday morning in July when the flowers and especially the roses, for which Portland is famous, were in full bloom. I found the sexton and asked him if he knew where Mrs. Sue Pettengill's grave was. He said "I'll take you to it." I had one of the happiest moments of my life awaiting me, for instead of finding the grave in disrepair, it was in perfect condition. The grass had just been mown, the flowers were in bloom, and the morning dew was on the grass.

For the first time in my life I realized the benefit of perpetual care of cemetery lots.

A few months before my mother's death, Father went to Tacoma, Wash., to become editor of the Tacoma Daily News and Ledger. Previously he had been managing editor of the Portland Oregonian and before that publisher and editor of the Portland Standard. In Tacoma he kept house for me and my elder brother Harry assisted by various Clagett girl cousins, among them Sarah and Lavinia, Uncle Tom's children, and Idaho and Mary, daughters of Uncle Will. To these girls, then in their late teens and early twenties, I owe a debt of gratitude for acting in the place of my mother.

Unfortunately I have scarcely any memory of my mother. She was a remarkable woman. It seems as if everyone who came in contact with her was invigorated by her presence, which made a lasting impression. For example, shortly after she and my father were married she visited in Grafton, Vermont, my father's birthplace and where his ancestors had lived since 1787. She gave a lawn party at the family homestead and among the guests was Miss Ella Dwinell of Grafton, then a young woman. Yet when she was over eighty she would talk to me about my mother and remembered almost her exact conversation on that occasion. John Barrett also told me what an impression she had made on him when he met her when he was a young man.

Mother's great social forte was as a conversationalist. She was remarkably well read and I have heard it said that when she was to give a party she prepared for the conversation as carefully as for the dinner itself. The result was that she was the life of the party, and if she had never done anything else she would have left her impress as a living ornament to the society in which she moved. Her conversation was sprightly and gay, but never chaff. She probably read more serious books than almost any woman of the time. Books of hers which I still possess are dog-eared and marked, showing attentive reading.

*Susan G. H. Clagett in 1877.*

She was the author of one full length novel that I know of, "Her Lovers," a story of antebellum days in the South which is somewhat autobiographical. I have a newspaper clipping describing her appearance which was written by a correspondent of the St. Louis Herald after he had interviewed her at the time the book was published. After saying that the book had been so favorably received that the second edition was all sold out before it was printed, he went on to tell of her previous accomplishments as a writer (which I will speak about later) and then described her appearance. At that time she was about thirty-four, was "of medium height and size, with regular features, brown hair just turning gray, with large and extremely black eyes. Her face, almost devoid of color, is one that would strike any person as a remarkable one. A pensive look seems to shadow it at first, but is immediately dispelled when she speaks. She is given to story-telling, often illustrating her stories by voice and gesture, in a manner that is very humorous."

Mother's father was Judge Thomas W. Clagett. He was born at Weston, the family estate near Upper Marlboro, Maryland, of a slave-owning family, but moved to Keokuk, Iowa, in 1850 when about thirty-five years of age. His wife, my grandmother, was born Susan Guigir Harry, whose ancestors were originally natives of Normandy, France, and spelled the name Harrie. They were Huguenots and upon the revocation of the Edict of Nantes in 1685, removed to Holland. Two grandsons of the French emigrant to Holland, Martin and Jacob Harrie, emigrated with their wives and children to Maryland in 1745 and settled near Hagerstown. Martin, born in 1720, died in 1788 and is buried in Hagerstown as is his brother Jacob. Jacob's third son, Martin Harrie, was born in 1755 and like his father and uncle was a very prosperous farmer and merchant and is said to have served in the Revolutionary War. In 1782 he married Susan Sailer, a Hollander born in 1761.

Their son was George Harrie, born in 1786. He moved to Georgetown and married Sarah Chesley, daughter of John and Anne Chesley. Anne was the daughter of Thomas Clagett of Piscataway, Md. a great-grandson of the Thomas Clagett who emigrated to America in 1670. He was always called "the Emigrant." George and Sarah Chesley Harrie's only child was my grandmother, Susan Guigir Harry, born October 14, 1814. I have never known why the spelling of the name Harrie was changed.

On December 24, 1833, when she was nineteen, Susan married my grandfather, Thomas William Clagett who was eighteen at the time. They had six children; three sons, Thomas, George and William, and three daughters, Sarah, Lucy who died in infancy and Susan Harry, the youngest, who was my mother. All were born at Upper Marlboro and their mother died there on November 18, 1843, and is buried at Weston in the family graveyard.

On July 6, 1844, my grandfather married Sarah Blanchard Lewis who had been born in Malden, Mass., on November 18, 1821. She was the "dear stepmother" to whom my mother's book was dedicated. She died on July 10, 1887.

*Thomas W. Clagett, from a daguerreotype made in 1840 when he was 25 years old.*

At the age of twenty-one, having studied law in the office of Reverdy Johnson, Attorney General of the United States, my grandfather entered the field of politics and was twice elected to the legislature. A prized possession of mine is a daguerreotype taken of him when he was a young man, supposedly by Daguerre. It was said that M. Daguerre had come over from France about 1840 to promote his new picture taking apparatus. According to a letter my mother wrote in 1887, her father was in Washington one day conversing with Henry Clay and Gov. Sam Houston of Texas on the steps of the Capitol when they met M. Daguerre. He invited all three of them to have their pictures taken by his new process and I have the one of my grandfather.

> It is historically incorrect that M. Daguerre came to this country. Although Samuel F. B. Morse, then President of the National Academy of Design in New York wrote to him in May, 1839, extending an invitation to come and introduce his new process, Daguerre did not come but sent a friend and pupil, Francois Gouraud, to represent him. It is possible that this was the man who made the three daguerreotypes and over the years his name was forgotten and it was thought to have been Daguerre himself. (Ed.)

The Clagetts originally spelled their name with two "g's." The first Claggett to emigrate to America was Capt. Thomas Claggett, born about 1635-40, who was an officer in the British navy. After leaving the service and his inherited estates in England he arrived in America in the autumn of 1670, and in 1671 settled in the lower part of Calvert County in Maryland. He is considered the founder of the family in America and is called "the Emigrant." It was at that time that he dropped one of the "g's" from his name. Apparently he was possessed of considerable means as he at once purchased, and also received by royal grant, large tracts of land in Maryland, such as Goodlington Manor of one thousand acres on the Eastern shore; Weston, an estate of eight hundred acres near Upper Marlboro; Greenland, and then Croome with five hundred acres in Prince George's County. The latter estate was eventually inherited by his great-grandson, the famous Bishop Thomas John Claggett, born on October 2, 1743.

Thomas John Clagett, as he then spelled his name, was graduated from the College of New Jersey (now Princeton University) in 1764. His father, Samuel Clagett, had been a minister and it is possible that he might have had some thoughts of following in his father's footsteps. While he was at Princeton he came under the influence of Rev. George Whitefield, the great evangelist, and it was then he determined to enter the ministry. On his graduation he returned to Maryland and studied theology under his uncle, Rev. John Eversfield, in preparation for holy orders. In 1767 he went to England and was ordained a priest in the Church of England. He did not sail for home immediately after his ordination but remained two or three months to study in the English libraries and to visit family connections. It was then that he decided to restore the second "g" to his name, since it was so spelled by his English ancestors. In early 1768 he returned to Maryland, never to see England again.

In 1775 he married his first cousin, Mary Gantt, born in 1752, and they had six children. When the American Revolution broke out Thomas Claggett felt that in conscience he could not openly support it since at the time of his ordination he had solemnly sworn allegiance to the king and loyalty to the British government. He therefore resigned his parish in 1776 and retired to his estate of Croome, where he remained for two years.

Writing in after years, Claggett referred to the Revolution as a "glorious cause" and it was always felt that he was truly in sympathy with his American brethren, but because of his sacred calling he was compelled to be neutral. He was always held in great respect by his parishioners, although few were Tories and his own family and that of his wife supported the war. It is evident that his delicate position was understood, for in 1778 he once more resumed his episcopal duties and became rector of several churches. On September 17, 1792, by unanimous vote of the convention called for that purpose, he was consecrated a Bishop in Trinity Church in New York City. He was the first Episcopal Bishop to be consecrated on American soil. When the government moved to Washington in 1800, he was the first Chaplain of the United States Senate. He must have made an impressive figure as he was six feet, four inches tall, an unusual height for those days. He was Bishop of the Maryland Episcopal Diocese when he died on August 2, 1816. He was buried in the little private burial ground at Croome which he had himself consecrated for family use. His wife survived him for ten years.

In October 1898, by order of the General Convention of Bishops and Clergy held in Washington, it was decided that the bodies of Bishop Claggett and his wife should be removed from the obscurity of the little country graveyard and be reinterred on the site where the Episcopal National Cathedral was to be built. There, on November 1 of that year, the mortal remains of the first Episcopal Bishop of Maryland, and the first Episcopal Bishop to be consecrated in America, were deposited under the chancel of the chapel on Mount St. Albans. Later the bodies were removed and interred under the floor of the Bethlehem Chapel of the Washington Cathedral Church of St. Peter and St. Paul. The marble slabs which had been placed over the graves at Croome were brought to Washington and placed temporarily in the crypt of the Cathedral with a view to being incorporated into the structure at some future time. The epitaph of Bishop Claggett was written in Latin by his dear friend and fellow churchman, Francis Scott Key, the author of the "Star Spangled Banner." The translation is as follows:

Thomas John Claggett, D.D.
The first Bishop of Maryland
born October second
in the year of grace
1743
Ordained Deacon and Priest in
London
1767
and consecrated Bishop
1792
Departed in the Peace of Christ
August Second
1816

With faithfulness and according to Law he ruled the Church and by his character he adorned it. To his wife, children and friends he left a most distinguished remembrance and to his Country and to his Church an honored name.

There is a woodcarving on the Bishop's Stall in the Washington Cathedral depicting the consecration of Bishop Claggett. The figures were carved from actual portraits and from left to right they are Bishops Provost, Seabury, White and Madison. Kneeling is Bishop Claggett.

On November 11, 1934, more than a hundred years after his death, the Maryland State Roads Commission erected a marker in honor of Bishop Claggett. It is located in a corner of the graveyard of historic Trinity Church which Bishop Claggett organized in 1810 in Upper Marlboro. When he died he left sufficient money in his will for a communion service for the church which is reported to be the most valuable in the United States.

I have written at length about Bishop Claggett because a story has come down in the family as to why the name has been spelled by some members with two "g's" and some with one. It was said that at the time of the Revolution the family divided for and against independence, and that those who took the side of independence dropped one of the "g's" so that they would not be considered Tories. However, since there are today many descendants of the several generations of Clagetts in this country before Bishop Claggett added the second "g" to his name, knowledgeable members of the family think the difference in spelling is really to be attributed to the fact that present day Clagetts and Claggetts are descended from just these two branches, or the latter possibly from English Claggetts who kept the original spelling.

The Clagett family is one of the most ancient and honorable in the annals of Maryland. All of the Clagetts, regardless of the spelling of their name, are said to have sprung from Norman stock, the progenitor of the race having landed in England with William the Conqueror in 1066 and participated in the Battle of Hastings. The name Clag(g)ett means Clay-gate and is derived from a tiny village called Claygate in Kent County, England. The first example of its use can be traced back with full proof, to one Robert Claygate or Claggett of Malling, Kent, who was born about 1490. From then on down the line is definite and certain. Capt. Thomas Clagett ("the Emigrant") was the great-great-grandson of Robert Claggett of Malling. He has many descendants not only in Maryland, but also in Virginia, Kentucky, Missouri, Tennessee, Ohio, California, Oregon and elsewhere. A great-nephew of Captain Thomas was Wyseman Claggett who was sent by the British government in 1750 to be Commissioner to New Hampshire. He served there as Attorney General under both colonial and state governments and was noted throughout the Revolutionary period. He has many descendants in New England and other northern states.

A Caleb Claggett settled in Rhode Island about 1708 and a William Claggett, born 1696, died 1749, came to Newport from Boston in 1716 and united with the First John Clarke Baptist Church in Newport in 1733. He was noted as a master clockmaker and when I was in Newport with my wife in 1952, we saw hanging in the Seventh Day Baptist Church a magnificent clock made in 1730 by William Claggett. It still keeps good time. William Claggett was also a good friend of Benjamin Franklin, having anticipated him in some of his experiments in electricity. When Dr. Franklin was in Newport some time prior to his death he visited him and was much interested in a machine he had made. Later his son, Thomas Claggett, also a clockmaker, wishing to make a machine with the improvements suggested by Dr. Franklin, and finding it impossible to get the material he needed in Newport, wrote to Dr. Franklin asking him to procure what was needed. Dr. Franklin complied and learning it was for the son of his old friend William Claggett, he refused to accept the money sent for its purchase.

A letter from a cousin tells me that while wandering through Westminster Abbey he ran across an ancient plaque bearing the information that the land on which the Abbey stands was donated by a Thomas Claggett.

In this chapter I am concerned only with the direct ancestry of my mother, which traces back to my ten-times great-

*Clock made about 1730 by William Claggett, Newport, R.I.*

grandfather, the aforementioned Robert Claggett. However I found the story of Bishop Claggett so interesting, especially as it seems to lay to rest the tradition that the two spellings of the name came about at the time of the Revolution, that I felt I should include it, even though he was only a collateral relative.

It will be noted that after Capt. Thomas, "the Emigrant," every descendant who inherited the family estate of Weston, was named Thomas. This was because of the law of entail, by which property could not be sold out of the family but descended to the eldest son. It was therefore the custom always to name the first son of each generation Thomas. They all had large families and I have been told that they were so zealous in preserving the name Thomas, that sometimes they would name more than one boy Tom with a different middle name, so that if one of them died there would still be another Thomas left. Of course entail was abolished in this country after the Revolution, but the custom of having a Thomas in each generation continued.

1. *Robert Claggett,* born 1490, at Malling, Kent, England.

2. *Richard Claggett,* born 1525, married a daughter of Sir Richard Gouder.

3. *George Claggett,* born 1570, three times Mayor of Canterbury, England.

4. *Col. Edward Claggett,* born 1605. An ardent Loyalist, he held a commission in the army of Charles I and at one time was imprisoned in the Tower of London by the Puritans. He married Margaret, daughter of Sir Thomas Adams, Lord Mayor of London, in 1646, who was a direct descendant of Charlemagne. (This information was obtained from English records and authenticated. I have in my possession the genealogical record, embracing every generation back to Charlemagne's grandfather, Charles Martel.) While Lord Mayor, Adams was sent on a mission to the Hague, and was there knighted by Charles II. Sir Thomas Adams' brother, Henry, emigrated to

America in 1634, and among his descendants was John Adams, second President of the United States. The names of Edward Claggett's children are recorded, three daughters and two sons, Richard and Thomas. Thomas emigrated to America to be known as

5. *Capt. Thomas Clagett "the Emigrant."* (1) He was born April 18, 1635-40. He was an officer in the British navy and leaving it and his inherited landed estates, came to America in 1670 and in 1671 settled at St. Leonard's Town, Calvert County, Maryland. He is considered the founder of the family in America and was the first to drop one of the "g's" in the name. As stated previously, he at once purchased and received by royal grant large tracts of land in Maryland, amounting to over four thousand acres. His first wife was Mary Hooper, widow of Lt. Richard Hooper. His second wife was Sarah Patterson of London. She joined him in a deed of entail to their son Thomas Clagett, Jr., of the estate known as Weston. This had first been surveyed in 1671 for a Charles Boteler and sold by him to Capt. Clagett. Capt. Clagett's signature and that of his wife, spelling the family name with one "g" is found on a parchment deed of entail for Weston, the original document being now in the Maryland State Hall of Records in Annapolis.

Capt. Clagett's name frequently appears in the early archives of the colony and he is always spoken of as "Captain Thomas Clagett, Gentleman." In 1683 he was appointed Coroner of Calvert County. He was one of the commissioners appointed to lay out towns in Calvert County and was a vestryman of Christ Church, Calvert County. In 1689 he is mentioned as one of the prominent Protestants who refused to participate in a revolt against the Roman Catholics.

Capt. Thomas Clagett died in 1703 and is buried in St. Leonard's Town where he had lived since coming to Maryland. In his will he left his English property to his son Edward; his son Thomas, having had Weston entailed to him, was not mentioned; Greenland was left to his son John, land in Calvert County to his son Charles, and another tract to his youngest son George. To his fourth son, Richard, he left Croome Manor. Richard married Deborah Dorsey, widow of Charles Ridgley, and had six children. His second son was the Rev. Samuel Clagett, whose son became the famous Bishop Thomas John Claggett, and inherited Croome on his father's death.

6. *Thomas Clagett (2)*, born 1675 and was married to Mary Keene about 1700. He received the estate of Weston from his parents about 1702, it having been entailed upon him and his heirs "forever." He built a large dwelling on the property between 1690 and 1702 and surrounded it with a park in the English style which included a number of deer. He was a member of the House of Burgesses in 1712 and a county commissioner and judge of the Orphans' Court in 1730. In Maryland archives he is styled "Captain" and probably held that rank in the provincial militia. He died in 1732, the first of a long line of Thomas Clagetts who lived and have been buried at Weston. His wife survived him until 1759 and is also buried at Weston. He left four sons and five daughters.

The house he built was destroyed by fire at the time of the Revolution and replaced by the handsome brick mansion now called Weston. This has always been the family homestead and estate with the exception of twelve years when it was owned by Charles J. Bonaparte, Attorney General of the United States under President Theodore Roosevelt. He was the grandson of Napoleon's youngest brother, Jerome Bonaparte. After this short period it was repurchased by the Clagetts and has been occupied by Clagetts ever since.

7. *Thomas Clagett (3)* born at Weston in 1702; died August 5, 1737. About 1724 he married Ann Belt, daughter of Col. Joseph and Esther Beale Belt. He was a vestryman of Christ Church, Judge of Land Commissioners and superintended the laying out of lots in the towns of Upper Marlboro and Nottingham. Upon his marriage his father conveyed to him two hundred acres of a tract called Clagett's Purchase, and at his father's death he received another farm of two hundred acres, in addition to the Weston estate entailed to him. It is believed he

Weston, the home built by Thomas Clagett (6) before 1815 in Upper Marlboro, Maryland.

The heart-shaped boxwood hedges at Weston.

never lived in Weston, as in his will dated August 5, 1737, shortly before he died, he devised to his younger son "the farm on which I now live" which was the same land his father had given him upon his marriage. His widowed mother and unmarried sisters were then living at Weston and apparently he did not wish to disturb them by taking actual possession of his entailed inheritance after his father's death in 1732. He is buried in the family graveyard at Weston.

8. *Thomas Clagett (4)* born in Upper Marlboro in 1726. In 1749 he married Rachel Magruder and his second wife was Mary Toogood. In 1774 he died and was buried at Weston. There were six children.

9. *Thomas Clagett (5)* born at Weston in 1750 and in 1785 married his cousin, Sarah White. He was Purchaser of Provisions for Prince George's County during the Revolution and also one of the three Provincial Judges. In 1774 he inherited Weston and it was during his occupancy that the large old dwelling built by his great-grandfather was destroyed by fire. He then lived in a smaller house some distance back of the original house. He died in July 1790, leaving a daughter and an infant son only six months old.

10. *Thomas Clagett (6),* born at Weston, January 16, 1790, the year of his father's death. Although the law of entail had by then been repealed, as the son he inherited the estate. In 1798, when he was eight years old, the county records state that Thomas Clagett (6) is "the ward of Sarah Clagett" and describes their home as "a small dwelling house, weatherboarded with plank and covered with lap shingles in tolerable good repair, and outbuildings." By the time he was twenty-five he had built on the site of the original house the fine brick dwelling also called Weston like the earlier houses. A wing of this house burned in 1938. When I last visited Weston in April, 1960, I took some photographs of it. It is approached by a long driveway leading down a hill from the main road, with parks on both sides, then up a hill to where the beautiful brick mansion stands, mellowed by time. Here the driveway divides in

front of a double planting of boxwood hedges. The middle one is in the shape of a heart, and my wife, being a romantic, decided that the hedges must have been planted by people who loved each other very much.

Thomas (6) served in the War of 1812 and was wounded in the arm. In 1812 he married his double first cousin, Harriet White, by whom he had nine children. Their first son, Thomas, born in 1813, died in infancy, so when their second child, a son, was born, they named him Thomas William Clagett. He became my grandfather. Harriet White Clagett died in 1836, and on November 12, 1838, he married Adeline Hodges Mundell, widow of Dr. Benjamin Mundell. By her he had five more children, a total of 14 children by his two wives.

Thomas Clagett (6) was noted for his fine business ability and strict adherence to what he believed to be right. His word once passed, he was never known to swerve a hair's breadth from his promise. He was one of the most successful planters who ever lived in Prince George's County and was considered one of the wealthiest men in Maryland, owning twenty thousand acres of land and several hundred slaves. At the outbreak of the Civil War he was supposed to have been worth nearly a million dollars. A man of a cold, undemonstrative manner, he was, however, a devoted father, and richly endowed each of his children when they became of age. When he died on August 27, 1873, his large estate was divided among his many children, some of whose descendants still live on land that has never been out of the family in over three hundred years.

11. *Thomas William Clagett (7)* My grandfather. Born August 30, 1815. He married on December 24, 1833, Susan Guigir Harry, born October 14, 1814, at Hagerstown, Md. She died at Upper Marlboro, Nov. [May] 18, 1843 and is buried at Weston. On July 6, 1844, he married Sarah Blanchard Lewis, of Malden, Mass., born on November 18, 1821. She died July 10, 1887. My grandfather died on April 14, 1876, and is buried in Keokuk,

*Thomas Clagett (6) of Weston, Upper Marlboro, Maryland, my great-grandfather.*

Iowa. Later I will write further about my grandfather's life and about his children. This list is just to show the line to which I belong.

12. *Susan Guigir Harry Clagett,* my mother. Born at Weston. March 13, 1843, the last of the six children of Thomas William and Susan Geigir Harry Clagett. Married my father, Samuel B. Pettengill, of Grafton, Vt., on December 22, 1880, at Louisville, Ky. She died at Osburne, Idaho, August 15, 1890, and is buried in Riverview Cemetery, Portland, Ore. My father died at Saxtons River, Vt., October 21, 1909.

13a. *Harry Clagett Pettengill,* my brother. Born at Portland, Ore., September 30, 1884. Married Elizabeth Love of Cambridge, Mass., September 8, 1926. Died at Somerville, N.J., February 20, 1963 and is buried there. Had one son, Harry Clagett Pettengill, Jr., born at Roselle Park, N.J., July 24, 1933. Married Dolores Serna of Chicago on September 16, 1967. Has two children, Rachel and Eric.

13b. *Samuel Barrett Pettengill.* Born at Portland, Ore., January 19, 1886. Married Josephine Strahorn Campbell of Napoleon, Ohio, June 1, 1912. She died June 26, 1948. Married Mrs. Helen Charles of New York City, July 16, 1949. By his first wife he had one daughter, Susan Harry Pettengill, born at South Bend, Ind., June 21, 1917. She married Thomas B. Douglas at Washington, D.C., on Novermber 28, 1949. No children.

## II

## MY GRANDFATHER, THOMAS CLAGETT

Since I have gone into so much detail about my Clagett forebears, I'll stay with the Clagetts before starting to write about my own life and my Pettengill ancestors.

When I went to Congress in 1931, I became well acquainted with all my Clagett relatives in Washington and Maryland, and have kept in close touch with them ever since. Consequently I believe I know most of the family history. I have many letters and clippings that have been sent to me from time to time from which I can quote as I go along in order to be as accurate as possible. Extremely valuable has been my correspondence with my first cousin, Lavinia Clagett, daughter of my mother's brother, Thomas Clagett, and with her niece, my second cousin, Mrs. Ruth Bowie Houghton of Washington. Another of Uncle Tom's daughters was Sophie Isham Clagett, the wife of Charlton Clark of Washington, who with her daughter, Elizabeth Clagett Clark, have helped me with their memories.

I have a letter from Cousin Lavinia dated April 28, 1950, in response to some of my questions, in which she tells of my grandfather's marriage. In the same letter she explains why he left his ancestral home in Maryland when he was thirty-five years of age, and moved with his family to Keokuk, Iowa, where he lived the rest of his life.

"Grandfather was eighteen years old, living at home at Weston and studying law in the law offices of Reverdy Johnson, who was Attorney General of the United States at that time. On Christmas Day, with a young lady of nineteen, he walked into the living room at Weston and said 'Father, this is my wife, Susan.' As this was news to great-grandfather,

*Thomas W. Clagett (left), my grandfather, and his wife, Susan Harry Clagett, painted about 1837.*

he was taken aback and angry and said, 'Well, Thomas, as you felt yourself enough of a man to take a wife without telling your family, I suppose you feel man enough to take care of her.' Grandfather said 'Come, Susan' and left the house. He now had no home and no money. But he knew of a farm in the vicinity that was called Starvation Farm because the owner, who had a very large family, had made a will directing that none of the slaves nor the land should be disposed of until the youngest child was twenty-one years of age. He then passed away leaving an infant. The population of the plantation multiplied so rapidly that long before the baby became twenty-one, it took all that could be raised to feed the people and there was not enough work for all to do. That was the situation when grandfather decided he would take over. There was need of extra labor on nearby farms, and grandfather hired out the surplus to those in need. He put the blacksmiths, wheelwrights, carpenters, spinners and weavers to work in like manner, and his management was so successful that in two years he had the place self-supporting and earning. Great-grandfather had been watching and was so pleased he gave grandfather Oakland, which at that time had a beautiful Colonial house on it and the farm was a going concern. So grandfather and his wife Susan moved there to live. I guess the roads must have been very bad, for during the winter many planter families moved to nearby Upper Marlboro and maintained winter homes there. Grandfather had a town house there in addition to Oakland plantation, and it was so large that it was later used as a hotel and is still standing on Main Street, ready to fall down.

"The babies came in due time. Thomas, George and William, Sarah, Lucy, who died in infancy, and Susan. They were as close together as nature permits, and grandmother Susan, who was still little more than a girl, could stand no more, and passed away to a good rest, I hope! Grandfather, even with the help of good nursemaids, had more than he could manage, and so on July 6, 1844, he married Sarah Blanchard Lewis, born in 1821. She was a governess in one of the county families and a woman of beautiful character. Her stepchildren always declared that they never missed their own mother, and as you know, your mother dedicated her book, Her Lovers, to her with the words 'To my own dear stepmother, to whom I owe everything but my birth, I fondly and gratefully inscribe this volume.'

"You asked if I know why your grandfather left Maryland to move west to Iowa. There were two important reasons. One was that there had been so much marrying and intermarrying for generations that the Clagett family was connected or related to nearly everyone in Maryland. With his children growing up he wanted to take his family among new people and get new blood, so they all went to Keokuk. The other reason was that he considered the system of slavery as a wrong, an evil and a curse — wrong to the slaves, evil to all in its tendencies and a curse which sooner or later would engulf the nation in disaster and ruin. He therefore went to his father and asked that he be

*Sarah Blanchard Lewis Clagett, the second wife of Thomas W. Clagett (7), and my mother's "own dear stepmother."*

given in money the value of his inheritance, which as the oldest son included Weston and many slaves. His father, being a wealthy man, was able to do this and so grandfather moved to Iowa with ample funds to begin a new life."

From other sources I learned that my grandfather, a lawyer, entered the field of politics when he was only twenty-one, and was twice elected to the Maryland Legislature. He was particularly interested in trying to establish a system of common school education for the youth of the state. When he moved to Keokuk in 1850 his ambition to do good led him to invest largely of his ample fortune in every enterprise which promised to advance the best interests of the community. He was active in promoting increased transportation facilities and there was probably not a church in Keokuk which did not benefit from his generosity. Many other public enterprises, especially the State Agricultural Society and the West Point Agricultural Society, both of which he organized and of which he was president, owed their continued existence to his interest and liberality. He practiced law in Iowa, was elected to the Legislature as he had been in Maryland, and was elected judge of the District Court, after which time he was always known as Judge Clagett.

He was a Democrat, but differed from most southern Democrats in that he hated slavery and was opposed to secession. On December 1, 1861, to further promote his views, he purchased the Keokuk Daily Journal and renamed it the Keokuk Daily Constitution. He edited it until his death and the publication was recognized as one of the ablest journals in the West. He fought the secessionist movement and was strongly in favor of colonization for the slaves. When the Civil War broke out in 1861, it was a serious question whether Maryland might join the Confederacy. He happened to be visiting in Maryland that year, and as a strong opponent of slavery, he stumped the state to persuade it to stay in the Union. For this he was thanked by President Lincoln. Although he was a Democrat he was always a Union man. However, he bitterly denounced measures of the administration which he regarded as subversive to the Constitution and dangerous to the personal liberty of the citizens. He favored the vigorous prosecution of the Civil War as the best, safest and surest means to accomplish a lasting peace. It was said that "he wielded a pen of fire, being fearless and leaving nothing to the imagination of the reader, because he put what he desired to say in print."

Keokuk had military forces billeted there and some very large military hospitals for wounded men of both the North and the South, some ambulatory, and his fiery editorials infuriated them. An editorial he wrote early in 1863 created a sensation in Keokuk, and on the night of February 10, 1863, a band of soldiers raided his publishing house, broke up the presses with sledge hammers, threw them into the Mississippi River and then looted the office and demolished it. Since no effort was made to stop them by the military or local police, it was believed that this attack had the tacit approval of the military commander of the district. A similar thing had happened to Elijah P. Lovejoy at Alton, Ill., in 1857. Fortunately my grandfather was not murdered as Lovejoy had been. The next morning the town was astounded when the paper came out as usual, unsparingly denouncing the leaders of the mob. This was due to the courtesy of the editor of the opposition paper, the Gate City Daily, who, although he disagreed with grandfather's philosophy, felt that the freedom of the press had to be upheld. Therefore he offered to print the Daily Constitution until new presses and type could arrive, which they did in about six months. The better element of the town was with Judge Clagett, and his paper was not again molested.

However some time afterwards his home and family became the objects of an angry mob, and here I shall quote from a very interesting letter written by my mother to her brother Will, describing the events. She was then just twenty years old.

July 31, 1863

"—— Upon the reception of some false intelligence of the capture of Richmond, we were awakened one night by the most infernal noises. Up we all jumped and of course couldn't find a

*My mother, Susan H. Clagett, at age 20 and at the time she wrote the letter of July 31, 1863, to her brother, Will.*

candle for love or money. By the time I had got to the front window the mob had partly demolished the fence and were bringing the cannon into the yard. Then you may be sure there was much hurrying to and fro, while one of your unhappy parents was eagerly demanding the restoration of his boots, the other was mildly requesting the possession of her dressing gown, and your poor sister was distractedly inquiring for some precise information as to the location of her garters which by some sad accident had been mislaid.

This little excitement over, we all acted in the most heroic manner, particularly your mother, who gathering around her her scanty habiliments, projected her head from the window and gave utterance to the following noble burst — "is there any man among you?" To this apparently unnecessary inquiry, as there were evidently about a hundred too many, a member of the bifurcated species satirically replied "nary a man." After firing off the cannon between the two houses, breaking in so doing about seventy-five panes of glass, this patriotic crowd finally departed.

Upon another later occasion, a mob came up to our house and took away from the porch Henry Clay Dean who had unexpectedly arrived half an hour before. (Note: Henry Clay Dean was a

Methodist clergyman, long time friend of Judge Clagett, and had been a chaplain of the U.S. Senate in 1855.) They afterwards surrounded the house, and a small body of them came up to take possession of Pa, who was fortunate enough to escape from what might have been fatal violence, after resisting arrest by two men in the alley. But during the whole night our house was invaded by successive bands of marauders who searched it from garret to cellar, stealing in so doing, Ma's watch and chain, which however have since been restored.

After this alarm we all went out into the country where we remained five or six weeks, but Pa being obliged to go to town to attend a court of inquiry, which he had requested of Gen. Pope, we all came back again and have stayed ever since.

The Democrats all say that the evidence completely convicted the commander, Lt. Ball, but the commissioners (being all abolitionists) in their report to headquarters which decided the matter, dismissed Ball with a very slight reprimand which was quite smothered in compliments and excuses. Pa is going to publish the evidence to show the injustice of the decision, and being a man I believe will never say die, has also instituted a suit against Lt. Ball in the civil courts. A few nights ago a party of Ball's friends after a wine supper which they had enjoyed with that gentleman, came up in front of the house, groaning in the most distressing manner, and threatening (there were only seven or eight of them) to raze our poor little edifice to the ground.....

Sue"

Feelings ran high in those days, as was evidenced by William Lloyd Garrison being tied to a cart and dragged through the streets of Boston, and another anti-slavery editor, Lovejoy, being shot and killed at Alton, Ill.

In his social life, my grandfather was a gentleman of the old school. He had a cheerful disposition and was a cordial and genial host, fond of entertaining his friends and the many relatives, who as in Maryland, would come with the whole family and stay for days on end. He was a cultured and interesting companion who loved children and flowers and had a strong attachment to household pets. Yet he liked nothing better than to engage in a sharp, active and keen contest with anyone whose ideas or principles differed from his. A man of brilliant abilities and unflinching courage, he was universally

*My grandfather, Judge Thomas W. Clagett (7), in 1875.*

admired by both friends and adversaries, and when he died on April 14, 1876, of a stroke which had come without warning forty days before, the press of the entire state united in paying tribute to his character, both public and private. It is from some of the many newspaper articles which appeared at that time that I have taken some of the above descriptions of him, for of course none who knew him personally are alive today.

Grandfather is buried in Oakland Cemetery in Keokuk, Iowa, having died on the twenty-sixth anniversary of his arrival from Maryland. He and his second wife had no children, but by his first wife, Susan Harry Clagett, who is buried at Weston in the family graveyard, he had six:

Thomas Clagett (8), born Sept. 21, 1834; died May 8, 1910.
George H. Clagett, Born 1836; died 1861.
William Horace Clagett, born Sept. 21, 1838; died August 3, 1901.
Sarah Clagett, born Sept. 17, 1840; died July 27, 1865.
Lucy Harriet Clagett, born March 24, 1842; died March 30, 1842.
Susan G. H. Clagett, born March 13, 1843; died Aug. 15, 1890.

## III

## MY GRANDFATHER'S CHILDREN

*Thomas Clagett* (8), my grandfather's eldest son, was born near Upper Marlboro, Md., on September 21, 1834. He died May 8, 1910. He went with his father to Keokuk, Iowa, when he was fifteen years old, arriving there on April 14, 1850. On December 13, 1855, he married Elizabeth Sophia Eichar, daughter of Peter and Sophia Isham Eichar. Peter Eichar was an early Iowa pioneer and farmer. In 1869, Thomas and his wife decided they wanted to live in Maryland, and his grandfather, Thomas (6) of Weston, gave him a plantation nearby which he called Keokuk. As there were several Thomas Clagetts in the neighborhood, he adopted as his distinctive signature "Thomas Clagett of Iowa." He had eleven children. The oldest, Susan Eichar Clagett, became a writer like her aunt, my mother, but as she lived twice as long, was more prolific and wrote many historical works and short stories over the years. She died on August 20, 1952, aged ninety-four, on the same day as her sister Lavinia, aged eighty-seven. The funeral service for both was conducted on August 22, in Trinity Episcopal Cemetery in Upper Marlboro. Uncle Tom's eleven children were:

Susan Eichar Clagett, born March 10, 1858, died August 20, 1952. Unmarried.
Thomas Clagett, Jr. born March 3, 1860, died 1932. Unmarried.
Elinor Clagett, born July 20, 1862, married Walter Worthington Bowie, Sept. 23, 1885. Died December 19, 1956.
Lavinia Klem Clagett, born December 25, 1864; died August 20, 1952. Unmarried.
Sarah Chesley Clagett, born Feb. 28, 1866, died September 8, 1963. Unmarried.

Charles W. Clagett, born September 3, 1869; married Catherine Beale, July 12, 1904; died July 11, 1958.

Sophie Isham Clagett, born November 14, 1871; married Charlton Clark, Sept. 9, 1903; died December 14, 1954.

Harry Guigir Clagett (Gui), born January 24, 1874; married Margaret Wilson, September 29, 1923; died February 15, 1954.

George Maxwell Clagett (Max), born ~~May 30, 1879~~ July 3, 1876; died February 1, 1963 ~~and his twin~~

Elizabeth Yates Clagett, born May 30, 1879, died November 20, 1889.

Royden Douglas Clagett, born September 3, 1880; married Alice Caldwell Clagett, his third cousin, July 20, 1911, died October 23, 1937. They had seven sons.

2. *George H. Clagett,* second son of Thomas Clagett (7) was born in 1836. He and his brother William H. Clagett, left Keokuk on April 30, 1861, to go to California. The route led through Nevada where George was taken ill and died on the trail near Carson City, in the fall of 1861. He is buried near where he died and I have been told that they ran a wagon back and forth over his grave so the Indians would not know where it was.

3. *William Horace Clagett,* my "Uncle Will", third son of Thomas Clagett (7). He was born on September 21, 1838, near Upper Marlboro and died at Spokane, Wash., on August 3, 1901. He had such a full and interesting life that I shall give him a chapter of his own.

4. *Sarah Clagett,* fourth child of Thomas Clagett (7) was born near Upper Marlboro on September 17, 1840. She was brought up as an Episcopalian, but became a convert to Catholicism and shortly afterwards entered a Roman Catholic convent in Keokuk. She died on July 27, 1865, two months before her twenty-fifth birthday, presumably from contagion from nursing Civil War soldiers during an epidemic.

5. *Lucy Harriet Clagett,* born March 24, 1842. Died "seven

days later. She was not christened." (This from family Bible)

6. *Susan Guigir Harry Clagett,* the sixth child of Thomas Clagett (7), was my mother. She was born near Upper Marlboro on March 13, 1843, and died at Osburne, Idaho August 15, 1890, aged forty-seven. Like my Uncle Will, she also deserves a chapter in addition to what I have already written about her at the beginning of this book.

William H. Clagett

# IV

## MY UNCLE WILL

William Horace Clagett was born on September 21, 1838, near Upper Marlboro, Prince George's County, Maryland, the third son of Thomas Clagett (7). When twelve years old he went with his father, step-mother, two brothers and two sisters to settle in Keokuk, Iowa.

There is an interesting family story about him which has a strange and amusing ending. When he was about ten years old, before the family left Maryland, he was staying at Weston and his grandfather sent him to Upper Marlboro with one hundred dollars in gold with which to pay a debt. Little Will went there on horseback and when he got to town a slave auction was going on and he stopped to watch. Negro children were often sold very cheap because it was an expense to keep them until they could work. A little negro boy was being offered for sale, and looking at the crowd around the auction block he saw Will sitting on his horse and recognized him. He called out "Massa Will, will you buy me?" Everybody in the crowd knew who Will was and thought it a good joke when the little white boy offered to buy the little black boy for one hundred dollars and then handed over the gold. The little black boy got on the horse behind Will and they started for home. One can imagine how with every step back to Weston, Will's heart sank, realizing that his grandfather had too many slaves as it was, and that he had disobeyed the instructions about using the money to pay the debt.

When they arrived home his grandfather gave him a hearty scolding, but perhaps taking pity on the little black boy and realizing that he might otherwise have been sold to someone who would not be kind to him, as he himself always was to his

35

slaves, he decided to let the purchase stand. However, Will was given to understand that he alone would be responsible for the little boy's welfare. The boy became Will's personal slave, saddling his horse and being with him much of the time. As so often happened in the old South, strong friendships developed between whites and blacks, and that was true of Will and the little boy he had befriended. However, when he went to Iowa with his family a couple of years later, he had to leave the little boy behind as his father took no slaves with him.

Years passed. In the meantime, Will had grown up in Keokuk and on April 29, 1861, he married Mary Hart, a niece of the famous anti-slavery Democrat governor of Indiana, Oliver P. Morton, who later was elected to the Senate. Will left his bride the very next day and started out for California with his brother George to seek their fortunes in the West. They travelled on horseback with emigrant trains and the route led through Carson City in Nevada. On the trail near there, George was taken sick and died and was buried nearby. Will went on to Carson City and there he encountered Samuel Clemens, later known as Mark Twain, and his brother Orion, both former residents of Keokuk. Since they were old friends, he decided to join them. The Clemens brothers had left Keokuk for Nevada after the departure of Will and George Clagett, but they went by stagecoach and made a hundred miles a day, while the Clagetts, traveling on horseback and slowed up by the emigrant trains, made at the most twenty-five. So the Clemens got to Carson City in twenty days and it took Will Clagett four and a half months.

In late 1862, Uncle Will had some business to attend to in San Francisco and went there on horseback. It was then a rough frontier town in which few decent white women could be found. To his astonishment when he went into the front room of one of the hotels, he saw his wife sitting there. He thought she was still in the East. She had written to him that she was coming to join him, but the letter never reached him. Traveling from Keokuk to New York by train, she had gone by boat to the Isthmus of Panama, crossed it, and taken another boat to San Francisco where she expected her husband to meet her. It was just by the strangest of coincidences that they met, and then the question was how to get her to Nevada. Their funds were low and neither had enough money to buy another horse and saddle for her.

So Uncle Will set out to see if he could find an acquaintance in San Francisco who would lend him enough money to make the purchase. Going into a saloon, he saw a negro behind the bar who somehow looked familiar, and on closer inspection and conversation the black man turned out to be the little boy he had bought at the slave auction. There were glad greetings between the two and when my uncle told him of his problem, the negro pulled out a buckskin pouch full of gold dust and handing it to him said "Massa Will, you bought me once when I needed buying bad, and now I'm going to buy myself back again."

There is another interesting anecdote of my Uncle Will's life. While still living in Keokuk, he had gone to the Albany, N.Y., Law School for a year and then came back home in 1858 and was admitted to the Iowa bar when only twenty years old. After he went to Nevada he started practicing law again and in 1863-64 was a member of Nevada's Territorial Legislature in Carson City, and his friend Samuel Clemens was a reporter covering the legislature for the Virginia City Territorial Enterprise. Clemens had a little outfit for making tintype pictures, and from time to time he would send stories and pictures back to the newspaper in his former home town of Hannibal, Missouri. On one occasion he heard that three horse thieves had been captured about twenty miles away and were being brought back to town for a "necktie party." Clemens wanted his home town paper to have this choice bit of news, but since the pony express which was the only means of communication with the east would be leaving before he could get a picture of the doomed culprits, the irrepressible future Mark Twain found this opportunity for a practical joke too hard to resist. He got two of his friends, Will Clagett and Major A. J. Simmons, Speaker of the House, to pose with him for a picture of the three horse thieves, and sent it back to Hannibal with the story. Under the picture he wrote "three of the suspected men still in confinement at Aurora." Of course when published back home, the readers of the paper recognized him and knew it was a hoax, and it is said that this is what started Clemens on his career as a humorist. When Mark Twain died, the picture was widely published and an enlargement of it is in Mark Twain's boyhood home in Hannibal, now a museum.

"The Three Horse Thieves," from left: William H. Clagett, Samuel Clemens (Mark Twain), and Major A. J. Simmons.

As it happens this is the only picture of my Uncle Will as a young man. He was twenty-five at the time and the only other photographs of him were taken in later years when he was famous as the "Gray Eagle of the North" and also called the "Silver Tongued Orator," for he was considered the equal or better of any speaker of the times. The Indians called him "White Feather," not as a symbol of cowardice, for he was exactly the opposite, but because of his magnificent shock of white hair, and his mustache and goatee. It is a Clagett family trait for hair to turn white early in life.

It was in Nevada that Clemens went through some experiences chronicled in his book, "Roughing It," a humorous account of his adventures. In it he refers to Uncle Will as "young Clagett," although he himself was only three years older. Uncle Will said that Clemens was the laziest man he had ever known. In camp and on the trail he unblushingly permitted others to perform all the hard work that was to be done. When beds of evergreen boughs had been made by others, Clemens would sneak in and occupy one of them, trusting to his droll wit to keep his more industrious associates in good humor, which it never failed to do. As a practical joker and camp wit, Clemens had no equal in the West. On one prospecting trip to gold country, Clemens had contributed a lean horse. "Young Clagett" drove, and when Clemens's horse frequently refused to move, they all had to get the eighteen-hundred pound wagon going by pushing and profanity, as Clemens later related. One December night the prospectors were encamped when they were awakened by the whoops of Indians. "Boys," said Sam Clemens, feeling of his hairline, "they have left us our scalps. Let's give them all the flour and sugar they ask for."

In this rough environment Uncle Will had many experiences. On one occasion a prospector came down from the mountains having cut his thumb practically off with an axe. He had tied his wrist tightly and his hand was black. There was no doctor. Uncle Will washed the wound with whiskey to kill the germs, tied his thumb together and wrapped it in wet paper, which of course hardened like a plaster cast. He slowly let the blood back into the man's hand and sent him on his way to a distant town where there was a doctor. The man recovered and the doctor later told Uncle Will that no one could have done a better job.

On another occasion when Uncle Will and a party of white men were out in the mountains, they came upon an Indian camp which for some reason had been suddenly abandoned. Perhaps the Indians thought the white men were coming to attack them. In their hurry to get away, the Indians left a papoose only a few weeks old. Uncle Will and the rest of the party did everything they could to keep the papoose alive until they could get back to civilization, but as there was no milk, they were unable to save the child.

These stories and many others were told me the year Uncle Will spent a month with us on the old farm in Vermont.

He was respected by the Indians as much as by the whites. He was always just in any dealings with the Indians. Whenever any of them came by where Uncle Will was living, he always shared whatever food there was in the house. On one occasion when my Cousin Mary, Uncle Will's oldest child, was about eight years old, an Indian Chief asked if the little girl could live with him and his squaw that summer. Uncle Will had not the slightest fear of treachery or harm to his little girl, and so for two or three months she was actually the guest of the Indian Chief.

Cousin Mary had some extraordinary experiences going with her father from place to place wherever there was a gold or silver strike. When she was about eighteen, Uncle Will left some papers with her which he told her to guard with her life. One night when she was alone in the house, she was awakened by a noise at the window, and in the dim light saw someone trying to get in. Mary was used to firearms and shot at the shadowy figure with her rifle. She never knew positively whether she killed or even wounded the man, but the next day some little distance from the house a dead man was found with a bullet through him. She kept her mouth shut and the papers remained safe.

Later on when I met Mary, she told me other stories. She remembered well things that happened when Uncle Will was practicing law in Deadwood, Dakota Territory. Those were the days of Calamity Jane and Wild Bill Hickok and both of them are buried in the cemetery in Deadwood. One of Uncle Will's children, Grace Septiana, who was five years old when she died, is buried in the same cemetery.

While a member of the Territorial Legislature of Nevada, Uncle Will wrote the state constitution which was adopted when Nevada became a state. He next went on to Montana and while its delegate to Congress, he wrote the bill by which Yellowstone National Park was created. He was thirty-three years old on December 18, 1871, when he introduced the bill in the House of Representatives. I have a photostatic copy of the bill penned in his own handwriting. It contains the historic phrase that the Park is to be "set apart as a public park or pleasuring ground for the benefit and enjoyment of the people." The House bill was HR 764 and the Senate bill S 392, 42nd Congress, both identical and both introduced the same day. While later some other members of Congress at that time claimed credit for originating and proposing the legislation, their claims have since been proved to have been unfounded. Uncle Will always gave credit to N. P. Langford the explorer, and Frederick V. Hayden the geologist, for exploring and setting the boundaries of the park, but he wrote the bill and I have a letter from N. P. Langford dated September 13, 1894, testifying to the fact. The Senate bill, introduced by Senator Pomeroy at Uncle Will's request, passed first, and then the House passed their bill, thus establishing the first of our great national parks through the Yellowstone National Park Act. In 1930, the U.S. Geological Board named Clagett Butte, about one and a half miles west of Yellowstone's Mammoth Hot Springs, in his honor. Previously, Fort Clagett on the Missouri River was named for him in 1870. This may have been because when he first went West he organized the first, and I think the only, company of Union troops that came from beyond the Rockies to join the Union army.

In 1962 Uncle Will's picture was on the cover of the Idaho Historical Society's Journal in tribute to his services as president of Idaho's 1889 Constitutional Convention which wrote the constitution of Idaho. It was admitted to statehood the next year. In those days, United States senators were chosen by the state legislature, and Uncle Will was chosen as one of the first two Idaho senators. However, his seat was contested and although he was given the privilege of speaking on his own behalf on the floor of the U.S. Senate, an honor never before extended to a man not sworn in, the Senate decided against him. He spoke for two hours. I have read the speech and it was a notable one. In it he said "I have spent my life on the frontier and have helped to bring more than one state into the union." He was again a candidate in 1896. The legislature was tied in a deadlock for over a month and finally through a technicality his opponent was chosen. These two defeats were great disappointments. Years before when he was territorial delegate from Montana, he introduced a bill to prohibit polygamy among the Mormons. He incurred the bitter hostility of the leaders of the Mormon church which endured as long as he lived, and it has been said that this was a factor in determining the results of his two failed elections. Finally such a bill was enacted after being sponsored by Senator Justin Morrill of Vermont. As both Brigham Young and Joseph Smith were born in Vermont, it is ironic that the polygamy founded by the latter in 1830 was finally ended by a bill introduced by another Vermonter, which became law in 1896.

Uncle Will participated in many of the biggest mining lawsuits ever tried in the West. His legal talents, his logic and his mastery of oratory were important factors in the results achieved. Wherever he went in the rough mining country of Nevada, the Black Hills of Dakota, in Montana, and the Coeur d'Alenes of Idaho, he stood for law and order. A man of irreproachable integrity, he was a very striking figure physically.

A book called "Silver Strike," written by W. T. Whicker as told him by William T. Stoll, an associate of Uncle Will's in the Gold Rush days, has much to say about the "Gray Eagle." It describes "his flashing eyes, the grace and proportion of his body . . . the personification of physical and intellectual power. . . . No voice was comparable to his, none approached its perfection, none was possessed of its appeal. His English was pure, his reasoning broad and extensive and his influence among his fellows at the bar and in public life were immeasurable. . . . Men like Clagett are gone like heroes of myth." I have a letter from Mr. Whicker written to me in 1932 which in part says as follows: "Let me say that I know much more of Mr. Clagett's life than appears in 'Silver Strike.' For many years I have knocked about in the West, probing about into its documents, striking up acquaintanceships with its old timers, and wherever I turn, in history or otherwise, I find Mr. Clagett's name honorably written and reverently remembered . . . He was the greatest prophet of law and order this country has ever known, for he had the greatness of spirit and the intelligence of heart as well as mind, to make it articulate. More than any other man in western life, William H. Clagett deserves to live in history and literature."

Is it any wonder that when I was fourteen and Uncle Will, then sixty-two, came to visit us at the old farm in Grafton in 1900, he left such an indelible impression on my life? It was, in fact, my admiration for him which caused me then to determine to be a lawyer rather than follow my father and mother in the field of journalism. No boy ever loved a man more than I did my uncle. His last words to me when he left the farm were "Hurry up, Bobby, come out West and help me practice law." The reason why he called me Bobby is because, according to my Cousin Lavinia, I was as broad as I was long as a little chap, and greatly resembled my great-uncle Robert Clagett. We each had "big girth." The name stuck with me until I was in my teens. You can imagine the thrill it gave me to think that I might actually *help* this distinguished lawyer practice law! The result was that I did not have to spend years of indecision in planning what I wanted to be, like so many youths.

*William H. Clagett, my Uncle Will.*

In 1938, my daughter Susan got a job working in one of the hotels in Yellowstone. At the end of the summer we drove out to get her and on the way back east we stopped at Deadwood. The car needed some attention and I drove to a garage. Outside on a bench was an old man with long gray hair and a beard. I asked him if he had lived in Deadwood long and he said ever since he was a boy. I said "Did you ever know William H. Clagett?" He said "Billy Clagett?" I answered "Yes, I'm his nephew." He was pleased as punch to meet anyone related to Billy Clagett, and we had a good talk.

On that same trip West, going out, we stopped at Keokuk where my grandfather had founded the Keokuk Daily Constitution. By accident we got to talking to some elderly people who knew of him and remembered my mother having lived there. They pointed out Grandfather's house which was still standing, and the little building next to it where my mother and her step-mother had conducted a private school for girls. I also went down to the newspaper office and introduced myself. It is now known as the Keokuk Constitution and Gate City.

While I was in Congress, I had an oil portrait of my Uncle Will made from a photograph, paying three hundred dollars for it. I took a snapshot of the portrait and sent it to Uncle Will's son Horace in Kellogg, Idaho. He liked it so much that he wanted the artist to paint two more, one for himself and one to be hung in the Capitol at Boise, where it can now be seen just outside the Supreme Court Room. Earlier, in 1927, Uncle Will's daughter Ida, donated a portrait of her father to the Montana Historical Library at Helena.

Uncle Will and his wife, Mary Hart Clagett, had nine children. The hardships of her life, following her husband all over the West, living in mining camps and bearing nine children must have been severe. Yet she outlived him for twenty-three years, dying in Boston on January 16, 1924, and is buried there. Uncle Will died in Spokane, Wash., on August 3, 1901. He is buried there.

Their children were:

Mary, born August 4, 1864. Married Dr. John Cornell in 1903. She was herself a physician, specializing in women's and children's diseases, and was much beloved by all who came in contact with her. She practiced medicine almost to the day of her death, May 13, 1926.

Idaho, called Ida. Born in April, 1866. Died in Spokane March 20, 1927.

Thomas W., born March 24, 1868. Called Billy. Married Louise Frazee on July 6, 1893. Studied law, but his health failing, he took up farming in Ontario, Ore. He died October 3, 1929.

Mabel, born April, 1870. In 1889 she married Frederick E. Lucas of London, England, and she died there April, 1929. Her daughter, Mabel Ellen Lucas, became head of the Christian Science Church in Boston during the 1950's. She died October 18, 1961.

George Dixon, born March 4, 1873. Married Ermina C. Heyburn, related, I believe, to Governor Heyburn of Idaho. They had three children. He died October 6, 1927. He was a twin of

Emma Genevieve, born March 4, 1873. She lived in Boston. Never married. She died January 20, 1956.

Grace Septiana (the seventh child), born January 10, 1875. Died November 22, 1880. Is buried in Deadwood.

William Horace, Jr. Always called Horace. Born July 7, 1877 at Deer Lodge, Montana. Died December, 1950 at Kellogg, Idaho. He married Mabel Theodora Sauer on October 17, 1908. She was born February 20, 1885 and died October 5, 1952. They had three children:
    William H. Clagett III, born September 9, 1909
    Frederic Clagett, born April 7, 1912.
    Virginia Clagett, born February 12, 1923.

Grace Morton, born 1880. She was named Grace after her sister, Grace Septiana, who died shortly after she was born. She was given Morton for her middle name. She married Frederick Ranney, July 25, 1915, and they had one son, Garner Ranney. She died on October 16, 1957.

*The home of Thomas W. Clagett (7), built in Keokuk, Iowa, about 1851.*

## V

## MY MOTHER

Susan Guigir Harry Clagett, my mother, was born near Upper Marlboro, Maryland, on March 13, 1843. She was first named Ann Elizabeth, but after her mother's death, she was renamed for her when she was three years old, by act of the Maryland legislature on March 6, 1846. She was seven years old when her father moved his family to Keokuk. Because of her delicate health she did not go to school until she was eleven years old and then only for six weeks. Her stepmother was a well-educated woman who had been a governess, and undoubtedly taught her at home. Her father built a large brick house in Keokuk, and nearby another house where later Susan and her step-mother taught school for some years after his death. It was in this smaller house that my mother did much of her writing, beginning when she was about twenty-five years of age. She was an authoress of note and wrote many short stories, essays and book reviews for magazines and newspapers as well as editorials for her father's newspaper. She sometimes used the name of Elizabeth Waking. I have a letter in my files, dated September 25, 1869, from Edwin L. Godkin, editor of The Nation in New York City, offering her ten or fifteen cents a page for any articles she might send him, and "even more if they are of extraordinary excellence." He also wrote that he would be very glad to engage her as a regular contributor as "with one exception you are the only female writer in America who gives evidence of real power and culture." I have often wondered who was number one!

I have already written about her appearance, character and accomplishments in the first chapter of this book and in this chapter will add all else that I know. I believe her to have been a remarkable woman and it has always been a matter of regret to me that I was so young when she died that I have had to rely on what writings of hers I could find and the memories of people who knew her for whatever knowledge I have of her.

When her father died in 1876, my mother managed the newspaper for three months, and wrote editorials for it as she had done in his lifetime, and thus she became the first woman to edit a newspaper in the United States. She then sold it in order to settle the estate. I have a copy of the last issue dated Saturday, July 15, 1876, wherein she explains the sale of a newspaper which had prospered under her administration and which she had hoped to continue to manage permanently. The discovery of more creditors than had been known at the time of her father's death made the sale necessary in order to take care of all obligations.

In an editorial on the first page she wrote about happiness and in it occur the words which I have always cherished and which I have framed in our home. "Happiness is not necessary. The performance of duty alone is necessary, and it alone is always possible. Other opportunities fail us, but the opportunity to do the right thing is the inalienable prerogative of human life."

After selling the paper she concentrated on writing the novel "Her Lovers" and it was published in 1877. It was very successful, going through two printings that I know of and possibly more. I understand that she wrote another novel called "Christian Grey" but I have never seen a copy and know nothing about it or when she wrote it. I do know that she was a prolific writer and wrote editorials, articles and book reviews until her death, many of which I have read.

My mother loved to entertain friends in her home and her letters mention interesting visitors and parties. She evidently enjoyed dancing. But she could be intensely serious when the occasion called for it. An interesting thing about her was that she apparently was much like her father in enjoying nothing better than a lively discussion of a controversial subject. When she was a young girl and attended a Bible class conducted by the minister, he said she drove him almost to desperation by introducing at every class arguments to substantiate the doctrine of predestination!

About 1872, my mother paid a visit to the Garden of the Gods near Colorado Springs, and there by chance met my father, who was also sightseeing on vacation from Vermont. They were immediately attracted to one another and started to correspond. This continued for five years and in 1877 he travelled to Keokuk to see her and they became engaged. However they did not marry for another three years. Her letters during that time show her to have had a gay and sprightly personality with a fine sense of humor and a warm, affectionate heart. A touching poem to my father shows this side of her nature.

### My Valentine

Dear heart, if love might strike the golden lyre
Of poesy, then mine 'twould be to fire
The heart with strains so tender yet so strong
They would to all times and all tongues belong.

But those high powers that rule our fates above
Denied me genius while they gave me love.
Not mine the laurel crown, the world's acclaim,
The splendid lustre of an immortal name.
The happier fortune they bestowed on me
To give my love, my life, myself to thee.

Mother and Father were married in Louisville, Ky., on December 22, 1880. From 1870 to 1879 my father was editor of the Rutland Herald in Vermont, and from 1877 to 1879 was also its publisher with Albert H. Tuttle, owner of the well-known book publishing company in Rutland. At the time of their marriage my father had become publisher and editor of the St. Albans Messenger and they went to live in St. Albans in northern Vermont. But my mother could not stand the severe winters there, and for the sake of her health they moved to Portland, Oregon, in 1883. There my father became publisher

*My mother, Susan, and my father, Samuel B. Pettengill, at the time of their marriage in December, 1880.*

and editor of the Portland Standard, and later chief editorial writer for the Portland Oregonian, one of the most important papers on the west coast. My mother continued with her writing and wrote many editorials and articles for both papers.

My brother, Harry Clagett Pettengill, was born in Portland on September 30, 1884, and sixteen months later I was born on January 19, 1886. All her life my mother had greatly admired Sir Philip Sydney, and because of this she named me Sydney Barrett Pettengill. But she always said that a person had the right to choose his own given name and when I was fourteen years old I took my father's name and became Samuel Barrett Pettengill, Jr.

My mother's step-mother, Sarah Blanchard Lewis Clagett, whom she dearly loved, seems to have lived with us until she died July 10, 1887. She was buried in Riverview Cemetery in Portland, Oregon, and three years later my mother was laid beside her. She had not been well for a couple of years, and finally went to stay with her brother Will and his family in the little village of Osburne, Idaho, where at that time he had a home, and she and her two little boys could be cared for by loving relatives. Several months later, when she knew the end was near, she wrote the following two letters to her husband and her sons. The one to my father, with the words on the envelope "to be opened when I am at rest," gave some necessary directions as to personal property, and then went on to say:

"Adieu my heart. I have tried to get well for your sake and my precious children's but it was not to be. Tell my little ones Mama said never to forget the "other shores" without the vision of which these are barren indeed. Keep them with you. Perhaps after a while, you can find some woman more intelligent than an ordinary servant who can take care of them as well as keep house.

"God bless you, dearest one, and grant that we may all meet again in peace. I fling my dying arms around you and my little ones. Do not grieve for me. I have suffered so much I am glad to go. The descent into hell may be easy, but the descent into the tomb is not — not for me.

"Brother has been so good to me. Adieu my dear, my dear. Oh this is the last dearest I shall ever write to thee.

Forever, fondly, Sue"
(S)
(H)     (B)

The (B) meant me, always called Bobby. On the envelope containing the letter to her children, she wrote, "Mama's last letter to Harry and Bobby." The letter is as follows:

"My own dear little children: Mama is dying but though she is hardly strong enough to hold her pen she cannot leave this green earth where she has loved you so much without telling you how she has clung to life for your sake, and how dearly she loves you, and how it is her chiefest hope that when the Great Summons shall come to you too, my precious lambs, we shall meet again with Papa, where there is no sorrow or sighing.

"I have so longed for the opportunity to assist you in your rearing and education and to enjoy the opening prospect of your minds, but since this has been denied to me, I pray God that you may sometimes feel my presence in the moment of temptation and turn away from the deceitful allurements of sin for God's sake, for your own sakes and for your dead Mother's sake.

"A great poet has said "Love virtue, she alone is free." Every time you do wrong you begin the weaving of a fatal chain of habit which I trust you will never rivet about yourselves.

"Strength fails me. Adieu my dear, my dear little ones. You are constantly in my thoughts. Oh may God grant that I shall see you after you have spent a life of usefulness, in the fair courts of heaven.

"I send you kisses which I have touched with my lips. Goodbye, my own. Goodbye.

(H)    (B)<br>From Mama"

These are such personal letters I have hesitated to copy them, but I feel they should be in these recollections so they may be preserved — the originals which I have carefully kept might some day be lost. The letters show my mother's beautiful character and I have always loved her deeply, although I was not yet five years old when she died and have little memory of her. However, young as I was, I had already learned the following verses from my mother, the first thing I ever learned by heart. I have the original in her handwriting in my files.

### Fritz on the Battlefield

When Fritz was quite a little boy
His mother used to say,
"Remember, Fritz, where 'ere you are,
The watchword is 'Obey'"

And now that he must face the foe
In battle's dangerous hour
That little simple household word
Has never lost its power.

The bayonets' flash, the cannons' roar,
Were fearful on that day,
But through it all he seemed to hear
That little word "Obey."

> And as he sank upon the field,
> "God calls, perchance" thought he,
> "If it be so, I must obey
> E'en though it leads through death's dark way
> The end is victory."

My mother died on August 15, 1890, and is buried next to her stepmother in Riverview Cemetery, Portland, Ore. At the time of her death, my father had left Portland and gone to Tacoma, Wash., where he had become the editor of the Daily Ledger. Two of my girl cousins, Mary and Idaho, Uncle Will's daughters, who had been at Osburne with my mother when she was so ill, brought my brother and me back to join him and kept house for us for a while. Two other cousins, Lavinia and Sarah, Uncle Tom's daughters, also took care of us for some months. At other times, Father hired a housekeeper but did not think this arrangement was good for his motherless boys, and after two years he thought it would be better for us to be brought up in Vermont on the family farm where his brother John was living. So in 1892, he brought us back to Grafton and then he returned to Tacoma where he remained until 1895. Then, since during the Cleveland Panic he had lost all the property he had invested in, and being in poor health and missing his children, he too came back to Grafton to live out his life.

# VI

# BOYHOOD IN VERMONT

Among my father's papers was my report card from the Tacoma Primary School in 1892, when I was in the first grade. I received a HIGH rating in both Industry and Scholarship but my Deportment only merited GOOD! Late that summer he brought my brother and me to Vermont.

I can still remember the trip from Tacoma to Grafton. It was a six day trip and I was six years old. I remember the large hamper as big as a bushel basket, which Father filled with food for the trip. At that time there were no Pullman dining cars, but we did get some quick snatches at train stops. Otherwise the hamper had to see us through. I have a very poignant memory of once being on the train when it began to move and I saw Father out on the platform. He knew, of course, that the train would again back up into the station. But I thought I would never see him again and if I live a thousand years I will never forget the agony that came over me thinking that my brother and I, like two little orphan waifs, would have to wander alone through the world from that time on.

For some reason we came by way of Montreal. On the way down from Montreal we stopped at Rutland where Father had been editor of the Herald for many years, and we went to the Bardwell House, presided over by one of Father's old cronies. He was an immense, rotund man named Crampton, with a fog-horn voice. We sat at Mr. Crampton's table in the dining-room that night. This was long ago when victuals were victuals, and besides it was near the fall of the year. The waiter handed me a bill-of-fare, the first I had ever seen, and at the bottom there were listed about eight kinds of pie. I passed up everything else and in my squeaky voice which was heard all

*Sam Pettengill (left) and his brother, Harry, in 1891, the year before they moved to Vermont with their father.*

over the dining-room, I said, "I'll have apple pie, mince pie, squash pie, pumpkin pie, cherry pie" and so forth. This set the dining room off in a roar of laughter, and Mr. Crampton, in his big booming voice, also heard throughout the room, boomed out "That's right, Bobby, eat plenty of pie." This was a favorite story of Father's as long as he lived.

Next day we got off the train at Chester where Uncle John met us and drove us over the Grafton hills to the old farm. The date was the first Monday in September, 1892. The next day was Freeman's Meeting Day at the town hall and we all went down to my first New England town meeting. However, I had not slept much for a week and soon fell fast asleep. I was carried across the street to the Phelps Hotel, now the Grafton Tavern, and laid on top of a big wood-box in the hotel parlor. Father told me that I did not wake up for three days except for a few minutes at a time. But he did not worry about me, knowing I was exhausted from the long trip. Years later after a hard political campaign I was able to do much the same thing — sleep solidly for about three days.

Uncle John had been married, but when my brother and I came to Grafton he and his wife had been separated for some time and she was spoken of only in whispers. On June 18, 1883, he had married Helen Bradford, daughter of Rev. Moses Bradford, fourth Congregational minister in Grafton and considered its most able. He served for twenty-seven years, from 1832 to 1859. In spite of her upbringing, Uncle John's wife would fly into fits of ungovernable rage during which she became dangerous. On the door of my grandmother's bedroom there was the mark of a flatiron, which she had used trying to break down the door. After that, for fear of physical injury, Grandma lived with Uncle Ed in Saxtons River, until after the separation when she came back to Grafton and kept house for Uncle John until she died in 1889. I never saw Uncle John's wife, as they were separated before I came to Grafton. But they were never divorced. In fact, I know of no divorce in my family. There were religious scruples against it. Fortunately they had no children.

As housekeeper, Uncle John had Mary Emma Diament, daughter of his half-sister Mary Altha. Cousin Mary stayed on the farm for about two years after we came, when she left to go out to Indian Territory to teach in an Indian school. Father had returned to Tacoma where he continued as editor of The Ledger until 1895, when having lost everything in the Cleveland Panic and being in poor health, he returned to the farm to live.

The relationship between my father and mother must have been a truly beautiful marriage. For years Father always choked up when I asked him something about my mother, and because I saw how it affected him, I stopped speaking of her and as a result was never told the many things a little boy would like to know about his dead mother. As I was just a little over four when she died, about the only faint recollection I have of her was of her giving me a pair of new shoes on Christmas or my birthday. This seems strange to me because in one of Cousin Lavinia's letters in which she was reminiscing about my mother, she tells of the time when she was staying at Uncle Will's house in Osburne, while my mother was there for some months before she died. She wrote, "Sam was dead in love with his mother and would never willingly let her out of his sight. She used to walk back and forth on the road that led from the house to the stable, with her hands clasped behind her, thinking, and he would walk quietly behind her with his hands clasped behind his back, imitating her exactly. When she turned, he did too." Yet I do not remember this at all.

After Cousin Mary left and Father came to the farm, we lived for many years without a woman in the house except occasionally for two or three weeks during haying time when work was heaviest. It was pretty bleak for two little boys to grow up without a woman to care for them. Once I banged myself pretty badly and Father and Uncle John tried to comfort me, but I said between my tears, "I want somebody with dresses." Those were hard scrabble days but they did not hurt me.

We were twelve miles from the railroad. The only money crops were the wool in the spring and the Baldwin apples in the fall. I have no recollection of prices, but I doubt if Uncle John took in more than four hundred dollars a year. My father's only cash income was his Civil War pension of twelve dollars a month, paid to all veterans regardless of whether or not they had service connected injuries.

We made our own soft soap with the lye from the wood ashes and hog fat. This soft soap was a great cleaner all right, but it practically ate the skin off your hands.

We grew everything we ate except salt, pepper, a few spices, and occasionally a little white flour. We bought cream of tartar and saleratus separately in paper bags, and mixed the two to make baking powder. Maple sugar and syrup sweetened everything we ate. We grew corn, barley, oats, rye, buckwheat but no wheat. We raised potatoes, turnips, squash and so forth. We would roast barley in a pan in the oven, grind it in an old fashioned coffee grinder and have barley coffee. We nearly always kept bees, and one reason for growing buckwheat was for its honey which we ate in the comb. Then too buckwheat flour did something special to griddle cakes, even though it was supposed to make the skin of growing boys somewhat blotchy. The swarming of bees was a fascinating sight. We used to put the hives in the attic during the winter and I can still remember hearing the humming of the bees over my head as the attic started to warm up in the Spring. If we had left the hives out of doors during the winter, the bees would have frozen to death. In the attic, although it was cold, they survived and let us know when it was time to put them outdoors again.

There was no way to keep green, leafy vegetables, such as lettuce or spinach, for winter use. Consequently we had none for seven months of the year. Turnips, carrots, beets and potatoes, buried in earth on the cellar floor, were our winter vegetable diet. I learned to eat without question whatever was put on the table, with the exception of boiled turnips. Even today turnips make me gag.

Cornmeal ground from our own corn was the staff of life — flapjacks, Johnny cake, hasty pudding and fried mush. In the summer we killed a chicken now and then. This fare was supplemented with woodchuck meat, squirrels and an occasional partridge in the Fall. I hope before I die to have another good mess of young woodchuck. It is truly excellent. In the late Fall we always killed a pig, smoked the hams, made sausage and head cheese, and kept the chops frozen out in the back room, or buttery, as it was called, sometimes all winter if there was no real thaw. The rest was preserved in the salt brine barrel down in the cellar. Of course we made our own butter and always had plenty of eggs.

Sage and other herbs used in curing meat and making sausage and for cooking grew in the garden. We had of course our own firewood, and water was pumped into the kitchen from a well beneath the house. The well was our refrigerator; in it we hung the milk and cream and butter in pails. As there was no pond nearby we never attempted to cut ice and keep it in sawdust through the summer.

In order to save matches, Uncle John cut long slivers of basswood and tied them up in bundles. By sticking one end into the embers of the kitchen stove, we lighted the kerosene lamp and lanterns with the burning sliver and Father used them to light his pipe. As a result we never used a store match unless the fire went out completely. One sliver could be used a dozen times. Friction matches were not invented until 1827, so we just went on doing what our ancestors had done.

Our kitchen stove burned wood and had a hot water heater in the rear. Unless it was too hot, our cats and kittens curled up under the stove, and our collie dog, Jack, would put his nose under it when he came in from the cold out-of-doors. At lambing time, we brought the frail, wet little fellows in from the barn, wrapped them up, and put them down by the stove to dry.

On winter nights, Father, Uncle John, Harry and I sat

around the kitchen table in front of the stove and read or studied our lessons by the light of the kerosene lamp. Father smoked a clay pipe and read Shakespeare, Uncle John chewed and spat, and if Harry and I had no lessons we read the Youth's Companion. The cats and Jack arranged themselves close by the warmth. The kettle always had water in it, steaming and bubbling away. It all felt very snug and safe as the blasts of zero wind rattled the windows and the trees soughed in the storm outside. Except on rare occasions, this was the only heat in the house. There were four chunk stoves in the house but they were seldom used. The old time fireplaces had been bricked up. One of the big jobs on the farm was to saw up the tree trunks with a cross-cut saw in lengths short enough to go into the kitchen stove after they were split. On winter nights after we went to bed, everything froze in the kitchen, including the water in the kettle. In the morning the first job was to start up a fire, unfreeze the kettle, and use the hot water to prime the pump in the kitchen sink. And so started the day. We never felt sorry for ourselves. Work was hard and hours were long, but the tensions and irritations of city life were far away. In a self-contained economy such as ours, there were many compensations wholly missing today in city life. There never was any feeling of insecurity in a job, because there always was a job. The rest of the world outside of Vermont could vanish, but we could manage to live.

We always had plenty of apples, and in order to have some fruit in the spring and summer, we followed the practice of generations. We cut the apples into quarters or eighths, strung the pieces on string, and hung them on a rack suspended from hooks in the kitchen ceiling. These dried, kept practically forever, and after being soaked overnight, were good for pie or apple sauce the next day. It pleases me that in the old house in which we now live, the hooks are still in the kitchen ceiling, reminding me of the old days. In the summer wild strawberries were an occasional dessert, and there were lots of blueberries and blackberries. A couple of bushels of butternuts were a staple. For a great many years Uncle John kept bees, and honey supplemented our maple sugar for sweets. We made candy out of maple syrup and butternuts. We never saw a lemon or an orange, except perhaps at Christmas.

Due to old-time religious feeling against unnecessary work on Sunday, practically everything for Sunday was cooked on Saturday, such as a big bowl of hasty pudding or an old-fashioned New England boiled dinner. In Grandma's time, the Sabbath began at sundown on Saturday and ended at sundown on Sunday.

Of course we always went to church and Sunday school. Grandfather had helped build the Congregational church in 1833, and was a deacon. Uncle John was secretary of the congregation for many years, and Father, who had been educated for the ministry and preached for three years before he went into newspaper work, was also a deacon and a highly respected member. I joined the church when I was twelve years old and have always continued my membership. One of my first Sunday school teachers was Miss Ella M. Dwinell, a distant relative, whose home in the village I acquired after her death in December, 1947.

At that time there were two churches in the village with different ministers. Difference of dogma still prevailed and it was seldom that a member of one congregation attended the other church. One year my teacher at the Pettengill school was Miss Haskins, the daughter of the Baptist minister, and it seemed an act of great tolerance to permit Congregational children to be taught by the Baptist minister's daughter. However, due to financial difficulties, in time the community was able to support only one minister, and for a number of years services have been held in the Congregational church in the summer and in the Baptist church in the winter, because it is easier to heat. For a while a Congregationalist would be chosen as minister, and then a Baptist would be chosen. Nowadays the two churches have united and are known under one name, the Grafton Church. In 1933 the Brick Congregational Church was one hundred years old and in response to an invitation from Hon. John Barrett, Grafton's foremost citizen, I gave the centennial address. Years ago my father wrote a history of this church and Miss Lou Daniels had it published in pamphlet form. I have copies.

With no movies or automobiles, the social events of the year largely centered around the church and the Sunday school. The chief one was at sugaring time in early spring. Everybody brought big pans which were filled with snow on which was poured the thick hot syrup. This congealed to wax and together with dill pickles, coffee, sandwiches and cookies completely filled the stomachs of all small boys.

The only minister I remember from my early days in Grafton was Alfred Leach, who lived in Saxtons River and was related to my cousin George Pettengill's wife, Jennie Louise Bunnell. His sermons were very weary affairs and the only bit of truth in all of his preaching which I remember was his statement, apropos of something, no doubt, that "you can't pick your teeth with a crowbar." As I pictured in my imagination a man trying to do that very thing, it made quite an impression on me, but even now I can't see the connection with my soul's salvation.

The main part of the house where I was raised was built in 1815 by Grafton's second minister, Rev. Mr. Goodell. It originally stood across the road from the old Middletown cemetery, and was known as the Minister Farm. He built it because the first minister, Rev. William Hall, was still living in the old parsonage on the Middletown Road when Mr. Goodell came to town, and did not wish to move from the place that had been his home for so long. In 1833, a new church had been built in the south village and my grandfather bought the Minister Farm. The frame of the main building, a two-story and attic house, 36 by 26 feet, was made of heavy timbers mortised together with big wooden pegs, and was fully finished inside with every room and closet plastered. My grandfather took down the ell that was attached to the house and in 1835 moved the house down the cemetery hill, across the brook and up the steep hill on the other side, and then down the road to the south, a distance of about a quarter of a mile. There he had built a cellar on the property once owned by Rev. William Hall, and there he set up the house. Moving the house was considered the greatest feat of engineering in the history of Grafton, taking five days and the labor of about twenty men. Huge tree trunks were placed under the house to act as rollers, and two men were at the rollers at each corner of the building to force it up the hill, while twelve teams of oxen hitched together furnished motive power. The building was so sturdily constructed that they used to say it could have rolled over and over down the hill and would have held together. My grandfather built a large ell on the north side of the house which extended across the back, and here the kitchen and work rooms of the dwelling were located. He tore down the old Hall house where he had lived after buying the property a couple of years before and some of the material was used in the new kitchen. He also constructed a large barn and other outbuildings.

*The Jonathan Pettengill House in Grafton, Vermont. The photo was taken in 1897. Sam Pettengill, age 11, is seated on the fence. His father is at the center of the photo and Uncle John is at the left rear.*

I remember the house very well. Downstairs there was a large hallway, with some steps at the right going up to a landing, and then turning left continuing straight up to the second floor. There was a parlor, with Uncle John's bedroom back of it, and a large sitting room, and several closets. Off the sitting room in the ell, was a very large kitchen where we did most of our living. In addition to the iron stove it had a brick oven. A back staircase from here went up to the second floor. Beyond the kitchen in the ell was a big pantry, or keeping room as it was called, where the pans of milk were set. The well was in the cellar under the ell and in the kitchen was a sink with a pump. Next to the keeping room was a workroom with a churn, wooden washtubs and so forth. And along the whole length of the ell to the south was a big storeroom and a woodshed, with the "two-holer" at the end of the woodshed. There was a chunk stove in the parlor and one in the sitting room, used only if we had company. There was a chunk stove in Uncle John's room, too.

Upstairs there were five bedrooms and a hall, and stairs going up to the attic which covered the whole second floor. Father's bedroom, which had been my grandparents', had a stove in it. I slept in what we called the north bedchamber. It was totally unheated and no doubt got down to or below freezing on cold winter nights. Criss-cross ropes through the bed frame supported two mattresses filled with corn husks. On the coldest nights I slept between the mattresses! We all had pieces of soapstone which we heated in the kitchen stove before going to bed, wrapping them in pieces of flannel and tucking them into the beds as foot warmers. Except in the kitchen we used candles which we made ourselves out of hog tallow.

Our only bathing facilities were in the brook in the summer, or in the big washtubs set in front of the kitchen stove. However, in the summer when there was a heavy shower, my brother and I used to strip off and stand under the eaves of the barn where a torrent of cool rain water splashed over us. It was very delightful.

The barn was one hundred fifty feet back of the house and was two stories high, the second story being filled with hay throughout. The cattle stalls faced the barnyard and along both sides of the barn facing the barnyard were the calving room, sheep pens, horse stalls, shelter for the wagons and farm machinery, the buggy and the sleigh. There was an outdoor pig pen and a chicken coop next to the barn. The barnyard was very good as it was protected from wintry winds on three sides and faced southeast. If it was a sunny day the cattle loved to be out, even though the weather was freezing. Water came to the trough in the barnyard by pipe from a spring forty rods to the southeast. It was always left running so it never froze up but in the winter we had to break up the ice that accumulated in the trough every time the cattle were let out. The cattle were always glad to see us on a cold winter morning, as they were ready for breakfast. And we were glad to be with them, as the cow barn was always quite a few degrees warmer than outdoors due to their bodies' natural heat, and it was a long cold walk from the house to the barn. The intimate mutual fondness of humans and non-humans for each other can never be appreciated by those who never were children on a farm.

We had two horses, a team of big oxen, steers, heifers, about six cows, seventy to eighty sheep, several hogs, about forty hens, a collie dog named Jack, and cats. The cats always came at milking time to get warm milk squirted into their mouths. The hens had the run of the entire place and it was a constant job to find the new nests where they laid their eggs. Hens are very secretive about their nests, but their enthusiasm after laying an egg was noisy enough so we knew a nest was not far off.

The barn was a great place for rats, mice, squirrels and birds. By the time I was ten I knew by sight and song a dozen different varieties of birds.

Great-grandfather Peter came to Grafton from Salem, New Hampshire, in 1787. He was eighteen years old and walked the entire distance at the shoulders of the oxen drawing some of the belongings of the first minister, Rev. William Hall, while the minister's son William Jr., drove the team of horses. Later William Jr. worked for Nathan Wheeler, the storekeeper, on Middletown Hill, finally becoming a partner until he left to establish his own business in Bellows Falls, and became very successful. His younger brother Caleb became a prosperous farmer and town official in Grafton where he remained until 1835 when he moved to Springfield, bought a large farm, and became a prominent citizen. The Pettengills and Halls had been friends and neighbors in Salem, and when the minister received the call from Grafton to preach, Peter came with him as his hired man and settled in Grafton for good.

There being no road up the Saxtons River from Bellows Falls to Grafton at that time, they came into Grafton center from the northeast via the road from Rockingham to Chester. The center of Grafton, then called Thomlinson, was at that time on the hill one mile north of the present village of Grafton, and was known as Middletown or "middle-of-the-town." In 1798, Peter married Hannah Stickney, daughter of Deacon David and Keziah Butterfield Stickney who had come to Grafton in 1781 from Billerica, Mass. For quite a few years Peter and Hannah lived in a house that he built on the Stickney farm and their three children, Abbott, Jonathan and Eliza were born there. I have a letter dated October 23, 1926, from a William C. Putnam whose family had settled in Thomlinson in 1783, saying that fifty years before, the cellar walls of the first Pettengill house were still standing. It was located about an eighth of a mile southeast of the brick house Peter built in 1820, and the first Middletown road went by it. I have since found the cellar hole.

Deacon Stickney's barn had been used for a meeting house before the erection of the first church in Middletown, in 1792. Peter was a carpenter by trade and took a prominent part in the building of the church, which according to Ella Dwinell, was larger than the second church built in the village in 1833. He was a very strong and powerful man and it was said that he would hew a 40-foot stick of timber and in framing it, when it became necessary to turn the log, would take hold of one end of it with his bare hands and flip it over, a thing which no other person in Grafton could do. Feats of strength such as picking up a blacksmith's anvil by the handle are part of the traditions which surrounded his name. The most remarkable one was about a time in winter, long after he was married, when a man he had hired to cut down trees failed to come home for dinner. Peter went to look for him and found him crushed to death beneath a huge tree. Peter lifted the tree, laid it on his knees and dragged the dead man out from under it. The man is believed to have been David Palmer. The tree was left untouched for years and all the strong men from miles around used to try to lift it, but no one ever could.

In telling me these stories, my father said that he had never forgotten one peculiarity of his grandfather's. In his time whiskers were almost unknown, and Peter would stand up before a bare wall, as if in front of a mirror, and shave himself without a looking glass. How much help it was for him to stand before a wall was always a matter of curiosity to his children and grandchildren.

Although my great-grandfather was noted for his strength, he was considered a very pleasant and agreeable man and very much devoted to religion. "Uncle Peter" as he was called, often took the place of the minister in giving advice and hope to his friends and neighbors. In church he sat in the same pew as Capt. John Barrett, one of his contemporaries, and it added to the seriousness of the service to see these two men, one at each end of the pew, receiving communion from the minister's hand. Peter was a regular attendant at church and prayer meetings, and was as noted for his piety as for any of his other characteristics. The letter from William C. Putnam, previously quoted, also said that he had in his possession a letter written by Peter Pettengill to his grandfather, Asher Putnam, about one hundred years before. He judged from it that Peter Pettengill was a "very strong character, but more interested in the welfare of his soul than current events."

The town meetings were held in the church on Middletown Hill for many years, as was the custom in most of the early communities. To enhance the formality of these meetings, many of the men occupied the pews they sat in on Sundays and their claim was recognized by everyone. It was during the latter part of the holding of the town meetings in the church that the practice of paying town officers for their services was inaugurated. The proposition was stoutly resisted by the older men but the "byes," as Capt. Burgess called them, carried the day and drew pay for services which had been gratuitous since the beginning of the town. In notes left by my father he describes what the center of the town was like in the early days. There was a store, owned by Wheeler & Barrett, the church, the parsonage, an hotel, a doctor's office, blacksmith shop, pound, a potash works, a tannery, and later a carding and fulling mill, and quite a number of residences. There was a brick schoolhouse which had taken the place of the first schoolhouse directly across the road from it. In addition to this road, which is still called Middletown Road, there was another road leading in to the center from the northwest. This road has long since been abandoned and overgrown by timber, and only the part between the present Gabriel place and Middletown Road remains. People came to the center from outlying farms to attend church and exchange news. It was the custom for practically everybody to attend church; in fact, to a considerable extent, it was compulsory.

Great-grandmother, and later my grandmother to a lesser extent, wove wool and flax into cloth. The attic in our house was full of spinning wheels and other accessories when I was a boy. I now have in my study one of my grandmother's spinning wheels with the flax still on it just as it was the last time she used it. It was given me by my cousin Fanny, daughter of my father's brother, Dr. Edward Pettengill, who lived in Saxtons River. A century ago, wool was the chief product sold for cash, and earlier still, around the 1840's, there were as many as ten thousand sheep in and around Grafton, and more than a half million in Windham County alone. These were the Merino sheep, famous for their fine wool and there were hundreds of thousands of them raised in Vermont, bringing much wealth to the state.

Both my great-grandfather and my grandfather did surveying in addition to farming, and I have the fine old compass they used, made about 1775, and still in good working order. My grandfather was fond of telling about being called to Chester to do some surveying for Hugh Henry who was pretty exacting with all who worked for him. He stood around and watched Grandfather go on with his work until he was satisfied that he understood his business, even if he did come from Grafton!

Peter and his older son Abbott made bricks in a brick kiln not far from where they lived. It was located a little west of the Pettengill Bridge on the road going to Houghtonville. A number of houses are still standing made of these bricks, among them my great-grandfather's own house which he built in 1820. It is located at the north end of Middletown Road, the last house on the left going down the hill to the Houghtonville Road. The present R. R. Barrett house on the hill was built of these bricks about 1815 by Benjamin Dwinell. The old Town Farm off the Kidder Hill Road which has long since fallen down, was also built of these bricks, and when I bought our River Mowing Farm in 1940, I bought the ruins for the bricks. I paid fifty dollars for them and we used the lovely old pink bricks for fireplaces at the farm, and there were enough left over so that later we were able to use them for some fireplaces at Robin Lawn. We found the impress of "P" and "AP" on some of the bricks, which made us treasure them even more.

Peter's first son, Abbott Pettengill, was born in 1799. He married the widow of Dr. Randall Clark of Windham. She was the daughter of Robert and Anna Gibson Park of Grafton, who built the house on Middletown Road in 1792, now owned by his direct descendant, Mrs. Martha Park Desrochers. Abbott and Martha Pettengill had two children, James Dascomb Pettengill and Martha, who died in Grafton in 1865. After the Civil War, James decided to move to Virginia. Riding horseback, he drove a flock of sheep all the way from Vermont to Virginia. It is interesting to think of him driving his precious flock of sheep through or around the busy streets of the cities along his way. I heard about this from Francis Palmer who was running the store in the village when I came back in 1940. He said his grandfather, Amos Palmer, had sold James the horse he used on the journey. He settled in Clarksville, Virginia, and his daughter married a Rev. Edgar Allen Potts.

My grandfather, Jonathan Stickney Pettengill, was born on July 26, 1801. When about eighteen, he went to Middlebury to live with Prof. Frederick Hall, a son of the Rev. William Hall of Grafton, and do chores for his board while preparing for, and later attending, Middlebury College. Prof. Hall taught Mathematics and Natural Philosophy, but in 1824 he left Middlebury to study medicine at Castleton Medical School, thus throwing Jonathan on his own resources. He hired out to Hon. Peter Starr, a prominent lawyer in Middlebury, and he worked on his farm for some years. In 1832 he married Mary Altha Foote, daughter of Martin and Hannah Dean Foote and they moved to the Foote farm. They had one child, Mary Emma, born in 1833, and two weeks after her birth, the mother died. About a year or so later Jonathan came back to Grafton with his young child and bought the old Hall farm on Middletown Road. It was to this land that in 1835 he moved the house in which I grew up. The next year he married my grandmother, Sally Barrett of Springfield. Their five children were all born in this house, my father being the second son.

The year his eldest son, Edward was born, my grandfather received a commission from Gov. Silas Jennison appointing him 2nd Lieutenant in the State militia, November 6, 1837. Subsequently he was appointed 1st Lieutenant and later Captain. On November 30, 1853, he was appointed Justice of the Peace in Windham County and I have in my possession the commission signed by Gov. John S. Robinson.

While in Middlebury my grandfather had joined the Congregational church and piety was one of the chief characteristics of the Pettengill family, as it had been in his father's time. Discipline was severe and the comments and warnings of the Scriptures were taken in a literal sense. In 1833, the new brick meeting house was built in the South village and the whole family attended church a mile from home every Sunday unless there was illness. It was far from being a day of rest for the children. They went to church carrying a doughnut or two for lunch and stayed through Sunday School, a short intermission and another service in the afternoon. There were two preferred seats; one by the side of the father and one by the side of the mother, where children could lean over and take a nap and there was quite a struggle on the part of the boys to get one of those seats. After returning home from church there was dinner which had been prepared the day before as no unnecessary work was allowed on the Sabbath. After that the children were obliged to read the Bible or a Sunday school book, or listen to reading by one of the older members of the family. Later they did the necessary chores.

One of the last services held in the old church on Middletown Hill was the funeral of my great-grandmother, Hannah Stickney Pettengill. She died in 1842 and some of the older grandchildren long remembered the smell of the coffin! In those days there was no such thing as upholstered coffins made long in advance of their use, and whenever there was need of a coffin the cabinet maker in town made it and painted it black. Later for some reason they were painted red and the smell of the freshly painted coffins was the same as many other articles similarly painted, and the odor became known as "coffiny." My father told me that the first "boughten" sap buckets were painted red and were first brought into town by a man named Campbell. Someone asked Campbell's hired man if he liked the new sap buckets and he replied that he liked them pretty well but they made the sap taste rather "coffiny."

The first school in the center had been succeeded by a brick schoolhouse on the lower side of the road across from our house. Here school was kept until 1855 when, because of much shifting of population, there was great agitation in favor of building a new school in the valley nearly a mile north, near the Pettengill Bridge. By this time many of the hill dwellers had moved down to the South village and had a school there for their children, and those who lived at the north end of the hill and down in the valley wanted a school more conveniently located for their children. Each school district at that time ran its own school and at the district meeting, opinion was almost exactly divided as to whether a new school should be built in the valley or the brick schoolhouse continued in use. My great-uncle, Abbott Pettengill, lived in the valley in a house now owned by Hardy Merrill, located across the meadow from the Pettengill Bridge. He had two children and favored the building of a new school nearer to his home, but when the matter was put to a vote, the result was a tie. By this time everyone was tired and hungry and they decided to go home for dinner and come back afterwards and vote again. Abbott went home and brought back his hired man whose name was Solomon Rhodes. With the hired man's vote, which probably was illegal as he was not a householder, the motion to build the new school was carried. The vote was not challenged and it was not until long after the new school had been built that everyone learned about it. By that time the passion had subsided between the two factions and the matter was good humoredly laughed off and the new school for many years was known as "Solomon's Temple." No one knew where Solomon had acquired the surname of Rhodes, for he was of unknown parentage and had been left as a baby on Abbott Pettengill's doorstep in a basket. He was found the next morning covered with snow and Abbott raised him, naming him Solomon. He made his home with Abbott most of his life.

Later the school was called the Pettengill School since the land on which it stood had been given by the family. My grandfather's elder children, Mary Emma, Edward and Samuel (my father) never went to this school. Mary had attended school for a year in Westbrook, Connecticut, living with an uncle, and then in 1850 returned to Grafton to teach school. She taught for several years and then married and left Grafton.

"Solomon's Temple," the Pettengill School in Grafton, Vermont.

The two boys had one term at Springfield Academy and then on December 9, 1855, left for Manchester to fit for college at Burr & Burton Seminary.

However, my Uncle John attended the one-room Pettengill School, as I did until I also went to Burr & Burton. I remember the school very well. The oldest boys took turns getting to the schoolhouse a little early and making a fire in the pot-bellied stove to take a little sting out of the wintry air. All of the children helped bring in wood to keep the fire going. The drinking water was brought in a pail from a spring about twenty rods away. The school never had more than twelve children at one time and often only eight or ten, but we had enough to play three old cat in a nearby pasture and we learned to swim in the swimming hole about a quarter mile down stream from the school. I doubt if it was ever more than thirty inches deep. In the winter we had homemade wooden sleds and old fashioned hand-me-down skates with a wooden platform and a big screw that screwed into the heel of our boots. We had homemade bows and arrows with which my brother and I played at attacking the enemy, who were always British redcoats rather than Indians. The school was abandoned in 1937 and I have the sign which formerly hung over the door. It had the name Pettengill painted on a large board and had been placed on the school by Mrs. Alger who then lived in the Zuill place during the summers. It was the small red brick house next to ours. Her husband was principal of Vermont Academy.

After the new schoolhouse opened in 1855, my grandfather bought the old brick schoolhouse across from our farm and fitted it up for a sugar house. It was used to make maple syrup and sugar until it burned down in 1896 at sugaring time. I was ten years old at the time and as far as I know the letter I wrote about it to Cousin Helen, another of Uncle Ed's daughters, was the first letter I ever wrote. My cousin kept it and many years later returned it to me. Here it is with the original spelling and punctuation.

Grafton, Vt.
April 30, 1896.

Dear Helen:

The sugar house burnt down the 9th day of April, in the morning.

My papa filled up the pans, and the heater, the night before, and put some snow in front of the arch, for the sparks to land on.

About 3 o'clock in the morning Uncle John got up to fix the fire in the sitting room, and as he was getting back to bed, he noticed a peculiar glow through the window.

At first he thought the kitchen was afire, but getting up he saw the sugar house was ablaze, so he called "Sam Sam" but I was quicker getting up, so Uncle John said "Go and call your papa" which I did.

When we got down there the roof was all afire, and the shingles just disappearing.

Hardly had we gotten down there ourselves when we saw a light moving from the west, and very soon Mr. Culver came with a lantern to see the fire, I s'pose.

The loss was two pans and a heater, a tin pail, and a wooden one, some timber, an axe, some old sleds, a scalding tub and a sap holder.

We had just enough strength to pull the sled and gathering tub away. Nothing is left now but the standing walls of brick.

We built an arch up in the woods and there we have carried on sugaring very nicely.

School began last Monday. I thank you very much for the card you sent up, and writing. Miss Mary Parks is the teacher.

Another little calf was born this morning making four calfs in our care.

I am very sorry that you are lame, and hope that you will be better soon. The Robins, Bluebirds, Linnets, Highholes, Barn Swallows, Phoebes, Cock of the Woods, Song Sparrows, Acadian Owls are here.

Harry and I have been sawing wood with the cross-cut, having sawed up a small pile.

Uncle John expected to go down to Saxtons River before school began but has not been well enough to go, he expects to go soon.

Tomorrow afternoon we will plant some trees down to the school house and make a flower bed.

Papa and Uncle John are going fishing tomorrow. Harry and I will take our poles down to the school house and fish noontimes.

Your loving cousin,<br>Bobby

P.S. I have finished reading the books which were very interesting.

---

As I said before, both my Uncle Ed and Father went to Burr & Burton Seminary in 1855 to prepare for Middlebury College. Uncle Ed was eighteen and Father was sixteen. They hoped they could receive scholarship aid there but knew they would have to work to pay their expenses, as my grandfather did not feel he could help much. However he did not oppose their going and at the beginning of the winter term in December, 1855, they set out for Manchester with young John driving the old mare. They had positive instructions not to let John go so far that he could not get back before dark that night. They expected to take the stage at Londonderry but on arrival found the stage had gone early that morning to return the next day and leave again for Manchester the following day. The boys agreed that they could not spend all that time waiting, so decided to go on, trying to plan what they would do when they reached the limit where John and the old mare would have to turn back. As they went by the town of Landgrove they saw where a building had fallen down with boards scattered around in the snow. This gave them the idea of making a sled out of the boards and putting their load on the sled and hauling it to Manchester. They piled some of the boards onto the wagon and when they got to the next town, Peru, they stopped at the hotel and borrowed a saw, axe and hammer. They unloaded the boards and got a piece of rope and some nails at the store. The old storekeeper asked what they wanted the rope for and the boys replied that they were going to Manchester. "Are you going to lead a calf?" he asked. "No, we are going to lead a sled." They finished the sled, tied their trunk on it and started walking to Manchester, while John turned the old mare around and headed for home. When the boys got to the foot of the mountain on the road to Factory Point, now called Manchester Center, the ground was nearly bare, but somehow they made it to the home of Leverett Spring. His family lived on an adjoining farm in Grafton and he had gone to Manchester to work in the store of one of his relatives. He drive Uncle Ed and Father from the Point to Burr & Burton. By later comparing the time, it was found that they had arrived at the Seminary within a few minutes of the time that John got back to Grafton. They had left home about three o'clock in the morning and reached their destination about six in the evening.

The boys found work sawing wood, sweeping the halls and taking care of the principal's horse and cow, and were able to pay a good part of their expenses.

While this was going on, Mr. Starr, the lawyer for whom my grandfather had worked while in Middlebury, came to Grafton with his son, Charles J. Starr, to pay Grandfather a visit. It was just after the completion of the Rutland Railroad, when the State Fair was being held at Middlebury, and they urged him to come back with them, attend the Fair and have a ride on the railroad, which he did. Charles Starr found out what Edward and my father were doing to get an education, became interested and told my grandfather that he would help the boys through the Seminary and then through college. He was as good as his word, and made their way easier. He sent each of the boys 125 dollars a year and so helped them do what otherwise might have been impossible. When Father was graduated from Burr & Burton, he delivered a Commencement oration in Greek!

Father left Middlebury in 1862 with other students to enlist in Co. B, 7th Squadron, Rhode Island Cavalry, the only company in the Civil War composed entirely of college students,

*My father, Samuel B. Pettengill, when he left Middlebury College in 1862 to fight in the Civil War.*

men and officers alike. He was mustered in as a private on July 24, 1862, to serve three months, and on August 12, 1862 was promoted to be a veterinary surgeon. This I could never understand! He was mustered out as such on October 2, 1862. Some years later he wrote a small book called "The College Cavaliers" telling how a company of college students offered their services to the Governor of Rhode Island who was raising a squadron of cavalry in response to Lincoln's urgent call for the defense of Washington. Their one provision was that they should remain as one unit and their offer was accepted. Eighty-two students from Dartmouth, Middlebury, Norwich and Bowdoin joined and saw service at Washington, Winchester, Harper's Ferry and Antietam. The only Grafton men in the company were Samuel B. Pettengill and Will L. Burnap.

In the meantime my father had decided to become a minister, and he attended Princeton Theological Seminary and then Andover Theological Seminary from which he was graduated in 1866.

A life-long friend of Father's was Wilder Luke Burnap, called Will, and born in Grafton. The two were in the same company during the Civil War. Mr. Burnap became the leading lawyer in Burlington, and every now and then came down to Grafton and stayed a day or so with us in order to visit Father and eat some of his salt pork and Johnny Cake. Father had a gift for Johnny Cake which I have never seen equalled. It must have been a little like the spoon bread of the South as it came out of the oven somewhat fluid. Burnap's grandfather had been a miller who grew up near Ticonderoga in New York. They came to Grafton to live when the town voted to exempt his new grist mill from taxes for a period of years. His wife had died and he brought Will's father as a little child about a year old in a hand sled in the dead of winter, walking about ninety miles from Ticonderoga. Will's son, Robert, an official of the Grand Trunk Railroad, became my life long friend. The encouragement to industry through exempting the Burnap grist mill from taxes, and contrarywise, the discouragement to business expansion through too heavy taxes, made a great impression on me.

When Vermont was first settled following the Revolutionary War, the first communities nearly always were built on top of hills rather than in the valleys. There was more sunlight and a better view on the hills, and the valleys were considered unhealthy due to malaria as a result of the dense primeval woods and underbrush. Consequently, my people were hill people from the beginning. The first settlement, Thomlinson, later called Grafton, was up on the hill called Middle-of-the-town, now Middletown, situated around our old farm. The first church built in 1792, stood on a common exactly one acre in size, and this later became a part of our farm. However, by 1830 people were moving down into the valley because of the mills that were being built along the river and so this became the village of Grafton as we know it. It was then called the South Village. The church was also moved at that time. By this I mean the congregation, not the building, for it remained standing until about 1858 and was used for town meetings until it was torn down. Also, occasionally an itinerant preacher was allowed to hold services there. The big granite steps that had been in front of the old church were salvaged by Deacon John Dwinell and are now the steps in front of our kitchen porch at Robin Lawn. Deacon Dwinell had sold his brick house on the hill and bought what is now our home.

By 1820, Grafton had its high point in population, 1,482 people. In 1900, Uncle John took the census and there were 804, a loss of about four or five hundred in his own lifetime. Today the population is even less, although it has climbed since its low point of 393 in 1940. Hillsides, once covered with houses and plowed fields, are now grown up to weeds and woods. We had about two hundred acres of land on the hill, one hundred of which were pastures on Spring Hill back of our farm, and named after the Spring family which had once owned them. Also there were four hundred acres on the other side of Houghtonville, where we used to pasture the sheep during the summer.

Uncle John had a little muzzle loading rifle. When I got old enough I was permitted to use it. It was loaded from a powder horn and with round bullets which we moulded ourselves from hot lead poured into a soapstone bullet mould. I used to carry it up to the hundred acre pasture on Spring Hill back of our farm. One time going up for the cows at night, I saw a fox and shot at it and broke one of its legs. It started to run and this being a muzzle loading rifle there was no time to re-load so I chased pell-mell after the fox. It came to a stone wall which it couldn't jump by reason of its broken leg. I caught up with it and in my excitement used the rifle to beat it with and broke the rifle in two. This was one of the poignant dilemmas of my youth — proud at bringing home a dead fox and grief over the broken rifle. It was never repaired.

When Father was a little boy, an old farmer living on the other side of Spring Hill used to ride over the hill to the Middletown road, and then on down to Grafton village to get his jug filled with West India rum. This went on year after year. As he became more dissolute he mortgaged his cattle, sheep and horses and finally the farm itself, until nothing was left. The neighbors said of him that "he carried his farm over the hill in a jug." Shakespeare could not have said it better than that.

Jim Zuill lived in the first house to the east of our farm, a brick Cape Cod type house, said to be one of the first brick houses built in Grafton. It was later owned by Professor Alger, principal of Vermont Academy and now by the William Herrlichs. Jim had a few acres of his own but also worked for us occasionally as a hired man. He was a bachelor, given to drinking whiskey and hard cider and was mean and dangerous when drunk. He chewed tobacco constantly and a big wooden panel over his fireplace was completely covered with little tin tags taken off of plugs of tobacco. At one time he took a poor old woman who had been living at the Town Farm and gave her bed and board for her services, thus relieving the taxpayers to that extent. He always spoke of her as "the people," never by name. When over at our place we would ask him to stay and have a bite with us, but he would say, "no, the people are expecting me." "The people" went barefoot inside and out most of the year. Jim finally fell off a sleigh in sub-zero weather when drunk and was found frozen to death in a snow drift. However, he had his good points. He had fought in the Civil War and always refused to take his soldier's pension even when it was no longer necessary to prove service disability. He took a fierce pride in refusing his pension, for which I admired him.

Jim Zuill's father had been Nathan Zuill who owned Four Chimneys, a beautiful Williamsburg type house of brick on Holmes Hill, north of the Middletown settlement across the Saxtons River. It has four chimneys, hence its name.

During my boyhood Vermont was a prohibition state. However, it was possible under the interstate commerce laws to have whiskey sent in from other states by express. At that time you could get four quarts of whiskey for three dollars and twenty cents or eighty cents a quart! Consequently anyone who wanted to get drunk was seldom prevented from doing so. The chief drink, however, was hard cider. When cider gets really hard it is almost pure alcohol. Men with hair on their chests would drop a raw egg into a tumbler of hard cider and took great pride in swallowing the egg at one gulp.

Deacon Park lived on the first farm west of us. He was a pillar of the church and as parsimonious as the most close fisted Scot. When his married daughter who had been living in Illinois for a number of years came to visit, Deacon Park drove to the railroad station to meet her, and in honor of the occasion wore a pair of brand new overalls.

Next above him, at the top of the road going past his house, was the home of A. B. Culver. His five children were the same ages as my brother and myself and went to the Pettengill school with us. The daughter, Helen, was my chief competitor for the best marks in school. She became Mrs. Frank Wilbur, lived in Grafton village, and died in 1954. Mr. Culver's father was a shoe maker and would go from house to house staying a week or more, making shoes and boots with bright red leather tops, for all the family.

Except during haying time, each farm family did practically all of the work the year 'round. However, hired hands were engaged at haying time and were paid a dollar a day. In many places the ground was so rough that mowing machines could not be used. The hay had to be cut by scythe. Every morning and afternoon the scythes had to be ground and it was the job of us boys to turn the grindstone until our arms nearly dropped off. Another minor job was taking drinking water out to the men in the fields. Occasionally we made a drink of water plus maple sugar with a few drops of vinegar. Bottled drinks such as we have today were wholly unknown and I think I was sixteen before I ever had a dish of ice cream.

I look back with the greatest nostalgia to sugaring time. Coming at the breaking of winter and with the sap rising in the tree trunks, there was an air of gayety and cheer at sugaring time, greater than at any other part of the year. We carried yokes on our backs from which hung two pails. We went from tree to tree gathering the sap which had collected in the pails previously hung on the trees, and poured it into a big hogshead strapped to a sled drawn by oxen.

It was the time when the first crows came north and even their harsh caws was a beautiful sound. But best of all was boiling the sap in the sugar house. We used four-foot lengths of cord wood and sometimes when the sap was running heavily we would boil all night long. It took forty gallons of sap to make one gallon of syrup. To fall asleep on a bed of spruce and hemlock boughs in the sugar house to the music of the bubbling sap with its sweet fragrance filling the air, is something one must live through to fully appreciate.

It seems strange to me now that I have no recollection of enjoying the beauties of the Vermont hills, especially in the fall of the year, which seem so magnificent to me now. I can't remember standing and looking at the glorious colors. I suppose being a little boy I just took them for granted.

One of Father's favorite stories was about my great-aunt, Betsey Barrett, a sister of my grandmother. She was born in 1794 in Springfield and had always lived there. She was a spinster and ate little more than a bird. One day an old lady friend came to call and staying late, Aunt Betsey asked her to remain for supper although she had prepared nothing special. There was very little in the pantry and great-aunt was constantly apologizing for this and that all through the meal. For dessert there was nothing but a thin sliver of a mince pie which great-aunt had been slowly consuming for over a week. This sliver was cut in two to make still narrower slivers and again great-aunt apologized. Her guest, a little weary of the apologizing by this time and perhaps of the food, said of the sliver of pie, "Oh, I know it must be very good, what there is of it." And then, taking a bite, she said, "And there's plenty of it, such as it is."

When she was younger, great-aunt Betsey was a school teacher. She possessed a very strong mind and had the courage of her convictions. One time on a Sunday morning, a fire broke out in Springfield near the river, and the men, not wanting to wet their Sunday clothes, were being pretty careful in handling the water buckets. Great-aunt Betsey, on her way home from church, thought they were much too slow, and taking a bucket she jumped into the mill pond where the water was waist deep, and filling the pail, called on the men to hurry the water along. She stayed in the pond until the fire was out!

Another story is about one time when she thought the tax on her homestead was too high and she asked to have it abated. This was in the days when the taxpayers outside the village paid their taxes by working on the highways. This was called "working it out." She lived then in the Eureka district and her request for abatement being refused, great-aunt declared she would work out the taxes with the men. She appeared with her hoe and worked so much harder than the men that it was too much for them. At noon they told her she could go home and they would work out the remainder of her tax. It was always said that they preferred to work out the additional tax, taking their own time about it, rather than try to keep up with great-aunt Betsey's quicker pace.

Great-aunt Betsey was an ardent foe of slavery. So deep seated was her abhorrence of human slavery that when she was compelled to use any product of slave labor she did so with the greatest reluctance. She used to say, "three things I hate, plants in houses, birds in cages and slaves in chains."

A couple of centuries ago all forms of decoration in the Congregational churches were frowned upon as resembling popery. This went on until one time some flowers were brought into the church and created a tremendous controversy. Great-aunt Betsey was asked her opinion and she said, "It's too diverting for the youth." I don't suppose she ever forgave the innovators for returning to popery.

A Grafton story going back to about 1840 was about the Deacon and the husking bee. Husking bees had disappeared when I was a boy but they must have been great events in the old days. All the neighbors gathered at one place and then husked corn out in the barn, lighted by jack-o-lanterns made out of pumpkins. Both men and women took part. And because it was one day in the year when a little jollity was permitted in that otherwise Puritan atmosphere, it was the privilege of a man who found a red ear to kiss the woman next to him. The old Deacon, filled with cider and doughnuts, was extremely fortunate in finding lots of red ears! So many in fact that some people suspected that he carried one around in his pocket and produced it at the right moment. Whether because he had better luck and the other men were jealous, or because they thought he was cheating, a scandal developed. Some days later the Deacon, who lived on a hill, saw the parson's old gray mare and buckboard slowly coming up the hill. The Deacon knew why the parson was coming and heated up some toddy in front of the fireplace. It was November, and by the time the parson had reached the house, his beard and mustache were full of icicles. The Deacon said, "C'mon in, Parson, sit in front of the fire and have a little toddy so you won't get lung fever." While temperance was a great virtue, nevertheless around 1840 it was still permitted even for the minister to have an alcoholic drink for health's sake. Consequently, after the icicles melted and the parson got warm, both from the fire and the toddy, it became increasingly difficult for him to bring himself to the point of his errand. At last the Deacon said, "Parson, I know why you came here today. You are going to remonstrate with me about that husking bee. But I am going to say this, Parson, if a Deacon can't have a little fun with the ladies once a year, in the fall of the year, at husking time, I'm going to resign my Deaconship." In short, he felt he had the right to blow off steam one day out of 365.

Lambing time was another great week on the farm. We had around seventy-five ewes. Their lambs all arrived during a period of ten days in the early part of April. As often it was very cold weather and freezing out in the barn, we would often stay up all night and bring the new born trembling wet lambs in from the barn, wrap them up and put them next to the stove to dry. We would feed the weakest of them by making a nipple out of a piece of cloth wrapped around a finger and soaked in warm milk, into which we would occasionally have poured a few drops of whiskey. By morning they would be dry and spry and we would take them back to their anxious, bleating mothers. In this way we saved a great many who otherwise would have died.

There were always little chicks, lambs, calves and once a colt, demanding the attention of us boys. I don't know of any better way to teach gentleness to growing boys than for them to have the responsibility of taking care of these babies of the animal world. The man who would actually abuse a horse or oxen was viewed with a great deal of disapproval in the community.

Each spring the sheep were washed before they were sheared. We made a little dam in the stream down hill from the cemetery into which the sheep were driven one by one. Uncle John stood in the water up to his waist and scrubbed off the accumulation of burrs and dirt as best he could.

I recently had a chance to see the List Book for 1858 which belonged to Frank Wilbur's grandfather, Ephraim Wilbur. Jonathan S. Pettengill was listed as follows:

```
2 oxen ..................................... $ 90
6 cows & 5 other cattle ....................  290
4 horses & "horse kind" ....................  165
100 sheep ..................................  190
2 swine ....................................   10
"Grain & forage not exempt" ................  100
                                             ----
                                             $845
```

The hill country in lower Vermont is much wilder now than when I was a boy. I don't remember anyone going deer hunting when I was a boy or killing any deer. Now hundreds of deer will be killed each year in Windham County during deer season. Today there are also bears in the woods and one weighing nearly six hundred pounds was shot on the Charles Wright farm around 1947. It was robbing some beehives. We never had the slightest fear of running into a bear up in the woods when I was a boy, but I do remember coming face to face with a big Canadian lynx. I was petrified with fear. But after we looked at each other a moment the big cat turned away and disappeared. On the other hand, I think there were more trout in the streams then than now, due to the fact that fewer fishermen came in from the outside. I well remember the first little trout that I caught and the immense pride I had in running home with it. We also caught minnows or dace, which we boys would clean, slit and eat RAW and think we were real he-men doing it.

In the old days, when the town had around 1400 people, the schools were crowded, especially in the winter months. At one time there were twelve one-room schools in as many districts. There was one school in Howeville that had ninety-six children in it, all at one time. And all of them came from just twelve families, an average of eight to a family. Today there is no school there and no children — Howeville has again become a forest.

When Father was a boy there was a family that had twenty-one children. The first name of the father was Noah, pronounced Nore. When he and his wife and twenty-one children came to church, it was quite a procession. On bitter winter days, everybody took foot warmers to church, filled with coals from the fireplace to supplement the big stove in the church. When a great many people with foot warmers were seated, the subzero temperature of the night before gradually warmed up, but with the wind howling outside a lot of cold air came in whenever the door was opened. So when Noah with his wife and flock arrived it kept the door open quite a long time as the procession entered. When the cold blast of air hit those already in their seats, they pulled their shawls closer around their shoulders and muttered, "Here comes Nore and twenty-two more!"

The minister used to conduct a bible class for the men of the village and Uncle Zeb, the village half-wit, but a harmless old man, attended with the others. It was the practice of the minister to expatiate on some subject and then ask each member of the class what he thought about it. One day the subject was the Apostle Paul and following his practice the minister said, "Well, Deacon Park, what is your opinion of the Apostle Paul?" Deacon Park replied that in his opinion the Apostle Paul was a very zealous man. And so it went around the class as each grave and reverent member expressed the opinion that the Apostle Paul was pious, courageous, a learned man, a teacher of men and so forth, until all the adjectives in the English language had been used up. Finally it was Uncle Zeb's turn. Uncle Zeb had a short, explosive manner of speaking. The minister said, "Uncle Zeb, what is your opinion of the Apostle Paul?" Everybody waited with bated breath for the words of wisdom to come from the half-wit. He thought a long time and finally exploded, "Well, in my 'pinion, the Apostle Paul was an APOSTLE." That summed it up. This was one of Father's favorite stories.

When I was a boy, every man twenty-one years of age was a member of the Vermont militia, and the younger and abler members were supposed to attend a muster and drill once a year. It would last several days and one of the great events of my boyhood was attending a muster near Springfield. President McKinley's Secretary of War was there and I am almost sure the President himself. The rapid fire Maxim gun was brand new then and I recall seeing the bullets in one of the Maxim rifles mowing down the underbrush up on the hillsides.

Another great event was Memorial Day, then called Decoration Day. Everyone participated. There was not only an address but the children sang and gave recitations of patriotic poems such as The Blue and the Gray. No grave in any cemetery was neglected. Some dated back to Revolutionary soldiers. I remember Father giving the address one year.

An event I remember well was the Fitzsimmons-Corbett heavyweight fight in Carson City, Nevada, in 1897. That fight was reported round by round in The Boston Globe, ending with Fitzsimmons' famous solar plexus punch that took the starch out of Gentleman Jim. I saved the report of that fight and read it over and over for months, and for a long time thereafter Bob Fitzsimmons was to me undoubtedly the greatest man in the world.

Uncle John died while I was at college in 1907, and a few months later the farm was sold. Counting a big pasture lot of four hundred acres in Houghtonville where we pastured the sheep in summertime, there was a total of six hundred acres. This sold, with all the buildings, for two thousand four hundred dollars. A great deal of cultivated farm land one hundred years ago could be bought when I was a boy for no more than one dollar an acre. After the sale of the farm Father went to live with his brother's family in Saxtons River, and half of the money received for the farm went to him, and half to Uncle Ed's children. Father died within two years on October 21, 1909, and what was left of his share went to Harry and me. My share, after paying debts and legal expenses, came to a little less than five hundred dollars. Except for my scholarship at college, this was the only substantial sum of money I received from any source during four years of preparatory school, four years of college and three years of law school. In 1912, the buildings on the old farm were struck by lightning and everything went, house and barns. If the house which had been hauled up the hill with twelve yoke of oxen, had been preserved, I would have been tempted to buy it when I decided to buy a place in Vermont in 1940. But with it gone and nondescript buildings erected in place of all that I remembered, the old farm had little appeal for me. So I was quite content to buy the old Charles White farm two miles east of Grafton village, and we called it River Mowing. It had two hundred fifty acres on both sides of the Saxtons River and a never failing spring up on the hillside back of the house, for which I had a large reservoir built, so we never lacked water. In 1951 I sold this farm as my wife and I decided we preferred

*River Mowing Farm, in Grafton, which Sam bought in 1940.*

living nearer the village in Robin Lawn, which I had bought from the estate of Miss Ella Dwinell, my old Sunday school teacher and distant relative. She had expressed the wish that I do so in her will. After passing through several hands and used mainly as a summer residence, River Mowing became a working dairy farm called Idyll Acres, and is owned by John S. Sidney.

When the farm burned in 1912 after we had sold it to a man named Howe, I wrote the following letter to members of the family, chiefly cousins, and again one of the cousins returned hers to me many years later.

March 9, 1912

To all the Pettengills:

The old homestead that has sheltered three generations of Pettengills and a parson or two before them was burned to the ground last Monday. It is now blotted from our lives forever. Though it passed from our hands by feoffment and grant some four years ago, it was still ours. And so the loss is ours — the loss of an image and ideal from the shrine of our hearts. "Be it ever so humble there's no place like home." Well, so it goes with the world. The gathering dust of the years is constantly sifting down and covering away old associations and memories.

Staunch old house. With its hand-hewn timbers, dove-tailed and foot-square, it was the queen of them all in its youth. Stories of wonderful charm were told by those who loved it — how grandsire Jonathan Pettengill bought it over seventy-five years ago and with twelve yoke of oxen and much shouting and tumult of men moved it upwards of a quarter of a mile. The better part of a week it took while all the town wondered. A great engineering feat, for the route was down and up a considerable hill, steep as Vermont hills go. No neighborhood husking bee or house-raising ever surpassed it for interest. And when, safe and sound, the old parsonage was laid on its new foundations, we can imagine the congratulations that were showered on the Deacon and his good wife.

Fine old house, typical of New England. Out from its kindly shelter went forth the boys to college and to war. There fond hearts waited for news from the front during the long and terrible years while spurs were won and Vermonters showed their mettle. There it remained, a Mecca for the loving pilgrimages of the ones who were out in the world. There lived the terrible termagent whom our uncle married, until toleration became intolerable.

Now it is gone — burned to the ground. No more apple explorations in its ghost-peopled cellar on wintry nights; no more butternut crackings on rainy autumn days in the garret, cluttered and cumbered with spinning wheels and wonderful chests; no more gathering of neighbors 'round the cider glass while things of local state were weighed and determined. The Harrys and Bobbys will never return again from Solomon's Temple, with dinner pails empty and minds full of questions and queries; never again will they climb the hill with Jack to call the cattle home; never again will the Doctor and the Editor and the Helens and Georges drive up to its door with their faces wreathed in smiles. The old homestead is gone. A blessing to those that loved it and in our hearts a solemn benediction.

Samuel B. Pettengill, Jr.

# VII

## MY FATHER

Father was the most just man I ever knew. This must have been due in part to his religious training, but I think it was largely a natural characteristic. I don't recall the slightest feeling of resentment for any punishment that he ever administered — either that I deserved none or got more punishment than I deserved. Slander and malice and criticism of others was foreign to his nature. He always tried to see the other person's point of view. I remember one time at church a young mother had a baby that cried all through the service. I was furious about it, thinking that she should have taken the child out regardless of the freezing winter weather. Father said, "She couldn't have come to church unless she brought her baby, and wouldn't you want her to come to church?" There were no baby sitters in those days unless it was an old aunt or grandma in the family who could take over. I never forgot that mild rebuke. I am sure that Father's attitude of suspended judgment as to the faults of others has influenced my whole life.

The defect of this virtue was, I think, that Father was sometimes too tolerant which led him to put off coming to a decision. He so often said, "With time you can do anything." Father was never in a hurry. Because of this and other characteristics, including great personal modesty, he lacked some of the drive that is so important in making a success of life.

His attitude towards my brother and me was of course largely influenced by the fact that he was both father and mother and for that reason may have been a little more kind than would otherwise have been the case. Even as I think about him all these years after his death, except for his lack of drive, he had no quality which I did not and do not admire. I do not recall ever hearing a profane word or an off-color story falling from his lips. He could, on very rare occasions, become extremely angry, but under such circumstances that you felt it was justified. One time when he was plowing with a team of oxen and the plow was in the furrow, the stupid oxen turned completely around and broke the plow in two. Father was quite furious at this.

As stated elsewhere, Father left Middlebury College to go to the Civil War with a Rhode Island regiment. For this reason his name does not appear on a bronze plaque listing the names of all the Grafton soldiers which is attached to a large rock in front of the Grafton Library. The names which do appear there were apparently taken from military records of Vermont regiments only. I have always regretted that I did not know about the plaque at the time it was being made and so was unable to have Father's name included.

When he returned from war, he spent a semester or perhaps a year at Amherst; then some time at the Theological Seminary at Princeton and later at Andover Theological Seminary in Massachusetts. One of his classmates there was Joseph Cook, who acquired international reputation in the theological world. Another was William Jewett Tucker, later the famous president of Dartmouth College.

Father's first religious work was as a home missionary in the upper Missouri Valley. This must have been about 1866-67. This section was very sparsely settled at the time, and Father drove vast distances like the circuit riders of a former generation. One time he was driving across the prairie in a buckboard when he came to a grazing herd of buffalo. The animals slowly made a path for the horse and buckboard, and when Father was in the center of the herd he said that they seemed to stretch to the horizon in all directions. Naturally this story made a great impression on me in my bow and arrow days. I could easily picture myself riding a broncho bareback and killing buffaloes with my arrows right and left.

Father's first parish was in the Congregational Church at South Royalton, Vermont, where I think he stayed for about three years. In 1954, Helen and I drove there and we took a snapshot of the church. Father was still single when he was there and one of his parishioners was a Mrs. Rix. Years later Father took a couple of days off and drove my brother and me fifty miles or so from Grafton to South Royalton where we stayed overnight with Mrs. Rix. This was in a lull of the Vermont farming in those days, between the end of haying and the beginning of 'tatering. Blackberries were ripe and Mrs. Rix was famous for her steamed puddings cooked in a bag. She had one for us stuffed with luscious blackberries. Of all the things I have eaten in my life, the thought of that pudding makes my mouth water the most.

Father was a profound student of the Bible. He studied Latin, Greek, Hebrew and Sanscrit at college and theological seminary. It would be wrong, of course, to say that he knew the Bible by heart, but I remember his saying at one time that if anybody gave him a brief quote from the Bible, he could identify the book in which it appeared and could give the substance of the lines preceding and following the quote. From the standpoint of his learning and his personal belief in the goodness of God and one's duty toward his neighbors, Father had the foundation for being a noted minister of the gospel. His self-restraint and modesty, however, prevented him from putting fire into his sermons. The ability to lift an audience which Uncle Will possessed, was not in Father's power. Consequently I think it was probably fortunate when he decided to give up the ministry, as his voice was failing him, and go into the editorial field, which was more congenial to his natural characteristics.

He was first editor of the Rutland Herald from 1874 to 1879 and then after his marriage was editor of the St. Alban's Messenger for about three years. Mother, however, could not stand the severe winters in northern Vermont, and this, together with the fact that Uncle Will was out West, led to their going to Portland, Oregon. There Father became the proprietor and editor of the Portland Standard, and later chief editorial writer for the Portland Oregonian, which at that time was probably the most influential paper on the West Coast. Then, just before my mother's death in 1890, Father became editor of the Tacoma Ledger and continued there until 1895, when failing health and the loss of his savings in the crash of all values in the panic of 1893 brought him back to the old farm in Vermont, where he had placed my brother and me with Uncle John three years before.

In reading my father's editorials and articles I have been constantly impressed with his clarity of expression. He was as lucid as a trout stream. He never used five syllable words or foreign phrases to show off his learning. He did not believe that a child needed to study grammar. He held that if a growing child heard good English in the home and read the masters of English prose, the grammar would take care of itself. But he did think it necessary to study words. In the old farm house, we had a big, unabridged dictionary. When I asked the meaning of a word he said, "Look it up in the dictionary." This was something of a chore for a small boy as the book was heavy, but I did as he directed. Then Father would go over it with me and explain the dictionary's explanation. Long before I studied a page of Latin, Father would talk in the most interesting way about the roots from which today's words grew.

In the long winter months Father would often read Shakespeare clear through and repeat a winter or two later. He took a great interest in the Grafton Public Library of which his brother had been an original subscriber and later Treasurer and a Trustee. He himself became a Trustee and when I came back to Grafton to live I gave a large number of books to the library in his memory.

While he shunned all purple patches and decorative writing, Father had a great feeling for words and phrases which were resonant, such as "Far Brought From Out the Storied Past." He loved the sonorous lines in Tennyson's "Ode on the Death of the Duke of Wellington." He said that was not only the greatest thing Tennyson ever wrote, but the equal of any poem in the English language.

Father had a quiet sense of humor which is well illustrated by an incident I heard about when I was in Congress. I received a letter from a gentleman who with his brother, went from Vermont to settle in the west in the late 1880's. I quote from his letter: "Among the fine letters of introduction we had was one from Gov. J. Gregory Smith of Vermont to your father, then editor of the Oregonian, one of the very best papers in that section of the country. Mr. Failing, who was president of the First National Bank of Portland, Oregon, told us to present our letter; that your father was worth knowing and was in contact with all that was going on, so we went. Your father had keen eyes, a shock of grey hair, a desk piled with papers, a big pair of shears, a paste pot, and a floor littered with papers of all kinds. Just the ideal editor's office we had read about. He read the letter, looked us over and said "Yankees." We said, "Yes, and proud of it." Then he started in and gave us the worst tirade against the Yankees and all New England people we had ever heard, so we naturally argued back at every point. We were much disgusted with our interview, but to show him we were game, we invited him to dine with us the next day. He cordially accepted. In the morning we read in the Oregonian, much to our surprise and pleasure, a fine, praiseworthy editorial upon the New England character, one that would delight any Yankee. It was grand. He wrote they were the best class of people in the world and most desirable for settlers in Oregon and the new state of Washington.

"Your father came to meet us, grinning. He had 'worked us' and used some of our arguments. He was freely forgiven and bygones were bygones. He was all Mr. Failing said he would be and proved a delightful and helpful gentleman. I thought perhaps you would be interested in this incident."

I was indeed and recalled with pleasure the many humorous stories Father used to tell about old Grafton when I was a boy, some of which I have written down in these pages.

Father loved books, but he was not a bookworm. He loved to fish and had a fine rod and tackle box. In the fall he was sure to take the old double barrel shotgun down off the hooks and bring back some grey squirrels or partridges. He had an almost telescopic eye for four leaf clovers and seldom walked anywhere along a country road without finding one to a dozen of them. He loved to talk with people older than himself about the early days. It is a pity that he never undertook to write a history of Grafton. No one could have done it better.

Brought up a Republican, he was one of thousands of that party who turned against Blaine in 1884 and elected Cleveland. "Credit Mobilier" and public scandals involving government contracts for levees on the Mississippi River were, he felt, in need of a good bath. After that he continued generally to support the Democratic cause, although he never let party loyalty overbear his own judgment of what was right.

Father was not a back-slapper, but he was always on the courageous and cheerful side of life. Whenever we parted and in all of his letters to me he nearly always said "Be a cheerful spirit."

Although my mother's death and his financial losses were grievous blows, he never complained. Self-pity was a vice unknown to him. His fortitude was like that of the old Romans. When I was a sophomore at college and he was sixty-seven years old, I received a letter saying he was going down to a Boston hospital for an operation and that he hoped I could come and spend a few days with him. These words conveyed a feeling that there was something very ominous and that we might never see each other again. It was in fact, a prostate operation. In 1906 that was considered a very serious operation. But knowing this, Father had put a few things in a satchel, got on a train alone in bitter winter weather and went to a strange hospital and a strange surgeon to face alone whatever might happen. Naturally I followed on the first train. When I reached the hospital, the operation was over and in a few weeks he was up and around again. This sounds pretty grim and bleak in the telling but that is the way Father faced life. Like Mr. Valiant-for-Truth in Bunyan's "Pilgrim's Progress" which he loved so much, he had a supreme confidence that everything would be all right "on the other side." When he died three years later I had inscribed on the marker at his grave the words "Soldier, Clergyman, Editor, Citizen." He was a CITIZEN in the finest meaning of that word.

President Taft said of his father, "My father used to say that the thing you could certainly say about the Vermonter was that he was a SAFE man, upon whom you could count for the things he OUGHT to do, and that he never failed."

This is as fine a thing as can be said of a man, living or dead, and it fits my father to a T.

When you know, without asking, that a man will do the RIGHT thing, even if it costs him some inconvenience in money or effort, you can feel safe with him at all times. I knew I could ALWAYS count on my father.

### DEATH OF SAMUEL BARRETT PETTENGILL
**Newspaper account in the Bellows Falls, Vermont, Times**

Samuel Barrett Pettengill, veteran journalist and clergyman, died at his home of apoplexy October 22, 1909, aged seventy years. He was the survivor of four sons of Deacon Jonathan S. and Sally Barrett Pettengill, and was born at Grafton, Vermont, February 7, 1839.

He had a good ancestry. On his paternal side it went back to a signer of the Declaration of Independence, and still further to a dissenting minister in the west of England. His maternal great-grandfather was Col. John Barrett, who served under General Gates in the Revolution and who was also a member and clerk of the first legislative assembly of Vermont and a founder of the Congregational Church in Springfield. Col. Barrett was one of the earliest settlers of Springfield, Vermont, going there in 1770 and was a large landowner.

While a school boy he helped feed and keep overnight a runaway slave. At that time the thrilling events which led to the Civil War occurred. He participated in a meeting of students to express indignation at the assault on Charles Sumner in the

United States Senate. The Representative John F. Potter who answered the brow beating of the south in Congress with a proposition for a duel with Roger Pryor was his relative. With such a heritage and surroundings it is not strange that he early developed and maintained throughout life a deep interest in all civic affairs and a sober sense of the obligations due from a citizen to the state. This idea, which was thoroughly characteristic, is well expressed in the freeman's oath of the older states, "to assist and be helpful in all the affairs of this jurisdiction, and by all means promote the public welfare of the same, according to your place, ability and opportunity."

He fitted for college at Burr & Burton school at Manchester. He attended Middlebury and Amherst colleges, a member of the D.K.E. and a high stand man. In 1876, Middlebury gave him the Master's degree and throughout life he held a warm interest in all the activities of his Alma Mater.

In 1862, he left the campus for the camp and became a member of Co. B., 7th Squadron, Rhode Island Cavalry. This was the only company in the Civil War entirely composed of college students, and maintaining its esprit de corps as such during the term of enlistment. After a brief but worthy campaign in the Shenandoah Valley in which they participated in the memorable flight from Harper's Ferry, they were mustered out and received in later years the commendations of their commander, General White and also of General Longstreet of the Confederate Army. Of this service Mr. Pettengill wrote a book called "The College Cavaliers." In his closing pages he wrote "In itself, war is simply a cruel handling of human beings by their masters in brutal struggles with each other. It is only when ennobled by a good and just cause, and undertaken as a last resort, that war is not a disgrace to civilized society. The results of the war in which these students engaged are all that makes a remembrance of their service a satisfaction; and this satisfaction is rendered doubly great because the vanquished share equally in these results with the victory. Their success was the triumph of civilization."

Returning from the war Mr. Pettengill studied for the Congregational ministry at Princeton and Andover Theological seminaries. From the latter he was graduated in 1866 and preached for a few years at South Royalton, Vermont.

His voice failing, he turned his attention to journalism and became editor of the Rutland, Vt. Daily Herald, a position he held for a number of years. Here, as elsewhere, he worked for civic betterment and served for some time as a member of the city school board.

In 1879 he became publisher and editor of the St. Albans Messenger. Four years later he went to Portland, Oregon, and became editor of the Portland Standard, and later chief editorial writer for the Portland Oregonian. In 1890 he left for Tacoma, Washington, where he edited the Daily News and the Ledger.

He was married in 1880 at Louisville, Kentucky, to Miss Sue Harry Clagett, a southern woman and gifted writer. Their union was most happy and her early death in 1890 was a blow from which he never recovered.

In 1895, broken in health and fortune, he returned to Vermont and has since lived in retirement.

He was an able writer and scholar, a public speaker who commanded attention, a charming story teller, and a good neighbor and citizen. His personal qualities were such that the things which should accompany old age, as honor, love, obedience, troops of friends, were his in full measure. He was ever loyal to church and state and maintained cordial relations toward his brother journalists and the ministry. Although he suffered many disappointments he never lost hope or faith. He received his hurts and so "God's soldier be he."

He is survived by two sons, Harry C., who had an engineer's training at the University of Vermont and at Washington D.C., and Samuel B. Jr., who graduated from Middlebury College last year and is now a student at Yale Law School.

The funeral was held at 3 P.M. Sunday at the home of Mr. Pettengill's nieces, Misses Fanny and Helen Pettengill of Saxtons River, where he had resided for the past two years and will be greatly missed.

Rev. G. F. Chapin of this place and Rev. Mr. Pennock of Grafton officiated. Two solos were rendered by F. C. Merrifield of Grafton, after which the remains were taken to the village cemetery for burial.

Father is buried in the Saxtons River cemetery in his brother Ed's lot. The latter was the father of my cousins Florence, Fanny and Helen, with whom he was living at the time of his death. Father died on October 22, ~~1910~~ 1909, of apoplexy during the night, apparently without any suffering. I was in my second year at Yale Law School and in New Haven at the time. I have sometimes thought that I would like to have Father's and Mother's coffins disinterred and buried together in Grafton in the same lot in the old Middletown cemetery where his parents

103

are buried, but so much time has elapsed that it probably would not be practical. When Helen and I came to live in Robin Lawn, we decided that we would like to be buried in the Village Cemetery just across the road from the home we love so much, so now we have a lot there where we shall rest, instead of up in Middletown with my ancestors.

*Note:* In the report of Father's death in the Bellows Falls Times just quoted, it said that his ancestry went back to a signer of the Declaration of Independence. This was perhaps on the authority of Cousin Fanny or Helen Pettengill, but I have no knowledge of the truth of this statement. A good many towns signed their own Declarations of Independence at that time. Chester, Vermont, was one. While my father's younger brother was named John Adams Pettengill, I never knew why.

It is a strange coincidence, however, that through my mother's family, I, personally, am connected in a most distant way and only collaterally, with a signer of the Declaration of Independence. Margaret, a daughter of Sir Thomas Adams, Lord Mayor of London, married Col. Edward Claggett and they became the parents of Capt. Thomas Clagett, the first of the name to come to America. His great-uncle, Henry Adams, who was a brother of Sir Thomas Adams, emigrated to this country in 1634, and among his descendants was John Adams, second president of the United States.

# VIII

## THE PETTENGILL FAMILY

The name is variously spelled Pettengill, Pettingell, Pettingill, Pattangill, and Pattangall. This is no doubt due to the fact that many of our ancestors could not write, or if they did, they spelled phonetically. It was not uncommon for them to spell their own names differently, not only on the same day but in the same document! It was the sound that was important, not the spelling. Regardless of spelling, all those bearing the name in this country trace back to the same progenitor, Richard Pettingell.

1. *Richard Pettingell* was born in Norfolk, England, about 1620 and came to Salem, Mass., sometime before 1640, for in that year he was a freeman in the colony. This was a dignity allowed only to members of the church after being recommended as worthy by the minister. Salem town records show him to have been the holder of considerable property. Around 1644 he married Joanna Ingersoll, daughter of the Richard Ingersoll reputed to have built the house which was the original of Hawthorne's House of the Seven Gables. They moved to Wenham shortly afterwards and their first two children were born there. In 1651 he bought a plantation in Newbury where he lived until his death in 1695, two years after that of his wife. They had four children who lived, Samuel, Matthew, Mary and Nathaniel, and Matthew is considered to be the direct ancestor of my line.

2. *Matthew Pettingell*, second son of Richard and Joanna Ingersoll Pettingell, was born in Wenham, Mass., about 1648. He married in Newbury on April 13, 1674, Sarah, daughter of Nicholas and Mary Cutting Noyes. They had seven sons and four daughters. Newbury land records show he was still living in 1710, but the date of his death is unknown.

We now come to a family mystery which has yet to be solved. The compiler of the Pettingell Genealogy, John Mason Pettingell, died before completing it and his brother, Charles I. Pettingell, arranged his notes for publication. He stated that he could not find the name of the third generation Pettingell who fathered my direct ancestor, Nathaniel, of the fourth generation, but was sure that his brother believed him to have been a son of second generation Matthew and a grandson of the first Pettingell, Richard. He said that his brother had carried many facts about which he was certain in his head instead of putting them in writing, and that there were several instances of this nature that were puzzling to him in getting the genealogy ready for publication after his brother's death. Then occasionally some casual note gave him the clue he needed. However, since he had no documentary proof of Nathaniel's parentage, he decided to give him a separate section in the book.

I have personally made many efforts to trace Nathaniel's parentage but have everywhere run into a dead end. Perhaps some time, some place, the puzzle may be solved. In the meantime I have a theory which seems plausible to me, as family tradition has always had it that Nathaniel was Richard Pettingell's great-grandson, and that Matthew was his grandfather.

3. According to the genealogy, the first child born to Matthew and Sarah Noyes Pettingell was a boy, born June 10, 1674, no name given and the remark alongside the date was "probably died young." However, since there is so much detailed information about all their other children, one may guess that this child, born too soon after his parents' marriage, might have been an embarrassment to them and was possibly given to a relative or friend to be brought up elsewhere. In 1676 a second son, Nathaniel, was born on January 21, and on November 18, 1678, a third son, Matthew was born. These were followed by four more sons and four daughters. All of these eleven children of the third generation were born in Newbury and with the exception of the first-born they all lived there and their lives are fully documented. But when my direct

ancestor, Nathaniel of the fourth generation, was married in 1720, he gave Marblehead as his home. To me this gives credence to my theory that the first born son lived and was brought up away from Newbury. Having been born in 1674, he would have been old enough to have fathered Nathaniel about 1700. Another mysterious fact is that when Nathaniel married Susanna Abbott in Andover, Mass., on July 14, 1720, the record of the marriage on file in several places gives neither the names of his parents nor his birthdate, although those of his wife are given.

So unless time disproves my theory, I consider it a possible solution to the puzzle.

4. *Nathaniel Pettengill* was apparently the first to spell his name Pettengill and his descendants all seem to have spelled the name this way. He was supposedly born about 1700 and on July 14, 1720, he married Susannah, daughter of Joseph and Sarah Devereaux Abbott of Andover. She had been baptized on August 10, 1701, at Marblehead, Mass., where her father was later Collector of Customs. Nathaniel and Susannah had five sons, and Joseph, the oldest, was my great-great-great-grandfather. No date is given for Nathaniel's death, but on July 5, 1763, "Nathaniel, gentleman, Nathaniel, Jr. yeoman, and John, cordwainer, all of Methuen, agreed upon the division of a farm." Also it appears that Nathaniel was still living in 1769, for in that year Methuen documents refer to a grandson, born in 1744, as Nathaniel, 3rd.

5. *Joseph Pettengill* was born at Andover, Mass., on January 30, 1720. On September 5, 1740, he married at Methuen, Mass., Elizabeth Lancaster. They had eight children, the third son, Abbott, being my great-great-grandfather, born February 12, 1746, in Methuen. The town records shown a Joseph and Elizabeth Pettengill selling land in Methuen on April 21, 1769. No dates are given for their deaths.

6. *Abbott Pettengill* born February 12, 1746 in Methuen, Mass. He married Hannah Page of Methuen, born about 1745.

They lived in Salem, N.H., which once was part of Methuen, and all of their eight children were born there. Land transfers are on record there in 1772, 1777 and 1792. In 1775 he was second Lieutenant of the South Company of the town militia, and served 26 days as sergeant in Capt. Gage's company of Col. Gates' regiment, which joined the Continental Army in Rhode Island in 1778. He was a Selectman of Salem from 1781 to 1783 and held other town offices. He died about 1797, and his widow several years later. They are both buried in the old Village Cemetery in the center of the town. Their graves are just inside the gate, straight back about 200 feet, and a few years ago I put a bronze marker "Soldier-American Revolution" at his grave. Their first son, Peter, was my great-grandfather. They had seven other children in addition to Peter: Eliza, Joseph, Sarah, Jonathan, Amos, John and Hannah.

7. *Peter Pettengill* was born in Salem, N.H. on August 5, 1769. I have already described in my chapter "Boyhood in Vermont" how in 1787, when he was only eighteen years old, he walked all the way from Salem to settle in Grafton, Vermont. On July 10, 1798, he married Hannah Stickney, born December 26, 1768. She was the daughter of Deacon David and Keziah Butterfield Stickney of Grafton, among the earliest settlers of Grafton. Keziah, who had been born in Chelmsford, Mass., on February 25, 1733, was the daughter of David and Keziah Shuttleworth Butterfield and in 1755 had married Benjamin Shed, born on December 17, 1727. In 1760 he died leaving her with three children, Benjamin, David and Keziah. She married David Stickney, born January 5, 1732 on January 3, 1765 and they lived in Billerica, Mass. where their six children were born. In 1781 they moved to Grafton, Vt., being among the first settlers to go there, and brought with them their own six children and the three Shed children.

Peter and Hannah Stickney Pettengill lived in a house he built on the Stickney farm on Middletown hill. Their three children were all born there; Abbott on April 29, 1799; Jonathan, my grandfather, on July 26, 1801, and Elizabeth on

*The Peter Pettengill House in Grafton, built in 1820.*

September 12, 1809. The house was located about an eighth of a mile southeast of the fine brick house Peter eventually built in 1820, and the original Middletown road went right by it. I have seen the cellar hole. The bricks for the new house were made by Peter and his son Abbott in their brick kiln nearby.

> Editor's note: Fortunately the brick house was always occupied and remained in fairly good condition until bought by its present owners, Mr. & Mrs. John Kenedy, who have restored it to its original appearance and it is now one of the most beautiful houses in Grafton.

Peter was a farmer, carpenter and surveyor and his fine surveyor's compass, made about 1775, is one of my most cherished possessions. He died on December 19, 1857. His wife Hannah had died fifteen years earlier, on May 21, 1842. Both are buried in the old Middletown cemetery.

8. *Abbott Pettengill* first child of Peter and Hannah Pettengill, was born April 29, 1799, in Grafton; died there December 7, 1867. He married Martha Park Clark of Grafton, born December 9, 1801; died August 14, 1868. She was the widow of Dr. Randall Clark of Windham, Vt., by whom she had two sons, Richard Clark, born December 20, 1824; married Lorane Fay of Boston on March 14, 1855. No children. He died September 20, 1894. The second son was Henry Miles Clark, born December 15, 1825; married Louisa Walker, daughter of Stephen and Louise Barrett Walker and a niece of Capt. John Barrett of Grafton. They had one son, Everett, born in 1860 who never married.

Abbott and Martha Pettengill had two children, James Dascomb, born January 9, 1838 and Martha Ann, born September 10, 1842, who died unmarried on October 10, 1865. Sometime after his mother's death, Abbott and Martha moved from his nearby farm across the river which is now owned by Hardy Merrill, to his father's house and lived there until his own death on December 7, 1867. His wife Martha died on August 14, 1868, and the homestead was then sold out of the family. Both are buried in the Grafton Village Cemetery.

*Jonathan Pettengill, my grandfather, and his wife, Sally Barrett Pettengill. From daguerreotypes taken about 1860.*

8. *Jonathan Pettengill*, my grandfather, son of Peter and Hannah Pettengill, was born in Grafton July 26, 1801. On January 18, 1832, he married Altha Foote, daughter of Martin and Hannah Dean Foote of Middlebury, who was born there on July 22, 1806. They had one child, Mary Emma, born March 3, 1833. Two weeks later, on March 19, 1833, his young wife died and a year or so afterwards he returned with his child to live in Grafton. On July 5, 1836, he married Sally Barrett of Springfield, Vt. She was born on September 8, 1806, the daughter of Thomas and Betsey Bates Barrett. Jonathan and Sally Pettengill had five children, Edward Henry, Samuel Barrett, John Adams, George Thomas and Sarah Elizabeth. Jonathan was a Deacon in the Congregational Church. He died on December 26, 1867, and Sally on October 24, 1889. They are both buried in Middletown Cemetery.

8. *Elizabeth Pettengill*, daughter of Peter and Hannah Stickney Pettengill was born in Grafton September 12, 1809. She married Merrick Larned and they had one child, William Larned, born near Toronto, Canada, on January 1, 1846. Elizabeth died at Judsonia, Ark., February 16, 1889.

9. *James Dascomb Pettengill,* son of Abbott and Martha Clark Pettengill, born January 9, 1838. On March 7, 1866 he married Celia Ann Burgess of Grafton, born January 6, 1845. They lived in the former Abbott Pettengill house until they moved to Clarksville, Va., about 1870. She died there on December 22, 1884, and he in January, 1901. Their daughter, Martha Maud, born in Grafton July 3, 1868, married Rev. Edgar Allen Potts in Clarksville. They had a son, Joseph Dascomb Potts, and a daughter who died in infancy.

9. *Mary Emma Pettengill,* daughter of Jonathan Pettengill by his first wife, Altha Foote Pettengill, was born in Middlebury, Vt., on March 3, 1833. She died March 24, 1866. She married Rev. Jeremiah N. Diament, a Presbyterian clergyman, who was born at Cedarville, N.J., October 4, 1829, and died June 22, 1894. They had two children, Mary Altha Diament, born August 10, 1861 and Calvin Edwards Diament, born December 29, 1863. He died at Stanton, Mich., February 15, 1871. Mary Altha Diament, lived with my Uncle John for three years, taking care of my brother and me when we first were brought to Grafton. Later she went out to the Indian Territory to teach. I don't think she ever married.

9. *Edward Henry Pettengill,* eldest son of Jonathan and Sally Pettengill, was born in Grafton on May 14, 1837. He fitted for college at Burr Seminary in Manchester, Vt., and entered Middlebury College with the class of 1862. A severe illness at the end of his second year prevented his graduation but in 1877 he was awarded a Master of Arts degree by the college. He enlisted in Company D, 16th Vermont Regiment, and served through the Gettysburg campaign. After an honorable discharge he began the study of medicine under Dr. Daniel Campbell in Saxtons River. He was graduated from Harvard Medical College in 1867, one of the signers of his certificate being Dr. Oliver Wendell Holmes. He then took courses at the University of Vermont and the College of Physicians and Surgeons in New York City. In 1869 he began the practice of medicine in partnership with Dr. Campbell in Saxtons River, and was continuously in practice there until his death on Feb-

Dr. Edward H. Pettengill

Dr. Ed's home and office in Saxtons River, Vermont.

ruary 8, 1900. He was a charter member of E. H. Stoughton Post, G.A.R. at Bellows Falls; was the first U.S. Pension Examiner in his part of the state and acted as sole examiner for four years until the formation of the Board of Examiners on which he served for many years. At one time he was President of the Vermont Medical Society. He occupied many public offices in town, among them Superintendent of Schools, Health Officer and Trustee of the Rockingham Free Library. (I recall with some interest that he was physician to the famous Hetty Green who had a home in Bellows Falls, and have often wondered whether she ever paid for his services.) On May 21, 1868, he married Rhoda Jane Wilder of Keene, N.H., born July 26, 1831, the daughter of Abijah and Rhoda Sanger Wilder. Dr. Ed's children were:

George Thomas, born July 11, 1869; died 1923. Married Jennie Louise Bunnell of New York City on December 28, 1898. They had two sons, John, born September 17 1902; died June, 1917, and Robert Bunnell, born March 6, 1904.

Fanny Mabel, born September 22, 1870; died December 18, 1958.

Florence Wilder, born January 23, 1872; died June 5, 1941.

Edward Barrett, born November 18, 1874; died January 19, 1917.

Helen Barrett, born August 4, 1878; died April 22, 1945.

None of the daughters ever married. Robert married and has a number of children.

9. *Samuel Barrett Pettengill,* my father, born February 7, 1839. On December 22, 1880, he married in Louisville, Ky., Susan Geigir Harry Clagett, born at Upper Marlboro, Maryland, on March 23, 1843. They had two sons, Harry Clagett and myself. She died August 15, 1890, at Osburne, Idaho. She is buried in Riverview Cemetery, Portland, Ore., in the lot she and my father bought in 1887 when her stepmother died. My father died in Saxtons River on October 21, 1909, where he had been living with his brother Ed's family. He is buried in the Edward H. Pettengill lot in the Saxtons River Cemetery.

*John Adams Pettengill, my uncle.*

9. *John Adams Pettengill,* born November 23, 1840, in Grafton. On June 19, 1883, he married Helen Bradford, daughter of Rev. Moses Bradford, Grafton's fourth Congregational minister. There were no children. The marriage was not a happy one and in a few years they separated and she went to Buffalo to live with her father. They were never divorced. My uncle John was a farmer and lived all his life in the family homestead on Middletown Hill. He was a stockholder in the Grafton Library Society until in 1874 it turned the stock over to the town and became the Grafton Public Library. From 1874 to 1892 he was the Treasurer of the Library and a Trustee. He was a charter member of the Grafton Grange and held a number of town offices. From 1900 to 1902 he represented Grafton in the State Legislature. He died on October 21, 1906, and is buried in Middletown Cemetery.

9. *George Thomas Pettengill,* born March 20, 1845; died April 10, 1867. He never married. After his father's death in 1861,

Major John Dwinell of Grafton, a distant relative, was appointed his guardian.

9. *Sarah Elizabeth Pettengill,* born May 12, 1847; died September 18, 1848.

10. *Harry Clagett Pettengill* born in Portland, Ore., September 30, 1884. Died in Somerville, N.J., February 20, 1963, and is buried there. He attended Vermont Academy and was graduated from the University of Vermont in 1907 as an electrical engineer. Married on September 8, 1926, Elizabeth Love, daughter of Rev. William W. Love, an Episcopal clergyman, and his wife Ann, of Cambridge, Mass. Their son, Harry Clagett Pettengill, Jr., was born July 24, 1933, at Roselle Park, N.J.

10. *Samuel Barrett Pettengill, Jr.,* born in Portland, Ore., January 19, 1886. Attended Burr & Burton Academy in Manchester, Vt. and Vermont Academy in Saxtons River from which he was graduated in 1904. Graduated from Middlebury College in 1908 and from Yale Law School in 1911. On June 1, 1912, married at Napoleon, Ohio, Josephine Strahorn Campbell, born there October 21, 1888. Practiced law in South Bend, Ind., and was elected to Congress in November, 1930. Had one daughter, Susan Harry Pettengill, born in South Bend, June 21, 1917. Josephine Pettengill died on June 26, 1948. On July 16, 1949, at New York City, married Mrs. Helen Ball Charles, born there January 30, 1897. Retired to Grafton, Vt., in June, 1956. Died March 20, 1974, and is buried in Grafton Village Cemetery.

11. *Susan Harry Pettengill,* only child of Samuel and Josephine Pettengill. Born in South Bend, Ind., June 21, 1917. Married Thomas B. Douglas at Washington, D.C. on November 28, 1949. No children.

11. *Harry Clagett Pettengill, Jr.,* only child of Harry C. and Ann Love Pettengill. Born in Roselle Park, New Jersey, on July 24, 1933. Attended M.I.T. and is a graduate of Rutgers College

and has a postgraduate degree from the University of Chicago. On September 16, 1967, married Dolores Serna of Chicago. They have two children, Rachel and Eric and reside in Chicago.

# IX

# MY BARRETT ANCESTORS

Both my father and I had Barrett for a middle name. His mother had been Sally Barrett, born September 8, 1806, daughter of Thomas and Betsey Bates Barrett of Springfield. She was the grand-daughter of the famous Col. John Barrett who once owned almost all of Springfield, Vermont. He went there from Connecticut in 1770, began buying land including a large tract along the Connecticut River, and by 1772 had built on it a large house on what was called the Blockhouse Farm. It is still standing and is the first frame house erected in Springfield.

The name Barrett came from the old French word "barat" meaning strife. The name has been variously spelled Barat, Baret, Beret, Barrit and Barrett. A Barat was on the Battle Abbey Roll as a follower of William the Conqueror. A coat of arms was assigned to the American colonist, Humphrey Barrett, who was born in England in 1592. He sailed for America sometime before 1639, and first settled in Plymouth, Mass. He brought with him his wife and three sons, John, Thomas and Humphrey, Jr. John later established his home in Marlboro, Mass., while Thomas and Humphrey, Jr. became citizens of Concord, Mass. The Barretts of Concord acquired a tract of land amounting to three hundred acres in what is now the heart of the city.

1. *Humphrey Barrett,* born in England in 1592. Came to Plymouth, Mass. sometime before 1639, and in 1640 settled in Concord. Was a Freeman in 1657. He died in November, 1662. He had three sons, John, Thomas and Humphrey, Jr. Dates of birth of John and Thomas not known, nor those of their descendants. Thomas drowned in the Concord River in 1660,

leaving a son, Thomas, and others. However, I am concerned only with Humphrey, Jr. and his descendants.

2. *Humphrey Barrett, Jr.* He was always called Deacon Humphrey. He was born in England in 1627, and died in Concord, Mass., in 1713. The records show a second wife named Mary Potter in 1675. He had three sons, Joseph, Benjamin and John. Joseph was born in 1678 and died in 1763. He was the direct ancestor of Grafton's Capt. John Barrett about whom I will write later. There are no birthdates for either Benjamin or John. John was my direct ancestor.

3. *John Barrett* married Rebecca Collins of Boston and apparently lived there, as their son, Col. John Barrett, was born there on December 3, 1731. He was a merchant. Historical records state "John Barrett & Sons' store in Boston was robbed, along with five other shops, of goods worth several thousand pounds sterling shortly after March 10, 1776. This was done under orders from General Howe to keep the goods from being used by the rebels."

4. *John Barrett (Col.)* born in Boston, December 3, 1731; died December 3, 1806. On June 19, 1755, he married Elizabeth Edwards, born in 1733. She was the daughter of Thomas Edwards of Boston, a descendant of Thomas Edwards, the original proprietor of Dunstable, Mass. About the time of their marriage they moved to Middletown, Conn., where he was engaged in trade. Later they moved to Wethersfield, Conn., and in 1770 he went to Springfield, Vt., and began negotiating for land. He bought, among others a large tract of land on the Connecticut River just north of the present Cheshire Bridge known as the Blockhouse Farm. Here he started the building of a large house which is still standing and was the first frame house erected in Springfield. In the fall of 1772 he moved to Springfield with his family and shortly afterwards completed the building of his house.

The land on which the house stands was first conveyed to a Gideon Lyman at a proprietor's meeting on November 10,

1762. On March 2, 1771, Lyman and others deeded this and many other tracts to John Barrett and Gale Bishop. Bishop conveyed his interests to several others who in turn conveyed their interests to Richard Morris on February 23, 1773, and on the same day Morris, by deed of that date, conveyed his interests to John Barrett. Some of these transactions had taken place partly under the original charter, but when the confirmation was obtained from New York in 1772, Col. Barrett was named as an original proprietor. There was much trading in land in those days, and Col. Barrett owned a great deal of land in the Skitchewaug meadows and on the mountain, as well as the Black River meadows on both sides of the river, timber lots and pasture lots, a grist mill and a saw mill. In 1772 he was the owner of the whole present center of the town of Springfield. That same year, however, he sold the portion on the west side of the river to William Lockwood. His real estate at the time of his death was appraised at $22,500, a large sum in those days.

Col. Barrett was a member and Clerk of the Cumberland County Committee of Safety in 1775. What was then Cumberland County consisted of the present Windham and Windsor counties. At Ticonderoga he was Captain in Colonel Seth Warner's regiment and took part in the Quebec expedition. He was commissioned Lt. Colonel of the Upper Regiment of the Cumberland on January 4, 1776. On September 7, 1776 he received orders from General Gates to construct a bridge over the Otter River at Rutland and build a road from the east side of Mt. Independence to join the old Crown Point Road at Castleton, and he completed this mission.

Col. Barrett took a leading part in the contests over the New Hampshire grants, the last titles and claims under New York not being cleared until 1795. He was a very active and influential man in the business and town affairs of Springfield, and held all the important town offices. In 1777 he was a delegate to the first Vermont State convention sitting in Windsor and in 1778, 1781 and 1782 represented the town in the General Assembly. He was the first Master of the first Masonic Lodge in Vermont which was located in Springfield in 1781. He was one of the original members of the Congregational Church and very active in its work.

Col. Barrett drowned in the Connecticut River on December 3, 1806, and was buried on his own land near the home he had built in 1772. Known as the Blockhouse Farm, it is located on Route 5, a little less than a mile north of the Cheshire Bridge between Springfield and Charlestown. Formerly the road ran between the house and the river; now the road runs in front of the house. It was called the Blockhouse Farm because a blockhouse had been built on the land in 1759 at the Wentworth Ferry, just north of the present Cheshire Bridge. The old stone blockhouse was sixteen feet high and was built as a protection for the eight hundred men building the nearby Crown Point Road under Lord Amherst and General Goffe. It was long ago washed away by the river together with the land on which it stood.

In 1966, my wife and I called on the present occupant of the house, Mrs. Stella Butterfield Walsh, then aged eight-five. Her grandfather, Jonas Butterfield, bought the property in 1854 from the son of Judge Jonathan Whipple, who had bought it from the Barrett estate in 1816. Thus only three families have lived in this fine old house since it was built in 1772.

> Ed. Note: Mrs. Walsh was still alive and living in the house in 1978!

The house was quite a pretentious one for its time. It measures 41 by 39 feet and there is a cellar under the entire house. There are two enormous chimneys, one of which measures five feet, three inches, by three feet, six inches at the attic floor. When in 1947 a fire destroyed a large two-story ell across the back which contained six rooms, and spread to the house, the front half of the house was saved by the huge stone chimneys. Mrs. Walsh had the rear of the house rebuilt as it had been originally, but not the ell. The house had seven fireplaces, four of which are in working order. There are four large rooms on each floor, and the center hall upstairs from front to back is

*Colonel John Barrett's house in Springfield, Vermont. Built in 1772, the house retains its original appearance except for the addition of a porch which is shown in the photo below. The lower photo was taken about 1890.*

twenty-eight feet long and eight and a half feet wide. In 1890 a porch was built across the front and left side of the house, but in all other respects it looks as it did when my great-great-grandfather lived in it.

The famous Crown Point Road went through Barrett woodland of which three hundred acres were sold in 1899 to the Diamond Match Company. There is a marker on the west side of Route 5 showing where the road started up the mountain. It was placed there in 1909 by the Lewis Morris Chapter of the DAR. General Lewis Morris was the son of Judge Richard Morris, an old friend of Col. Barrett and fellow investor in land. In 1795, General Lewis Morris built a fine home which is still standing on land which adjoined the Barrett property to the south, on what is called the Connecticut River Road.

When the Barrett property was sold to Judge Whipple in 1816, two rods square were reserved around the graves of Col. Barrett and his wife. Some time after his purchase, Judge Whipple obtained permission to have the bodies reinterred in the center, south side of Springfield's Summer Hill Cemetery. There, because of his foresight and care, their burial place is forever secure. Carved on a tall, grey, double stone are the words:

> John Barrett, Esq.
> died Dec. 3, 1806
> AE 75. also
> Elizabeth, his Wife
> died August 27,
> 1809, AE 76.
> While in one grave in
> Death they lay,
> Their spirits immortal
> We trust, in heaven rest.

When John Barrett moved to Springfield in 1772, he brought with him not only his wife and four children, all born in Middletown, Conn., but also a negro girl named Rose, bought by him in Wallingford, Conn., in 1770. She lived with the family for many years and later in a little log house which was all her own. She was known as "Old Rose" and much respected throughout the town.

5. *John Barrett,* son of Col. John and Elizabeth Barrett, born August 16, 1756. Entered Dartmouth College but left there and was graduated from Harvard College in 1780. He studied law with Benjamin West at Charlestown, N.H., and then located at Northfield, Mass., and died there in 1816. He married Martha Dickinson of Westfield, Mass., and they had four children:

*Mary,* born 1791; married Woodbury Storer of Portland, Maine.

*Another daughter,* married Franklin Ripley of Greenfield, Mass.

*Charles E.,* born 1803; graduated from Bowdoin College in 1822; lived in Portland, Maine.

*Another daughter,* married, Rev. Dr. Shepard, of Bristol, Conn.

5. *Thomas Barrett,* born February 10, 1760. Educated at Yale College; studied surveying with Col. Simon Stevens, and after the latter's death did most of the surveying in Springfield, besides being County Surveyor. He was Town Clerk and Selectman for several years and was prominent in town affairs and much respected. On July 25, 1791, he married Betsey Bates, daughter of Lt. Roger and Huldah Stoddard Bates. He died on May 31, 1838, and Betsey died September 23, 1850. They had eight children:

*Thomas T.,* born January 22, 1792. He graduated from the medical department of Dartmouth College, and studied medicine with Dr. Moses Cobb. He first located in Walpole, N.H., and then in Chester, Vt., where he became a successful practitioner and prominent man. He was Associate Judge of Windsor County Court from 1845 to 1849. He married Nancy Grout and they had three children:

Rockwood, born August 5, 1820
William G., born December 12, 1822
Juliette P. born August 30, 1826. Married Foster Howe.

*Elizabeth,* born August 7, 1794; died August 10, 1875. She was familiarly and affectionately called "Aunt Betsey" by young and old of two generations and was a noted woman in Springfield. She attended school on the Common and later the Eureka school, and became a teacher in the district schools for many years. She was a strong minded woman with the courage of her convictions and many stories were told about her, some of which, told me by my father. I have related in my chapter entitled "Boyhood in Vermont." She never married and lived with her sister Mary for many years. They died within three days of each other in 1875.

*Mary,* born March 24, 1799; died August 7, 1875.

*Sarah,* born May 20, 1802; died November 8, 1803

*Samuel,* Sarah's twin, born May 20, 1802; died August 24, 1888. He married Sarah Blake of Boston; they moved to New Orleans, La., where he became a prosperous cotton dealer, and mayor of the city.

*George Washington,* born August 4, 1804, died February 5, 1813.

*Sally,* my grandmother. Born September 8, 1806; died October 24, 1889. Married Jonathan Stickney Pettengill July 5, 1836. They had five children:
    Edward H., born May 14, 1837; died February 8, 1900. Became a doctor in Saxtons River, Vt. Married Rhoda Wilder, of Keene, N.H. Had five children:
        George Thomas, born July 11, 1869.
        Fanny Mabel, born September 22, 1870.
        Florence Wilder, born July 23, 1872.
        Edward Barrett Sanger, born November 18, 1874.
        Helen Barrett, born August 4, 1878.
    Samuel Barrett, my father. Born July 7, 1839; died

October 21, 1909. Married Susan Clagett. Had two sons:
- Harry Clagett, born September 30, 1884.
- Samuel Barrett, Jr., born January 19, 1886.

John Adams, born November 23, 1840. Died October 21, 1906. Married Helen Bradford.

George Thomas, born March 28, 1845; died April 10, 1867.

Sarah Elizabeth, born May 12, 1847; died Sept. 18, 1849.

*Nancy*, born September 21, 1808. Married on October 20, 1834, Thomas Harkness Smiley, born May 4, 1804. He was a son of Rev. Robinson Smiley, famous pastor of the Springfield Congregational Church for twenty-four years, and was always called "Father Smiley." His wife, known as "Mother Smiley," was a quiet woman who knew her own mind and usually got her own way. She was extremely well read, and when Father Smiley decided to build his new home above Summer Hill, she wanted it to stand true with the compass. When it was staked out, she went home and told her husband it was all wrong. He spoke to the workmen who maintained they were right and she was wrong. Father Smiley reported this to his wife, who said nothing. But that night, there being a brightly shining moon, she left her husband and all the little Smileys asleep in their beds, stole out of the house and up the hill, and moved all the stakes to where she wanted them. She said nothing until it was too late to change her civil engineering, and Father Smiley always delighted in telling how his wife got the best of him. The beautiful brick house was built in 1816, and its last occupant was Senator Ralph Flanders who modernized and made additions to it. Thomas Smiley was first a merchant in Springfield, but in 1842 moved his family to Knoxville, Tenn. He died August 2, 1866. They had two children:

George Robinson, born July 25, 1835; died October 20, 1844.

Harriet Elizabeth, born May 14, 1838. Married on

November 20, 1866, William Albert Henderson, a prominent attorney in Knoxville. They had two children:
    Mary, born September 4, 1867.
    Anne, born July 15, 1868.

5. *Elizabeth Barrett,* first daughter of Col. John and Elizabeth Barrett, born August 10, 1758. Married Rev. Isaiah Potter of Lebanon, N.H. They had three sons: John, who became a lawyer in Augusta, Maine; Barrett, a lawyer and later a judge in Portland, Maine, and Thomas who always lived in Lebanon. A son of John's, John Fox Potter, born in Augusta on May 11, 1817, was admitted to the bar in 1837 and moved to Wisconsin. He served three terms in Congress from that state, 1837 to 1863. Barrett Potter's second daughter, Mary Storer Potter, married Henry Wadsworth Longfellow, the poet, in September, 1831. They went abroad in 1835 and she died in Rotterdam, Holland, in November of that same year. Longfellow refers to her death in his poem "Footsteps of Angels."

5. *May Barrett,* the fourth and last child of Col. John and Elizabeth Barrett, was born October 27, 1765. She married Arthur McLellan of Portland, Maine.

# X

# ANOTHER ANCESTOR, LT. ROGER BATES

Roger Bates was my other great-great-grandfather in Springfield. He was the father of my grandmother's mother, Betsey Bates Barrett.

He was born in Scotland, on November 11, 1745, came to America and lived in Hingham, Mass., and later in Boston. Then he moved to Winchendon and finally to Springfield, Vt., about 1777 or 1778. He had served in the Revolutionary War and was always called Lt. Bates. He married Huldah Stoddard and four of his thirteen children were born before he came to Springfield.

He settled in the Eureka District, which until about 1800 was the center of the Springfield settlement, and bought the farm of Joseph Little, which was close to the old Crown Point Road. Little had built his frame house to be a store and tavern as well as his home, and Lt. Bates continued with these activities. Town meetings and church services were held there, and in 1781 the Congregational Church was organized there with sixteen members. Later that year it was voted to build a meeting house on Lt. Bates' pea ground which he gave for that purpose. The house was to be 28 by 26 feet with 14 foot posts. The men were to have three shillings a day for their work. After the frame was up funds were not forthcoming to pay the bills and the work stopped. By 1789 there was still no meeting house, but in 1790 it was decided to build the new meeting house down on the Common in the present center of Springfield, as people were beginning to move down there. Lt. Bates was so grieved that the meeting house was not set on his pea ground, handy to his store and tavern, that he finally sold his place to Joseph Ellis and in 1797 moved to Canada where he died in 1825 at the age of eighty. His wife lived to be over ninety. They had thirteen children, three of whom died in infancy. Their second child, Betsey, born on November 25, 1770, was my great-grandmother. She married Thomas Barrett on June 25, 1791.

# XI

# CAPT. JOHN BARRETT OF GRAFTON

It is a strange coincidence that a Capt. John Barrett settled in Grafton in 1805, coming from Mason, N.H. He became one of Grafton's leading citizens and his name is still a household word in town. I did not know there was any connection between him and my grandmother's Springfield family until I started looking up my Barrett ancestry and found that both branches were descended from a common ancestor, Humphrey Barrett. Because Capt. John Barrett's name is so well known in Grafton, my own home town, I think it appropriate to include his ancestry here, and show the relationship to my direct ancestor, Col. John Barrett of Springfield. Col. Barrett was a first cousin of Capt. John Barrett's grandfather. Their fathers were brothers, sons of Deacon Humphrey Barrett, Jr. Of his three sons, John was the father of Col. Barrett and Joseph was the great-grandfather of Capt. John Barrett. See foregoing chapter "My Barrett Ancestors." The line of descent is as follows:

*Humphrey Barrett,* born in England 1592; died in Concord, Mass. 1662. He was the father of

*Deacon Humphrey Barrett, Jr.* born in England, 1627; died in Concord, Mass. 1715. By his second wife he had three sons, Joseph, Benjamin and John. The direct ancestor of Capt. John Barrett was

*Capt. Joseph Barrett* born 1678; died 1763. He was a farmer in Concord, Mass. In 1701 married Rebecca Minot, born 1685; died 1738. He was the father of

*John Barrett* born 1720; died 1790. He was a farmer in Concord. His wife was Lois Brooks. He was the father of

*Capt. Joseph Barrett,* born 1745; died 1831. He was a farmer in Mason, N.H., and a prominent man in Mason at time of Revolution. By his first wife, Sarah Brooks, born 1751; died 1794, he had nine children. His second son was Capt. John Barrett.

> *Joseph Barrett,* born January 25, 1774; died November, 1852. Farmer in New Ipswich, N.H. had two daughters.
>
> *Capt. John Barrett,* born August 21, 1775; died August 22, 1857. Merchant in Grafton, Vt. Married Lucy Joslin on December 22, 1822. She was born 1785; died 1866. They had four children, Lucy, John Humphrey, Susan Hall, and Charles.
>
> *Elisha Barrett,* born December 7, 1776; died 1857. Farmer in Mason, N.H. Sons were George Minot Barrett and Brooks Barrett. George worked for his uncle in Grafton and in 1841 built his own store, present Grafton Village Store.

There were two more sons, both died young, and four daughters. By his second wife, Leah, Capt. Joseph Barrett had two more children, Asa, born April 5, 1800; a farmer in Harrisville, N.H., and a daughter Louisa, born September 26, 1810, married Stephen Walker, a farmer in Grafton, Vt.

## XII

## PREPARATORY SCHOOL

Father and Uncle Ed had gone to Burr & Burton Academy in Manchester, Vt., in the 1850's. At that time it was called Burr Seminary and I have a copy of the graduation exercises in 1857 when my father gave the commencement oration in Greek! So in the summer of 1900, the decision was made that my brother Harry and I would enter Burr & Burton. This we did. I was fourteen at the time and up until then had attended the one-room Pettengill school down the hill from where we lived in Grafton. Both Harry and I had to work at Burr & Burton in order to help pay our way. Harry fired the furnace in the boiler room and I sawed cordwood and mowed lawns and trimmed the walks on the campus.

At the end of the year I spent the summer in Manchester, continuing to work at the Academy for my room and working on other lawns in the village, for which I earned ten cents an hour. This enabled me to pay a few bills. And at the end of the summer, which was my first summer away from home, I had about thirteen dollars.

For our second year in school, it was decided that we should go to Vermont Academy at Saxtons River. It was agreed that at the end of my summer in Manchester, Uncle John would start driving towards Manchester on a certain day, and that I would take the stage from Manchester to Peru, and then walk until we met. But I wanted to save the stage coach fare and in addition wanted to surprise my uncle. So I got up very early that morning and walked the twelve miles up the mountain to Peru, where I went into the store to buy some crackers and cheese. I accidentally broke a pane of the old thin glass in the showcase on the counter by leaning on it. The owner said it would cost

*Harry and Sam Pettengill at Burr & Burton Academy in 1900.*

me seventy-five cents. This was a tragic event. I had hidden my precious thirteen dollars in my shoe for fear of robbers and had the humiliation of taking off my shoe and peeling off one of my hard earned dollar bills.

The store in Peru is still running and has been in the same family of Hapgoods since 1827, now 128 years as I write this in 1955. It is described in "Vermont Life" for Spring, 1955. This must be something of a record for a country store. I remember the breaking of the showcase glass as the first real tragedy of my life. It was such a useless way to spend money and it wiped out the stage coach fare I had saved by walking twelve miles. It was my first great frustration.

But I continued walking towards Grafton and because of my very early start, I met Uncle John just above Houghtonville with the horse and buggy, before he had gone more then four or five miles. I did twenty-six miles that day on foot and because I was hard as nails, I recall that the next day I was completely free from sore muscles or "charley horses" and was very proud of myself.

I want to record my memory of Dr. E. H. Hemingway, who was the village doctor at Manchester. He was in Middlebury College with Father and wrote Father that he would look after Harry and me without charge, which he did. He was a fine, wonderful man, the old country doctor par excellence, whose inner secret was kindness. We kept in touch even after I moved to South Bend to practice law. He died in Honolulu, where after he retired, he lived with his lawyer son.

That fall we went to Vermont Academy. I got a job working for Mrs. Hughes for my room and board. She had one cow which I milked, put the milk in tin pails and left the pails on the doorstep of her customers early in the morning. In addition I mowed the lawn and sawed and split her firewood. But chiefly it was the cow and Mrs. Hughes which saw me through my first two years at Vermont Academy. No big city milkman of today making thousands of dollars a year is any happier than I was.

The Vermont Academy baseball team in 1904 which compiled a 2-4-1 record. Front row, left to right: William Clift and Ernest Illingworth. Middle row: Hays Jones, Homer Hunt, Captain William Walker, Manager Burt Olmstead, and Assistant Manager Smith. Top row: Ray Leach, Ed Warner, Sam Pettengill, and Ed Boynton.

During my last year at Vermont Academy I had a room in one of the dormitories and I went back to my old work of keeping the lawns and walks in good condition, emptying the slops from the Academy kitchen and turned the crank when ice cream was made, a job for which there were always plenty of applicants.

I did the mile, two-mile and broad jump on the track team and played shortstop very badly on the baseball team, making seven errors in one game. Here I want to quote from an article about the 1904 Vermont Academy Baseball Team that appeared in the sport section of the Bellows Falls Times recently. After describing the various members of the team, it said this about me: "Samuel Pettengill played the infield and was fondly remembered for his graceful movements which caused much mirth. His baseball career can hardly serve as a barometer for his future success (his batting average was .066) as he went on to distinguish himself as a United States Congressman from Indiana."

I became editor-in-chief of the Academy's student paper, "The Vermont Academy Life," in my last year; was president of my class and of the student Y.M.C.A. and gave the class oration on graduation day. Father heard it and said, "It was very good — for a boy." This threw cold water over my spirits as I thought I had certainly equalled Daniel Webster if not Cicero. However, Father had a fine faculty for encouraging us boys to do our best, but at the same time kept us from getting swelled heads.

When I went to Vermont Academy it was a semi-military school. We wore uniforms, at least most of the time, and had about an hour's drill a day, which was under the direction of a retired army officer, Major Wolfe. We called him "Lupee" behind his back. It was not as strict as the top-notch military schools are today, but the little military education I got there I have always regarded as one of the best parts of my education. It taught us gawky, country boys to stand up straight, to be neat and alert, respect the flag, and take pride in the perfection of our drill. There were two or three old, unused cannons on the campus and we drilled with Springfield rifles. But so far as I can recall, we never even fired blank cartridges.

All of Uncle Ed's five children had gone to Vermont Academy before I did. My principal was Dr. Ellery. It was a co-ed school when I was there, with both men and women teachers, and supplied for the vicinity the place of high schools which were practically non-existent in Vermont at that time.

My teacher of Medieval History was Miss Julia E. Goodwin of Falls Village, Conn. She was a gentle, cultured New England spinster, who wrote poetry and painted in oil and water colors. Having been raised in a home without a mother, sister or aunt, she was the first woman who took an interest in me after my babyhood. She wrote me encouraging letters when I was later at college and law school, and continued as one of my most devoted friends until she died some years ago. When I was at law school she occasionally sent me a five dollar bill out of her tiny hoard, with strict admonitions to use it for nothing but milk and cream, and thus supplement my pinched rations. I was very happy to be able to write a foreword for her little volume of poems entitled "Singing Pictures" in 1937, and I treasure the copy she gave me with its loving inscription.

While Saxtons River was only seven miles or so from the old farm, I was tied to my job of milking Mrs. Hughes' cow morning and night for my first two years at Vermont Academy. But during my third year, when I roomed in the Academy dormitory, I occasionally went home on a Saturday afternoon or Sunday. I thought nothing of walking the distance to and fro.

Probably the red letter day of my years at Vermont Academy was the day I graduated. As usual there was quite a crowd of fathers and mothers to be provided for in the dining hall. It was a big day and ice cream was the dessert. It was my job, with a couple of the other boys, to make the ice cream in the old hand turned freezers. We got the ice from the ice house, washed it off as it was covered with sawdust, and made ice cream nearly all day for the big dinner that night. This ice

The Vermont Academy Class of 1904 of which Sam Pettengill was president. Front row, left to right: Ruth Randall, Homer Hunt, and Gertrude Johnson. Middle row: Clara Belle Alford, Leon Norcross, Sam Pettengill, Burt Olmstead, Lena Campbell, and Mary Parker. Rear row: Adelle Orton, Mabel Chase, Spencer Swasey, Walter Archibald, Ray Leach, Ellen Ward, Myrtle Powell, Alice Cole, and Kate Beach.

cream was made from milk with all the cream left in, and to this extent I think civilization has gone down hill since I was a boy, for no ice cream today could equal that. On the old farm after milking, we put the milk in pans to let the cream rise and after it had risen, one could run a knife around the edge and practically pick the cream off the milk with one's fingers. It was this kind of milk that was used that day. We never had a freezer at the farm, and ice cream was a real treat. The matron in charge was a kind-hearted soul and was not skimpy in letting us clean out the freezer every time a gallon was made, after which it was put in quart bricks for the dinner. The result was that I ate ice cream all day long, and after the dinner and the help had had all they could manage, there was still another quart which another boy and I finished. I don't remember the number of gallons of ice cream we made that day, but as there were two or three hundred people at the dinner it must have been a good many, and I suppose I must have consumed about two gallons all by myself! Those who have an idea of how to make a graduation day more memorable, please send in your suggestions!

Some years after I was graduated, Vermont Academy ceased to be a co-ed school and is now one of the very fine boys' schools in the country. The fiftieth anniversary of the ice cream was in 1954. I was the only member of my class present and made a response for my class at the dinner that night. I painted an optimistic view of the future and said that some of the boys present that evening would no doubt be coming back to the old school for their fiftieth anniversary in 2,004 A.D. and would, I hoped, have as happy a memory of their years at Vermont Academy as I have.

After finishing at Vermont Academy in 1904, a representative of a book firm seduced me into the belief that I could make a great deal of money acting as a book agent, going from door to door selling "The Life of Pope Leo XIII" who had recently died. The territory assigned to me was Holyoke, Mass., where I was told many people lived who would buy the life of the Pope as soon as I rang the front door bell. No hope was ever dashed to earth more than this. At the end of a month I had used up the few dollars with which I had started and had only a little over a dollar left, with room and meals still to be provided for. This was not enough money to pay my fare back to Vermont, so what to do? I looked at the help wanted ads in the newspaper and found that the Massachusetts State Agricultural College at Amherst needed a teamster. So I took the inter-urban there, taking all my belongings with me in a little valise, as I did not have enough money to get back to Holyoke.

Opposite me in the car sat a man and I wondered if he had seen the same ad. We both got off at Amherst and I heard him ask a cab driver how far it was to the college farm. It was about a mile, and he got into the cab and drove off without another word. I felt faint. I didn't have enough money for cab fare, so I walked, lugging the valise. It was an anxious mile. If the job was filled by the time I got there, what would I do?

When I got to the farm, a man was just leaving the Superintendent's office, looking mad. It was my traveling companion. We spoke not a word and now it was my turn for an interview. I asked the Superintendent if he needed a man and he said, "Yes, but not a boy." I said, "I am not a boy. I am eighteen years old and grew up on a Vermont farm and can do anything that any hired man can do." "Can you drive a team of horses?" I said I could. He took me to the horse barn and pointed to two huge Percherons, the tallest, biggest horses I had ever seen. Standing at their shoulders I could not see over them. He asked, "Can you drive this team of horses?" I answered that I could and the next question was "Do you drink?" I said I didn't and he said, "You're hired. I could smell liquor on the breath of that man who just left. The driver I fired was a heavy drinker and wasn't good to the horses. I'll have no drinking drivers."

I learned that the horses were the biggest in Massachusetts, if not in New England. I will never forget the feeling of awe and terror when I first crept into the stalls to harness them. Their harnesses were so heavy and the horses so high I had great difficulty in getting the harnesses over their backs and was afraid I'd be squeezed as flat as a pancake between one of them and the side of his stall. However, I patted them and talked to them and gained their confidence and got very fond of them.

Every load of hay that was brought in from the fields was weighed and the record kept. Before the summer was over my Percherons and I drew into the barn the heaviest load of hay in the history of the Agricultural College.

As I recall, I was paid twenty-five dollars a month plus room and board. With the proceeds of that summer's work, I bought a few absolutely necessary clothes and was ready for college.

My brother Harry, who was a year ahead of me at Vermont Academy, spent only two years there and then went on to the University of Vermont. While in Saxtons River he stayed at Uncle Ed's home and did garden work and odd jobs around the neighborhood.

*Samuel Pettengill, the budding lawyer, during his undergraduate years at Middlebury College.*

## XIII

## COLLEGE

Middlebury was decided upon for two reasons: first, Father and Uncle Ed had been there before the Civil War, and second, it was the only college I could afford to attend. After my mother died, and Father had lost everything he had invested in during the panic of the early nineties, and besides was in poor health and so came back to Grafton to live, he had no money income for a good many years before he died except his twelve dollars a month Civil War pension. He was able to help Uncle John with the farm work, but there was no money for college.

Professor W. E. Howard was the Dean of Middlebury and presented Middlebury's cause at various preparatory schools as against the claims of other colleges. Preference was given to the children of old Middlebury graduates. Father had left college without graduating to go to the Civil War, and in 1862 Uncle Ed did the same, enlisting in Company D., 16th Vermont Volunteers. Middlebury conferred the honorary degree of Master of Arts on him in June, 1877, after he had been practicing medicine for some years in Saxtons River. He had gone to Harvard after returning from the war and received his degree from Harvard Medical School in 1867. I have it in my possession, one of the professors signing it being Dr. Oliver Wendell Holmes. So between Father and Uncle Ed I was considered part of the Middlebury family and Professor Howard arranged that I should receive a scholarship which covered my tuition. He also arranged for me to have a job working in the Post Office at Middlebury, which would pay me three dollars a week.

When I got off the train at Middlebury to enter college, I had eight dollars as my stake. I went up to the Post Office and introduced myself to the Postmaster, a Mr. Skiff. He was a hunchback. He was also a very kind man. He asked when I was ready to begin work. I said "Right now." He asked, "Have you any place to sleep?" I answered "No." He said Professor Howard had told him I was a very poor boy so he had already arranged for me to sleep in an office over the Post Office in the Battell Building. It was used by the Vermont Merino Sheep Breeders' Association and where the records of pure bred sheep were kept. It was used only when the secretary came in for a few hours, once a week or so, to post the sheep records. The secretary of the Merino Sheep Breeders' Association was a Mr. Chapman, and he and Mr. Skiff had agreed that I could use the office for nothing. However, it had no bed. Therefore my first purchase at the hardware store was a folding canvas cot. This took about half of my eight dollars. I put the cot under one of the old-fashioned long, high accounting desks at which men formerly worked standing up, or sitting on high stools. There were, of course, no springs, mattress or pillow. But with the blankets I had brought with me and a bunch of newspapers for a pillow, I slept soundly through three college years.

All of my possessions were in an old sheepskin covered trunk at the railroad station. I found it would cost twenty-five cents to have it brought up to my office-apartment. Not wishing to spend this enormous sum I asked Mr. Skiff if I could borrow a wheelbarrow somewhere. He took me to a nearby grocery store and told the owner what I desired. I was ashamed to wheel my trunk up from the railroad station in the daytime, so waited until it was dark to do so.

With what was left of my original eight dollars plus the three dollars a week at the Post Office, plus about twenty-five dollars my father managed to send me, I went through my first year at college with all bills paid. For weeks on end I spent no more than one dollar a week for my food. I had no way of heating anything and except for an occasional bowl of hot soup at a nearby "greasy spoon" I ate everything cold. In time I met some Middlebury people who invited me to their homes for a good dinner every so often, and my boss was particularly kind to me in that respect. His wife also saw to it that I got a bowl of good hot oatmeal for breakfast at least once a week. I bought a quart of milk in a tin pail every day which cost five cents and the rest was mostly crackers and apples.

The Post Office staff consisted of the hunchbacked Postmaster, a young woman named Lewis who came in around nine every morning and handled the money orders, and once in a while Mrs. Skiff would come in for an hour or two. The mail for the day was tossed off the New York-Montreal Express at three in the morning. I went downstairs to the Post Office at five each morning and sorted the mail, which had been brought up from the railroad station by old Pat Mulligan, my devoted friend, who brought the mail in a one-horse buckboard and roused me from my slumbers on his arrival. Mr. Skiff came in around seven or eight o'clock. By that time I had the mail sorted, put in the boxes, and the rest ready for the three R.F.D. routes. I had swept out the Post Office, emptied the waste basket, and then was off to the campus. I returned to the Post Office at noon for an hour, and after classes ended in the afternoon, I stayed at the Post Office until it closed, around eight or nine o'clock.

During my first three years at college it is literally true that I did most of my studying standing up at the Post Office window. This, and the poor light when I sorted the mail at five in the morning, strained my eyes so badly that it became necessary to buy glasses, which I have worn ever since.

Thousands of poor boys have worked their way through college at Middlebury and elsewhere, and I was no different from others, although I do think I did with less during my four years than any other student on the campus. I had neither clothes nor money to go to a dance and so never attended social functions of that character. I never owned an overcoat until I was in law school. By modern definitions I was certainly included in the ill-fed, ill-clad and ill-housed group. But the point is that I never pitied myself or envied others. It never occurred to me to do so. I actually was quite proud of myself because I did not and would not write home for money every time I wanted something.

Years later, when I was in Washington, this experience which continued for many years, kept me from swallowing the false humanitarianism of the New Deal which pictured every worthless bum as an exploited patriot and considered that a Robin Hood Government which taxed money out of all pockets to support the favored charities of the politicians, was the highest form of statesmanship. More damage has been done to the moral fibre of the nation by these New Deal attitudes in fanning the flames of self-pity and envy than we will be able to measure for decades.

When politicians promote self-pity and envy they create arguments for social robbery. In the name of the welfare of the state, they destroy the conscience of the individual. When conscience and personal responsibility are destroyed, taxation and inflation run riot with the result that today the small, independent colleges like Middlebury are finding it increasingly difficult to survive, thus denying in the future the chance which I, as a poor boy, had before the Moloch of the Welfare State had so many worshippers.

Another point I would like to make here is the kindness of men and women as exemplified by Mr. Skiff and Mr. Chapman, who before they ever saw me had made the arrangements for me to get my sleeping quarters for nothing. Kindness is one of the greatest of our natural resources. It can be tapped by any poor boy or girl who wants an education. If God helps those who help themselves, the law works through human hearts. Everyone was kind to me during my years of schooling and the kindness had nothing to do with pity. I think it was a way of showing respect for ambition and elbow grease.

Another objection I have to state welfarism is that when people are taxed to death to support the favorite charities of politicians, now world wide, the inclination is to be less kind and to say "let the government do it." This is certainly shown today in the way in which people pass off their moral responsibility toward aged parents.

When the first college year ended, I spent the summer working in the Post Office, but with the students gone, the principal industry in the town, the work was lighter and I was able to do some odd jobs to supplement my federal salary. Saturdays I worked at the grocery store part of the day.

I remember one customer very well. He was a vestryman in the Episcopal Church. He and his wife and his wife's mother lived in a two-story house, with himself and wife in one part, and his wife's mother in the other, both having separate cooking arrangements. At that time Fleischmann's yeast was two cents a cake. He would come and lay down one penny for his half of the cake and had the remaining cent charged to his mother-in-law. This was not proof of a nasty nature, because as I have already mentioned, he was a pious and good citizen. It was simply old-fashioned New England thrift carried only a little further than was usually the custom.

In 1906, at the end of my second year, I got a job as utility man at Moosa-la-Moo Park at Lake Dunmore, some eight miles from Middlebury. It was a collection of three or four cabins and a boathouse, with a concentrated population of mosquitoes. D.D.T. was unknown. I did everything about the place that the cook didn't do, rented boats, cleaned fish for those who caught them, put up the horses of the guests who drove in, fed them, dug bait, painted the boats and so forth. It was there that I first saw an automobile. It was a French car that you got into from the rear like in the old-fashioned carry-all that took guests from the railroad station to the hotel.

It was there that I met Josephine, my first wife, and our romance began when she caught a five pound bass which I cleaned for her, with the idea of salting it so she could take it back to her grandmother in Ohio. We did the best we could, but she wrote me they had to throw the fish out of the railroad car window before they got halfway to Napoleon! It was the beginning of our correspondence which ended with our marriage six years later.

I continued to live in my sheep breeder's paradise for three years. In the meantime I had become a member of the Delta Kappa Epsilon fraternity, as was my father before me, and in my senior year the Dekes agreed that if another fellow and I, at our own expense, made a room in the attic of the DKE House, we could use it rent free. With a little help from a plumber, we did a pretty good job of carpentry and had a pleasant room.

As I recall I worked at the Post Office at least part of the time all through my four years. But after the first year, I began to do more odd jobs around town in order to earn more money. One year in spare time I was a telephone lineman. I will always remember how difficult it is after a bad storm to climb a telephone pole that is sheeted with ice, while standing at an angle. It requires as much skill as a tight-rope walker.

One of the telephone company's men showed me a switchboard that had been used when telephones first came to Middlebury. It was like a chess or checker board, with dark squares made of metal alternating with white squares made of wood. The metal squares had the numbers of the subscribers marked on them. Two small pieces of iron were linked together with a flexible wire. When subscriber Number 3 wanted to talk to subscriber Number 10, the operator connected the proper squares with the movable metal pieces and the conversation began. The man told me that the metal squares could be linked with the thumb and finger of the human hand. The thought of talking through human bone and flesh almost lured me into the world of science. But I stuck to my original goal of the law.

Despite all the time spent fending for myself, I got good grades and failed of making Phi Beta Kappa by only one point on my overall average.

*Sam Pettengill, seated at the extreme left of the front row, was manager of the Middlebury College football team in 1907.*

During my senior year I also found time to be manager and treasurer of the football team. College football then was not what it is today and especially so with reference to receipts. Except for a few hours after a game, there was seldom more than a hundred dollars in the athletic treasury. Consequently I was not required to put up a heavy fidelity bond. When we went out of town to play, the host college made a guarantee which was supposed to cover our traveling expenses. On one occasion, after careful figuring, it was ascertained that the guarantee would pay the traveling expenses of only twelve men. As there were no other funds available, the big question was who the twelfth man should be. As manager I was entitled to go, but patriotism and love of alma mater led me to think that we had better send one substitute in case of an injury! So the substitute went. Our opponents generally were the University of Vermont, Norwich, Williams, Amherst, Union, St. Lawrence, and Wesleyan in Connecticut. When we won, as we did occasionally, it was a great event.

I also became half owner of the college book store during my junior year. This had been a Deke monopoly for a number of years, and a room was given for it in the basement of the chapel. By opening it a few hours a day, the two partners generally made about a hundred dollars each a year, provided they were careful of their credits. My first partner was Lyman B. Tobin and he was succeeded by Carl J. Kilburn in my senior year. After I was graduated, Edwin S. S. Sunderland took over the book store. He later became a partner in the John W. Davis law firm in New York City.

Earning your way through college is generally regarded as teaching self-reliance, the value of a dollar and so forth. These are good, but as I look back upon it I believe the greatest benefit is learning to work with other people, to like them and to have them like you. I am sure that all of the things I did to earn my way through prep school, college and law school stood me in good stead later when I was pleading cases before juries or engaging in politics. I am quite certain that I learned more outside of books during my school years than I did in the classroom, at least until law school, when my books became bread-and-butter subjects.

I think the most valuable thing I learned outside of books happened at Middlebury at the beginning of a semester in college physics under Professor W. G. Bryant. After we assembled for the first day of the semester, we had a new text book, hundreds of pages long and looking exceedingly authoritative and formidable. Professor Bryant said, "I presume you are naturally impressed by this new text book written by men with almost world-wide reputations. I have just one thing to say about this book—*don't believe a word in it*," and then after a pause, "until after experiment or otherwise, you *have* to believe it." In short, he wanted us to think things out for ourselves and come to our own conclusions. The statement made a tremendous impression on me and I think did more than any other one thing in my life to make me cautious about swallowing bunk from any source. It is the thing said and not the person who says it that is important. The independent course that I followed during my years in Congress may be attributed in large part to what our professor said.

Two other professors I remember very kindly. One was Professor Howard who was responsible for arranging for me to receive a scholarship that paid my tuition. He taught economics and government. He knew what a struggle it was for me to get through school and was always a source of encouragement. A day or two after I graduated I met him on a path on the campus for the last time. We shook hands and he said, "Goodbye, Pettengill. Middlebury will be proud of you someday."

Another professor whom I remember best was C. B. Wright, who was head of the English Department. His criticism of my essays and papers greatly helped me to write clear English. He introduced me to poetry which I had never previously thought I would like. He used to read some of the best poetry aloud in class and was one of the few persons who *knew how* to read

151

poetry aloud. I remember especially his reading Wordsworth's "The Beggar on the Cumberland Road."

Professor Wright's daughter, Marjorie, married William Hazlitt Upson, author of the Earthworm-Caterpillar stories that appeared for so long in the Saturday Evening Post. He still makes his home in Middlebury and he and his wife are both my good friends.

The President of Middlebury was Ezra Brainerd. When he got my class graduated he considered that his life's work was done and retired! His son, Ezra, Jr., went to Oklahoma to practice law, was appointed a member of the Interstate Commerce Commission by President Coolidge, and I shared office space with him in Washington for a few years after I left Congress. The Brainerds were distantly related to the Barrett family of Grafton, and Ezra, Jr.'s sister, Miss Brainerd, occasionally visited them in Grafton.

There was very little drinking in Middlebury. The college authorities and the fraternities frowned on it. However the village voted to license one bar. I was offered the job of acting as bartender an hour or so at noon when the proprietor took time off for dinner. The offer of the job appealed to me tremendously as a delightfully wicked thing to do, but after writing Father to ask what he thought of it, he advised me to decline, which I did. I don't recall ever taking a drink of any alcoholic beverage until a good many years after I began the practice of law.

The first theatrical performance I ever attended, and the only one during my years at Middlebury, was a travelling show which put on Sherlock Holmes in the village Town Hall. The admission was twenty-five cents. I lived and dreamed Sherlock Holmes for months thereafter.

The only music I heard as a boy on the farm was the organ in the brick church, pumped by hand. Its only rival was making sounds with a piece of paper fitted over a comb. One of the things for which I have always been grateful to the Dekes was that at the DKE house we had a piano which one of the brothers played very well, and when our fresh, young voices joined 'round the piano, singing Deke songs, it did much to soothe my savage breast.

I won second prize of, I think twenty dollars, in a prize speaking contest, my first real oratorical effort. I selected a speech about Ann Story, one of the early Vermont pioneer women, given some years before by Judge Wendell Phillips Stafford, an old Vermonter, then on the Court of Appeals in Washington.

In my sophomore year, my Uncle John had to be in Montpelier on business and came to Middlebury for a day's visit. Except for going back to Grafton the following year to attend his funeral, I don't recall seeing home or any other relative during the four years I was at college until graduation day.

At the end of my junior year, during the summer of 1907, I was a policeman on the exposition grounds of the Jamestown Exposition, at Jamestown, Virginia. John Barrett was the Director-General of the Pan-American Union at Washington, and all of the Latin-American countries had exhibits at the Exposition. Mr. Barrett had the right to name some of the staff and wrote to me at Middlebury asking if I would like to be a policeman and wear a uniform and tell people what's what. Mr. Skiff agreed that I could take the summer off, so I answered that nothing would please me better than to go to Jamestown, and the result was that I had a very interesting summer.

The police force was about seventy-five in number. We slept in a little tent city on bunks and in tents furnished by the U.S. government, and ate at the mess of a regiment of regular U. S. Army troops just back from the Philippines. They paraded every fine day on the parade grounds and shot off blank cartridges from machine guns.

While we were called the Exposition police, what we actually did chiefly was to act as guides and tell people where buildings were, where various activities were and answer questions as best we could. I don't remember arresting anybody for disorderly conduct, but it was very pleasing to wear a blue coat and a badge.

On days off we took short trips to Hampstead Roads and Virginia Beach where I ate my first oyster, which I found in the sand.

The Baker Chocolate people had an exhibit which included a pretty lunchroom where chocolate was served by girls dressed just as they appear on the chocolate tins of today. I have always felt that American women have never looked more attractive than in those old-fashioned dresses and wearing sunbonnets. It was my favorite place for an inexpensive lunch, but I think I really went to look at the pretty girls.

Every day there was some important event on behalf of some state or some industry and a lot of VIP's came and went. Among them was President Theodore Roosevelt. I heard him make a speech. While there was a huge crowd, my badge got me up close to the speakers' platform. I have forgotten what the President said, but will always remember how ferocious he looked when he pounded the rostrum and showed his teeth. A gawky kid off a poor hill farm in Vermont, I was seeing the big world and some of the important people in it from an advantageous position. Cabinet officers, governors, admirals, generals and so on, all passed by and occasionally they would even ask the farm boy from Vermont where something was.

One of the exhibits was a small U.S. Mint where silver dollars were actually being made in honor of the Exposition. Nearly everybody wanted to see the Mint. One of my brother officers had a wise crack whenever people came up to him and asked, "Where is this place where they make money?" He would say, "Why, I am making three dollars a day here. Is that what you want?" Then he would direct them to the Mint.

When the summer was over I returned by way of Washington and made my first visit to Upper Marlboro in Maryland where my mother was born. Her brother, Uncle Tom Clagett, was still living and I stayed overnight with him at his farm that he had named Keokuk. During the evening we sat out on the lawn and he told me stories of the old days before the Civil War when the "quarters," a little distance from the big house, were occupied by the slaves. I guess there never were any Simon Legrees in the Clagett family. I will always remember Uncle Tom saying how happy the slaves seemed to be when he was a little boy. There was so much laughter among them. And on nights similar to the evening I was there, Uncle Tom said that in the old days he could always hear the singing and banjo playing down in the quarters. He said, rather sadly, "Even the dogs don't bark any more the way they used to." It was the first and only time I ever saw my Uncle Tom. He died two or three years later, but I have never forgotten the impression I got that night; how gentle he was, soft spoken and kind.

I was at Jamestown nearly three months. As I recall, I was paid seventy-five dollars a month plus keep in the tent city and the army mess. After paying my expenses down and back I must have had about two hundred dollars when I returned to Middlebury, the largest sum I had ever had at one time. At Middlebury I went back to my job at the Post Office.

When I graduated in 1908, I was class orator. My subject was "The Abolition of War" which I delivered in the Congregational Church. With youthful enthusiasm I confidently predicted that the human race had become too intelligent to engage in any more wars! Father came up to attend graduation and Professor Wright told him that my oration had saved the day from being a humdrum affair. I was certain that my oration had pointed the way to vast new vistas for mankind. Anyhow, I remember how happy I was with my speech and the acclaim it received. It pleased my father so much. And Miss Lucy Daniels had it printed in a small booklet, which was the

*Sam Pettengill when he graduated from Middlebury College in 1908.*

first time I was so honored. I was thrilled to see my name in print and have kept a copy ever since. This is the speech.

### The Abolition of War
Graduating Address Delivered by Samuel Barrett Pettengill Jr., at Middlebury College Commencement
June, 1908

Seventeen years ago Edward J. Phelps stood at the base of the Bennington battlefield monument and said these words: "History is full of battles. All her pages are stained with blood. There have been battles whose smoke went up like incense to heaven, but for the most part, they have been instruments of ambition, tyranny and crime. It would be well for the world to be spared the misery they wrought. It would be well for its history if their memory could perish."

I stand on this proposition. And I shall try to set forth some of the reasons for believing that the abolition of war will be a reality in a not-far-distant future.

War has been condoned in the past, largely I believe, because of the notion that somehow it is essential to a nation's life; that somehow it fosters manhood, and rears the strongest individuals. The world is learning that the contrary is true. The 19th century taught us that progress is secured only by the survival of the best and fittest of the race. Apply this law to nations. The historian says, "Greece died because the men who made her glory had all passed away. The Roman empire perished for want of men." "Spain," says President Jordan, "died centuries ago. She never crossed our path. It was only her ghost that walked at Manila and Santiago." And when we remember the fifteen million beings who have died on the battlefield since history began and realize that these men were not the weakest but the strongest men of their nation, we know that the law is true. The weakling is left to propagate the race and in the course of time, just as in a herd of neglected cattle, the aboriginal man appears in a wasted race of men. War is the destroyer, not the creator of heroes.

There is another illusion that is being swept away — that a standing army means peace. There is Russia with a standing army of a million men, a Cossack on the back of every peasant. What are the results? Externally, beaten by a third class power three years ago; internally, the world thought a second French revolution had dawned here. The time is not ripe for that but if that travail be necessary for the birth of freedom, God grant that the time soon comes. But there is no peace there. The torch responds to the torch. Dynamite answers dynamite. There are Ireland and France, shrinking in population every day. Why, friends, in the past fifty years twenty million of men have fled to this country to escape the militarism of Europe. Is this peace? A standing army does not spell peace. It never did except in the sense Tacitus meant when he said, "Where they have made a solitude that they called peace."

Another factor is the rapidly increasing cost of war. Where nations once fought for ten, thirty or a hundred years, they are now exhausted by a twelve months struggle. A decade ago we "benevolently assimilated" the Philippine Islands at the point of the bayonet. That was a small war, but it cost this nation a billion dollars and a half. The sum is so large that we need a yard stick to measure it by. Fifteen thousand million dollars would water every desert acre in our great West. Even in time of peace, our billion dollar Congress is appropriating forty percent of that sum in war expenditures. What does this mean? It means that every family in the United States, every household represented here, in the clothes it wears and the food it eats, is paying over twenty-three dollars per annum in support of our army and navy, and only eleven dollars for schools. The figures become significant when they strike home.

There are other influences, positive ones, that I can only briefly mention. There is the growth of international law which is unique in one great respect, that it has no material force behind it. It is proof of the supreme power of gentleness. There are the treaties of Paris and Washington, the Brussels declaration and only recently, the Hague tribunals. Towns are no longer plundered. Privateering is abolished. Neutral ships sail free. Poisoned wells, assassinations, and the dum-dum bullets have been thrown into the rubbish heap of the past. These are the splendid results of arbitration, pointing a better way than the arbitrament of the sword. There are the peace conferences, the interparliamentary union of two thousand statesmen, the federation of South Africa, the pan-American union of South American republics. There is the annihilation of space and time, the growing interdependence of nation on nation, making long wars absolutely unendurable. And lastly, there is the growth of international comity and humanity. The world is beginning to realize that divine truth, "He hath created of one blood all the nations of the earth."

Friends, these are the results. And you and I ought to be proud of them, not only for humanity's sake, but because they have been achieved largely by men of our own race. The Teutonic race has been the foremost champion of this great cause. We see the tide of Anglo-Saxon civilization, rising in those far-away forests on the German hillsides, gathering strength from Magna Carta, from Runnemede and Naseby, bursting into magnificence in our own great revolution, sweeping away the shackles of the slaves, and then rushing on to its final goal, to that bright ocean of universal peace that shall one day surround the world.

The good seed has been sown and the fields are white with the harvest. Who shall be the reapers? Here is America, the haven of the oppressed, chief of that great family of nations that shall one day become the federation of the world. What a magnificent opportunity awaits her! When our great peace-loving people once highly resolve, as the gentle Lincoln did on a different occasion, that "if they ever get a chance they will strike this accursed thing hard," then will the words of that prophet of old, that man of God, come true, "They shall beat their swords into plough-shares and their spears into pruning hooks. Nation shall not lift up sword against nation; neither shall there be war any more."

By the time I had concluded my senior year I had decided to go to Yale for my law course. That summer I worked as a bus boy in the dining room of the Equinox House at Manchester, Vt. This was a very swank hotel. The waiters got the tips and the bus boys carried out the dirty dishes. The hotel help had a baseball team, upon which I played second base and acquired a broken little finger on the right hand. When the doctor pulled this back into something approaching its former shape, I came nearer to fainting than I have ever done in my life.

In this elite and pampered age, I realize that the foregoing recital may call up a picture of grim, hard going for a boy. But as I said before, it never occurred to me that I was being abused by anyone or that the government owed me a living. My turtle-neck sweater kept me warm in winter and I don't recall having any sickness more than an occasional cold. However, it is true that I was at the point of malnutrition. I developed a sore spot under my right collarbone, which pained me for a number of years. But so long as a boy can maintain his health and reasonably good grades, I am a firm believer in all young people working part of their way through school.

Years later I served one term of three years as a Trustee of the college, elected by the alumni, but as I was not able to attend board meetings regularly, I did not stand for re-election. On June 14, 1941, I was awarded a large, very handsome pewter plate by the Alumni Association of Middlebury for "meritorious services" to my alma mater. In June 1949, I gave the Commencement address at Middlebury. My subject was "The Responsibility of College Graduates as Citizens." A good many thousand copies of this speech were printed by various groups in different parts of the country. At this same time, the college honored me with a Doctor of Civil Law degree. It was a very happy day for me, for attending the ceremonies, watching me receive my hood, and hearing my speech, was the lady who a few weeks later became my dear wife, Helen.

## XIV

## YALE LAW SCHOOL

I entered Yale Law School in the fall of 1908. It was the last class to be admitted without requiring a college B.A. degree, and for that reason was the largest in the history of the school. The school also permitted one to double up his courses and complete in two years rather than three. I was anxious to get my education behind me, so went to a member of the faculty, Judge Baldwin, then Chief Justice of the Supreme Court of Connecticut and later Governor, for advice. He said, "Young man, if you finish in two years you will, of course, be earning a little money practicing law three years from now. But if you take three years of law school you will be making more money ten years from now." So I decided on the three year course.

The financial problem was as acute as ever. Perhaps more so, as I now wanted to boil down on my books even more than at college. I got my room and board slinging hash at a boarding house down by the car barns. The people I slung hash at were street car motormen, conductors and right-of-way men, a rough and hungry crew. The landlady was a hard working widow by the name of Mrs. Cooper. This took care of my room and board but provided no cash, of which I was in great need, as at Yale I had no scholarship and had to pay my tuition, which then was a hundred and fifty dollars a year. I also had to pay for books and other necessities in real money.

One year I worked in the library where there were some fifty thousand volumes of law books, mostly sheepskin bound. I spent a year rubbing white vaseline into them and binding up their cracked backs with the result that I had an intimate knowledge of every book in the library! At another period I worked at the New Haven railroad freight offices after class and on Saturdays.

*Sam Pettengill during his first year at Yale Law School in 1909.*

At the end of my first year I went to the Bureau of Self-help on the campus run for Yale men in need of jobs. A Yale graduate, by the name of Perry, practicing law in Detroit, had written in that his uncle, Mr. Benjamin Bulkley of Southport, Connecticut, had a string of race horses that went on the road during the summer, and that he needed a secretary and bookkeeper. I took the next train to Southport. Mr. Bulkley was an unhappy old gentleman long separated from his wife and daughter and he found his consolation in his horses. He was living on money left him by his father and grandfather who had made a small fortune in the merchant marine. He was really generous at heart, but miserly in the way he lived. He wore celluloid collars and bragged of the fact that he seldom paid more than ten dollars for a suit of clothes. He hunted fire sales for bargains; never passed a piece of string or a pin on the sidewalk without picking it up, and yet, with all of his peculiarities, was kind to everyone except waiters in the hotels.

We agreed that I should work for him that summer for one hundred dollars a month, plus expenses. The stock farm was at Mt. Kisco, New York, where I reported as soon as school closed. His manager was Mr. F. H. Burgess. His widow is still living in Bennington, Vermont. He and Mrs. Burgess had no children and took me to their hearts almost as if I were their own.

It was my function to go with the race horses, trotters and pacers, from town to town; arrange for train movement; find a place for the men to board; pay the bills and collect the prize money when we won, and generally act as the owner's representative except in the actual training and driving. I did this for three summers.

To move the horses around the country we leased for the season an Arms Palace horse car. The first race meet we attended was in Oil City, Pa. We took twelve horses, twelve men or "swipes," one for each horse, Mr. Burgess and myself. Although I traveled hundreds of miles in that horse car, Mr.

Burgess and I roomed at a hotel or nearby boarding house. The men slept with their horses in the car, or in the stalls at the race tracks. It was quite an experience going to both the mile tracks on the grand circuit and the half-mile tracks at the county fairs. Some of the towns where we raced were Cleveland, Buffalo, Albany, Hartford, Goshen, Hagerstown and Bethlehem.

The next year the horses were moved from Mt. Kisco to Goshen, N.Y., which became our headquarters the last two summers I was on the road. It was near Goshen that Hambletonian, the greatest sire of trotting horses was raised and is buried. A big monument is over his grave. Hambletonian lived about 1850, and there is scarcely a harness horse in America that does not have his blood. He sired sixteen hundred foals.

The swipes or touts around the race track are kind to their horses, but are pretty rough. On one occasion two of our swipes got into a furious drunken fight. One knocked the other down and picked up a pitchfork to drive it through the back of the fallen man. I grabbed the pitchfork out of his hands, which made him as angry at me as the man he was fighting, and as there were plenty of pitchforks around, it was nip and tuck for a moment or two as to whether someone was going to get killed, including me.

We never won enough purses to pay much of the expense and each season wound up with a deficit of some thousands of dollars, which Mr. Bulkley cheerfully paid, however parsimonious he was in smaller matters. We got along all right, and for quite a number of years after I was in South Bend, the lonely old man paid us a visit of a day or so each year on his way north from Florida where he spent the winters.

A member of the faculty who did me the most good at law school was the Dean, Henry Wade Rogers. He had the ability to make all of us young fellows see the necessity of doing close and exact work. Other members of the faculty whom I remember well were Professor Vance, author of several text-

*Benjamin Bulkley with my daughter, Susan, during one of his visits to South Bend, Indiana, about 1918.*

books, Professor Wurtz, a retired lawyer who taught real estate law, Professor Corbin on contracts, and Judge Baldwin.

Despite everything, at the end of my first year I was close to the head of my class of about one hundred and fifty members, and was elected to Xi Tau Kappa, the honorary law fraternity equivalent to Phi Beta Kappa in college. I was also a member of the law inter-departmental debating team and an alternate on the university debating team. Lenn Oare, later Judge Oare, was also a member and our acquaintance not only led to my going to South Bend, but was a fine friendship for over forty years.

In my senior year I had begun to fall violently in love and did not do so well with my books! However I got through the entire three years without flunking a single course and was graduated eighteenth in a class of one hundred and twenty-six.

Two of my closer friends were Cowan of Sacramento and Bill Graves of Texas. Both were older than I, but the three of us formed a tight little group of our own. Cowan taught me to play chess and Graves, who had ridden the brake beams from Texas to New Haven to go to law school, got a job as night watchman in an undertaker's parlor, which contained a little chapel where funerals took place. Cowan and I often met there at night and practiced public speaking from the pulpit with corpses all about. Our custom was for one of us to go up to the pulpit, shut his eyes, open the Bible, put his finger down, read what his finger had touched, and then deliver an oration on the subject. The other two made up the audience with pungent criticisms of the stumbling efforts of the speaker. However, it was the best practice in thinking on your feet that I know of and I recommend it to all law students!

My last year I roomed with Mrs. Susan H. Burt, a fine woman who was raising three or four children and taking in students to help pay the bills. After leaving law school, Mrs. Burt and I wrote each other occasionally until she died in December, 1950.

In my senior year I had acquired something of a reputation as a poet, writing doggerel verse, lampooning the professors and other objects of student interest. The result was that I was asked to write the class poem, to be published in the year book. I sweated over this for some months, and when it was finished and appeared in print I felt sure I had written something that would echo down through the corridors of time. I was never good enough to play on the University chess team, but used to watch the matches with teams from other colleges. It was a great shock to me to find students with jaw-breaking Russian, Polish and other foreign names beating chess players with fine old Anglo-Saxon names. This did more than any other one thing to cure me of a smug feeling which I had acquired as a boy growing up in Vermont, that the only people who had real brains were the Anglo-Saxon race.

On Commencement Day, the Speaker was to be Attorney-General Wickersham of the Howard Taft cabinet. This was my first approach to greatness. I was standing on the sidewalk, twenty rods from the law school building, when a taxi drove up and a gentleman got out whom I thought from his picture must be Mr. Wickersham. He asked me where the law school was and I said, "I'll take you there." So we walked down together. Some fifty of my classmates were sitting on the law school steps. Mr. Wickersham and I marched through the crowd which opened up like the Red Sea to let the children of Israel through. It was a brief moment of glory for me.

In 1909 after returning from the races my first summer, I went up to Saxtons River for a short visit with Father, who was living with my cousins, Fanny and Helen Pettengill. It was the last time I saw him alive and I will always remember his telling me that night of his experiences in the Civil War, which he had described in more detail in his little book, "The College Cavaliers." Father's Company B of the 7th Squadron Rhode Island Cavalry was the only company in the Civil War that was made up entirely of college students. The reason Father got into a Rhode Island command was that in response to one of President Lincoln's calls for volunteers, the other New England states had filled their quotas, but Rhode Island had not. So men from Middlebury, Dartmouth, Bates, Colgate and other New England colleges helped fill the Rhode Island contingent. About a month after I had returned to New Haven, Father died in the night of apoplexy.

The political campaign in 1908 was the first in which I took a voter's interest. It was Bryan versus Taft. I couldn't afford to go back to Vermont to vote, but did attend some of the political rallies in New Haven. I especially remember one for Eugene V. Debs, Socialist campaigner for President. Like most young men who are naturally sympathetic to the underdog, I was much in favor of the brave new world which the Socialists promised and for some years subscribed to "The Appeal for Reason." However, if I had voted that year I presume I would have voted for Bryan, who not only was for the toiling masses of mankind, but his magnetic personality had a tremendous appeal to young men. Years later, I met Mr. Bryan two or three times, and liked him very much, just as General Dawes did who knew him when they were both young lawyers in Lincoln, Neb. Later too I met his daughter, a lovely lady, Mrs. Ruth Bryan Owen, who became Ambassador to Denmark. We became good friends.

Two days before I graduated from law school I wrote to my

cousins in Saxtons River about my plans. Several years ago Fanny returned the letter to me.

Dear Folks:

I have heard from all of you in the last few days from different parts of New England. Things have been humming with me for some time, the last month especially. The final exams took three weeks and I was about all in when they finished a week ago. It is a tremendous strain on one's nerves. I'm all right now but there were days when I was pretty shaky. But the eleven years of classic halls are at an end and I am sincerely glad. The three years down here have been a long, hard pull. You will be glad, of course, to know that I got through everything successfully. I feel that the year has been well spent. One hundred and twenty-six will get their LL.B's on Wednesday. My rank I was told, was eighteenth man — that is there are seventeen in front of me and one hundred and eight behind me. One hundred and sixty-five took the final exams and over thirty failed to pass, or about twenty-two percent of the class. So my stand is satisfactory to me considering the other things I have done and have tried to do during the year. I should have liked to have gotten a cum laude, but that was not to be. However I've tried for the University debating team, been on the law debating association, helped put out our class book, "The Shingle," wrote the class poem, a small effort of one hundred and seven lines, worked in the library, slung hash for three months, and I have sent off a few things for publication. That's my resume for the year's work.

Today was Class Day and Attorney-General Wickersham of Taft's cabinet gave the address of the day at the law school. It was very scholarly. I met him very informally on the street yesterday. President Hadley gave the Baccalaureate in Woolsey Hall to seven hundred graduates in the different departments. There was such a jam that I could hear very little. Tomorrow comes the Harvard baseball game and Wednesday we get our sheepskins. President Taft will be here for a few hours on that day. Then the latter part of the day I'm off for the Bulkley stock farm, where I expect to have my headquarters for the third summer. I'm afraid I shall not see you before autumn. I thought that would be the better arrangement as I shall have more time to see you then. During the summer I shall try to decide what part of the United States I shall practice law in, and then after a call all around, I'll be "Down, hull down, on the long trail" to which I have looked forward for so long. At present I have not the faintest idea where I shall go — possibly Vermont, Burlington or Rutland, possibly Texas, Alaska or Sacramento. It is a very unsatisfactory feeling — not knowing where to settle. Then in December or January I shall plan to take my bar examinations in whatever state the breath of destiny carries me to.

I'm glad to hear that the Academy is doing so well. Will write again from the farm and in the fall will show you our "Shingle" and send you one of my class photos.

    Ever faithfully,

    Samuel B. Pettengill.

## XV

## PRACTICING LAW

On the day of my graduation from Yale Law School, I received a telegram from Percival W. Clement, later Governor of Vermont, asking me to come to see him in Rutland, Vt. He said it was important. I knew he had been a close friend of my father's, but I hadn't heard anything from him in all the years I was at school and so I was surprised. However, since he had been Father's friend and said it was important, I decided to go and took the train to Rutland. I went to his office in a fine looking building where he greeted me cordially. He said, "You haven't heard from me at all, but I have been keeping track of you all through college and law school, and if you want to practice law in Rutland, there is a nice office in this building you can have rent free until you get on your feet, and I will throw all the business I can your way."

I told him that on account of my Uncle Will having practiced law in Portland, I had always thought I would want to go to the Pacific Northwest, but now that I had become engaged to Josephine Campbell, her people were reluctant to have us go so far away. I had also received several offers to go into one of the big New York City law firms, but I never liked the big city atmosphere and have always been glad that I did not get immersed in what has become the European annex of the United States. Since Uncle Will had died I had no relatives in the practice of law anywhere and had been giving some thought to several cities such as Dayton, Ohio, not too far from Josephine's home in Napoleon, Ohio.

After hearing me out, Mr. Clement said, "I will let you have five thousand dollars so you can take a year to travel around the United States and decide where you want to locate, and if you finally decide on Rutland, the offer I have made you still stands."

This was an astonishing and tempting offer but I felt I should consider it carefully before making a decision. I had already committed myself to working for Mr. Bulkley during the summer, so I told Mr. Clement how much I appreciated his offer, but that I wanted to think about it and if it was all right with him, I would let him know as soon as I had made up my mind. He said this would be satisfactory and I left to go to Goshen.

At the end of the racing season in 1911, I stayed on at the horse farm in Goshen for a couple of extra months compiling a genealogy of all of Mr. Bulkley's horses. By then I had decided that I did not want to wait another year before deciding to locate, as I was already twenty-five and was anxious to begin the practice of law. I had become engaged to Josephine Harrison Strahorn Campbell, whose step-father was William Wildman Campbell, Republican Congressman from Napoleon, Ohio, in 1905-06, and I wanted to make some money so Josephine and I could get married. I had also decided that because I had no family left in Vermont and Josephine's family wanted us to be nearer to them, the offer to start practice in Rutland was not for me, in spite of Mr. Clement's generous offer.

In the meantime my old Yale Law School friend, Lenn Oare, had settled in South Bend, Ind., due to the fact that his wife Edna, was a North Liberty girl. He had written me that if I had not yet come to a decision, why not come to South Bend and join up with him. So I wrote and thanked Mr. Clement and told him that I had decided to go into partnership with my friend, and after spending a week with Josephine and her family in Napoleon, I went on to South Bend, arriving on November 4, 1911.

I did not know a soul in the state of Indiana except young Oare and his wife. He had a little cubby-hole of an office in the J. M. S. Building, consisting of two small rooms, and it was there that we started out together for about two years. We had a second hand typewriter and no secretary. When one of us had a caller, the other had to go out into the other little room and cool his heels. However, this fact did not disturb us a great deal as we had few callers!

Oare's father-in-law, a well-to-do farmer, threw him a little business, but nobody threw me even a bone. My gross earnings my first year were ninety-five dollars, which of course, nowhere paid even my share of the office rent. It was only by reason of Grandma Harrison advancing me a hundred dollars now and then that I was able to hold on. For a long time she kept the wolf from coming right through the door.

The bar examination was an oral quiz by Judge Lucius Hubbard and Andrew Anderson, a grizzled old veteran of the bar. They asked me a lot of questions I could not answer. But with the kindness, already mentioned, with which I have always been treated, they gave me my credentials. Probably they soothed their consciences by realizing that I would not have an opportunity to do much damage to clients for some years, and in the meantime would have plenty of time to bone up on Indiana pleading and practice, as well as statutory law of which I knew nothing.

For a month I roomed at the Y.M.C.A. This was too expensive, and I got a room at the home of Mr. and Mrs. Gaston who lived on West Jefferson Boulevard. The Gastons were like characters from Dickens; neither of them much larger than a good-sized bird. But I went to church with them and slowly made a few acquaintances.

The first case I tried was in Justice of the Peace Court, on which I worked for weeks and got paid five dollars. I lost the case.

*Sam and Josephine Pettengill at the time of their marriage in 1912.*

Meantime Josephine and I had decided to get married. I found a widow, Mrs. Ella Hendricks, 1128 Portage Avenue, living alone in a little house with three rooms upstairs. The rent was sixteen dollars a month, but she had a nice garden and gave me the privilege of working it. I had plenty of time to do so with the result that I had some radishes and lettuce, with beans coming along nicely, by the time of our marriage.

We were married on June 1, 1912, at Grandma Harrison's house in Napoleon. We had no money for a honeymoon, so after shaking the rice out of our clothes we took the day coach to South Bend where some furniture had already been sent to us. I walked to the office as it was only about a mile away, and with so much time on my hands often walked back for lunch. A street car line was then running which made it easy for Josephine to get to town. It was a hard struggle but we were happy about everything except the failure of clients to realize what a valuable addition had been made to the South Bend Bar.

After one year, Lenn Oare and I decided to separate because we felt that by doing so we might better our economic plight. He went into partnership with Ernest Morris, who soon left the law and started the Associated Investment Company, of which they made a great success. I joined Charles Wiedler and a young lawyer, Orrie Parker, under the firm name of Wiedler, Parker and Pettengill in the Jefferson Building. Mr. Wiedler was in revolt against the machine running the Democratic party and ran for mayor on an independent ticket. They got me to run with him as candidate for state representative. We had a lot of fun peering into the cesspools of local machine politics, but were completely and almost unanimously slaughtered on election day, a fate that happens to most reform tickets.

From a memorandum in my files, I find that our first year's earnings, from 1913 to 1914, amounted to $2,698.89, or $74.97 per month per man.

Gradually my income picked up but I had a great many discouraging hours. I often thought that I would have to give up the idea of being a lawyer. I think it was a mistake not to have gone into one of the established law firms on a salary, small as it might have been. It would have paid something definite and given me much more practice than was possible waiting around for clients. It was only by reason of the encouragement given me by Josephine's step-father, W. W. Campbell, a fine old-fashioned lawyer in Napoleon, that I held on. I remember him saying to me, "Don't give up. It will not be long before you will make in a month what you are now making in a year." This seemed utterly fantastic to me at the time, but it worked out that way.

At this time I gave a course on Commercial Law for Business Men at the Y.M.C.A. It met every Tuesday evening for six months and added a few dollars to my income. On March 18, 1914, we bought the house at the corner of Riverside Drive and East Navarre Street, owned by a widow and her school-teaching daughter, Helene Siewertsen. The price was three thousand five hundred dollars. Grandma Harrison loaned us the five hundred dollars needed for the down payment. It was here that our daughter, Susan, was born, June 21, 1917. By the time Susan had arrived I had been able to buy a second-hand Ford for two hundred and fifty dollars. It had an "arm-strong" starter, magneto ignition and the spark plugs had to be cleaned every time I drove it. However it was a godsend in permitting us to take little drives in the hot summer evenings. Due to rising prices on account of the war, I sold the car a year later for two hundred and thirty-five dollars, so it cost only fifteen dollars plus the gas and oil during that year. Later I bought a new Ford sedan which was very comfortable in cold weather.

During our first years in South Bend, in order to develop acquaintances and build up a law practice, I began making speeches before little groups all over the county. There was no tuberculosis hospital in northern Indiana and a group of South Bend doctors and their women allies interested themselves in getting one established. I became chairman of our publicity committee at a salary of zero a year, but went hither and yon speaking before various groups such as the Parent-Teachers in behalf of the T.B. hospital, for which funds were finally voted by the County Board of Commissioners. In addition I developed a lecture on "The Trial of Jesus from a Legal Standpoint." I thought this would be an excellent way to impress the natives with my legal ability, and gave this talk wherever a group wanted a speaker but had no money with which to pay one. The older members of the bar thought this was rare stuff. And in bar association meetings for years the program nearly always had reference to Pettengill as "that Pettengill who would move for a new trial for Jesus."

The fall we were married I made my first political speech at a little school house in the county in behalf of Woodrow Wilson and the immortal principles of Thomas Jefferson. There were about fifteen in attendance, most of whom were the candidates. This was followed by many other talks during the campaign, and then I did some speaking in succeeding years for other presidential candidates, such as Cox, John W. Davis and

Al Smith. Actually I made my first real step into politics when I made a radio speech for Al Smith in the 1928 campaign. I was a Congregationalist and a 32nd Degree Mason, but in 1928 Indiana was largely in the control of the Ku Klux Klan; the state was violently anti-Catholic and a great deal of sentiment was developed all over the state against having a Catholic for president. But I liked Al Smith and I liked the things he stood for then and subsequently. So I made the speech, the theme of which was that religion should not have any part in the selection of a president.

I played a good deal of chess in the Y.M.C.A. and organized the first chess club in town and became chess champion of South Bend. I also began to acquire what became the largest chess library in the city. Over a period of years the club arranged for chess matches with Edward Lasker of Berlin, former world's champion; Capablanca of Cuba, world's champion at the time he visited South Bend; Alekhine of Russia, also world champion when in South Bend, and Frank Marshall, United States champion. I had the privilege of playing with each one of them and lost each time. After I played with Capablanca he gave me an autographed photograph of himself which now hangs in my study.

When World War I broke out, I was over thirty and a husband and father, and so was not inducted into the army, but was appointed to serve the U.S. government as a "Four Minute Man." In his citation President Woodrow Wilson wrote: "Upon you Four Minute Men . . . will rest . . . the task of arousing and informing the great body of our people. My best wishes and continuing interest are with you in your work as part of the reserve officer corps in a nation thrice armed because through your efforts it knows better the justice of the cause and the value of what it defends." I made countless speeches on behalf of the war effort and helped sell thousands of dollars worth of Liberty Bonds until the war ended and my services were no longer needed.

In the fall of 1915, old Judge Lucius Hubbard died and his son, Arthur L. Hubbard, invited me to join with him under the firm name of Hubbard and Pettengill in the J. M. S. Building. I had fought hard in a case in which he was the opposing counsel and attracted his attention. Mr. Hubbard was president of the First National Bank and was considered a wealthy man and through the bank and otherwise a good deal of business came into our office, most of which he was glad to turn over to me. It was only then that I felt sure I saw daylight ahead. His secretary was Miss Frances Rush, who stayed with me both in the law office in South Bend, and as my secretary in Washington while I was in Congress, and then again in South Bend as long as I was active there. We have always kept in touch with one another since.

About 1921, the First National Bank and the Union Trust Company affiliated and the bank and our law office moved to the Union Trust Company building. The firm's name by that time was Hubbard, Farabaugh and Pettengill and continued under that name until 1933 when Mr. Hubbard went broke and shot himself during the bank depression that swept over the country. After that the name became Farabaugh, Pettengill and Chapleau, and for a long time we were located in the St. Joseph Bank Building. Later Joseph Roper's name was added to ours as a fourth partner.

In 1920 we sold the Siewertsen place for five thousand dollars, at a profit of one thousand five hundred dollars over what we had paid for it, and bought a duplex at 129 W. Wakewa Avenue, taking the second story apartment. The price was ten thousand dollars which was too much for us to handle, even though I was making about six thousand a year by then. My practice was mostly banking and estate cases. So we sold the first floor apartment to another lawyer, William Betsch, who in turn sold it to still another lawyer, Otis Romine. It was from this home that Susan first toddled off to kindergarten at Harter Heights, her mother weeping copiously. An amusing recollection of that time is of a little four year old neighbor with whom the name Pettengill didn't seem to register and she used to call Josephine, "Mrs. Fingernail."

In 1926 we sold again and bought a new house at 310 Marquette where we lived for eighteen years. That place cost us twelve thousand five hundred dollars and I didn't get the mortgage paid off until after leaving Congress. Due to the fact that I was out of town so much and firing the furnace and shoveling snow was such a burden, we finally decided to sell the house and bought into a cooperative apartment at 128 South Scott Street where we lived for two years. In the meantime in 1940 we had bought the farm in Grafton which we called River Mowing, and in 1946 we sold the apartment and moved everything to Vermont with the idea of making the farm our summer home, and Josephine and Susan spending the winters in New York. I had to be in New York so much ever since 1944 that I had been staying at the Union League Club and wanted my family with me.

When Susan was three years old, she had a severe case of influenza complicated by pneumonia and wasted down almost to a skeleton. To get her out into the sunshine, Josephine took her to California in January, 1921, and they stayed until May. Susan made a good recovery but we worried about her every winter, and in 1925 Josephine and Susan spent the winter in Florida. In February, 1928, they went to Europe and did a lot of traveling, to Italy, France and to England in the spring and they came home the end of May. In January, 1929, they again sailed for France and Susan attended school in Cannes, until they returned to America sometime around mid-summer of 1930. In 1935 they went to Europe again, and Susan once more went to school in Cannes. During that summer Susan spent several months in Copenhagen after I had asked my friend, Mrs. Ruth Bryan Owen, then Ambassador to Denmark, to keep an eye on her, as her mother was remaining in France. In the fall, Susan went to Paris and attended classes at the Sorbonne while Josephine continued on in Cannes and later joined her in Paris. In June, 1936, they came back to America and Susan decided to go to summer school at Middlebury, and went back other years to attend both the French and Spanish schools and one summer the English school at Breadloaf.

As a budding lawyer I thought it wise to join a few organizations, chief of which was South Bend Lodge #294 of Free and Accepted Masons. I entered the Blue Lodge as Apprentice on April 11, 1913, and my Masonic record is outlined in the next chapter. Another organization in which I took great interest was the Round Table, a men's discussion group founded in 1907, its motto being "I am a man and everything human interests me." A speaker was appointed for each meeting and was free to choose his subject, and another member was selected to preside as chairman for the discussion which followed. During that period any member might offer his point of view provided he compressed it into seven minutes and refrained from personalities. An excellent dinner always preceded the program, conceding that enlightenment thrives in an aura of well-being. The possibility of controversy was no barrier. Religion, politics, education, law, ethics, social and labor problems were subjects touched on over and over again. In 1922 a Ladies' Night was inaugurated and the custom began of printing the paper voted the best of the year by the Committee of Judges. I was a two-time winner. My paper, "Poetry, and the Poet's Mission" which I consider one of the best things I ever wrote, was selected as the winner for 1929, and in 1933 my discourse on "Gold" was chosen. I have, of course, kept both and "Poetry and the Poet's Mission" will be found at the end of this book.

In 1925, Mayor Eli Siebert named me to the South Bend Board of Education and I became its Secretary. This was the only political office I ever held before being elected to Congress and it was not an elective office. Whether or not it was required by law, it was at least the custom to give both parties representation. A Democratic vacancy occurring, Mayor Siebert, a Republican, appointed me for a term of three years. He left the selection of teachers to the Superintendent of Schools, and kept free of other details normally belonging to his office. There was one exception. This was in connection with the purchase of coal to heat the school buildings. It ran into a sizeable sum much desired by the city's coal dealers and for a long time this plum had been given to one dealer who had an in with the political machine. I engaged in a real row with Chester Montgomery, a power in Democratic party politics in St. Joseph County. He disagreed with my view that the purchase of coal should be on a non-political basis and that separate bids should be made by all the city's dealers on the supply for each year. I won, and prosperity was passed around. During my three year term on the Board we built two fine new schools and I spoke at the opening of each. One of them at my request was named the Jefferson School. There were sixteen thousand children in the schools and I enjoyed speaking to them at their various events. While at that time I had no political ambitions, my name became well known in the city and I'm sure it helped when I became interested in running for Congress.

An amusing incident took place when I attended a meeting of the American Bar Association in Seattle in 1928. The first night we had all been invited to dinner and an entertainment at Vancouver and we went there by boat. On arrival at the hotel we found that our Canadian hosts had outdone themselves in providing alcoholic refreshment for the deprived lawyers from the dry United States. A few of us were personally dry but some were not and they took full advantage of the situation. The return trip left Vancouver at midnight, and a couple of hours later a distinguished member of the bar who had been practically carried on to the boat, awakened from a refreshing sleep on board and asked, "What time is it?" He was told two o'clock and suddenly remembering the big meeting that was to take place next day, exclaimed, "My God, we've missed the boat!"

In 1930 I was President of the St. Joseph County Bar Association. Its function was to promote high standards in the practice of law and to take action against those who were charged with violating them. Once a year we had a dinner meeting with an outside lawyer giving the address. At the end of my year as President, the invited speaker was Hon. James Hamilton Lewis, a noted lawyer from Chicago, who was later U.S. Senator. He was a very fluent speaker, who dressed meticulously on all occasions, including visits to the Chicago stockyards. The men employed there were a brawny lot, but when "J. Ham," as he was called, campaigned there, he dressed as well as he did when speaking to millionaires and their wives on Chicago's North Side. Other politicians felt that they would be called dudes if they did not dress like "one of the boys." But the "boys" felt complimented that J. Ham dressed his best for them.

I shall never forget that night at the dinner table. Mr. Lewis sat next to me and in talking about someone or other, I remarked, "He's nuts." Instead of responding "You're right," or "I don't agree," the famous man said, "Mr. Pettengill, it is a matter of infinite regret to me that I do not wholly concur in the opinion you have so admirably expressed!"

On May 30, 1930, I was the speaker at South Bend's massive observance of the day set aside to pay tribute to the living and fallen heroes of America's great wars. Because in it I traced the origin of Memorial Day, or Decoration Day as it was originally called when it was first officially observed on May 30, 1868, I think it appropriate to quote that part of it here.

> "When Lee surrendered at the famous apple tree of Appomattox, reason dictated that we should bind up the nation's wounds and care for him who had borne the battle, and again be brothers. But men did not feel like responding to reason. Lincoln had been murdered and Ben Wade and Stevens were insisting that the South should be treated like a conquered province; that Lee and Davis should be hanged as traitors. Then an event occurred such as those upon which the gods themselves throw incense. In the obscure town of Columbus, Mississippi, in 1867, only two years after Lincoln's death, a group of Confederate women went to the cemetery to lay wreaths on the graves of their fallen dead. As it happened, there were two or three Union soldiers in the same God's acre. With a divine inspiration one of the women suggested that they lay some flowers on these graves also. And so it was done. Just a few southern women, touched with that quality of mercy and tenderness for which their sex is honored.

"But it happened also that the crop of murders and divorces had been small that day, and so the press for want of something better, devoted a tiny inch of space to what they had done. This carried the news farther, but it would have been soon forgotten if it had not fallen under the eye of a poet, not one of the authentic poets, you understand, like Lowell or Longfellow, or Whittier, or Holmes, but an amateur poet. His name was Francis Miles Finch, a distinguished New York lawyer, judge and dean of the law school of Cornell University. He took the meagre prose item and transfigured it with a haunting rhyme and a magic melody. His lines have been recited hundreds of thousands of times.

'Sadly, but not with upbraiding,
   The generous deed was done;
In the storm of the years that are fading,
   No braver battle was won.
Under the sod and the dew,
   Waiting the judgment day,
Under the blossoms, the Blue,
   Under the garlands, the Gray.

No more shall the war cry sever,
   Or the winding rivers be red;
They banish our anger forever
   Who laurel the graves of our dead.
Under the sod and the dew,
   Waiting the judgment day,
Tears and love for the Blue,
   Love and tears for the Gray.'

"These beautiful lines did more perhaps, to heal the nation of its grievous hurt than all the labor of statesmen. They express the true meaning of Memorial Day. It is a day in which to remember. It is also a day in which to forget. A day to remember valor, a day to banish hate. Time that touches all things with mellowing hands causes us to forget the angers and passions that once divided us. It also causes us to recall the courage and devotion which unite us. When Charles Francis Adams, Lincoln's ambassador, was once twitted by a Britisher with the news of a southern victory, he pronounced these never to be forgotten words, 'Sir, the soldiers who yesterday defeated us, are our fellow countrymen.'

"Our fellow countrymen. Even in the heat of that terrible conflict we felt that the political division was somehow unreal and temporary, that the union of blood and race was a strong knot which no sword could cut."

# XVI

# MY MASONIC RECORD

### Blue Lodge
### South Bend Lodge #294 F and A.M.

| | |
|---|---|
| Entered Apprentice | April 11, 1913 |
| Fellow Craft | April 25, 1913 |
| Master Mason | May 16, 1913 |

Later I went through the chairs and became Master of #294 in 1921. Ralph Longfield was my Senior Warden, and Elias Strickland, Junior Warden. The year I was Master, #294 was the largest Blue Lodge in St. Joseph County, with over 1,000 members, and I think it was the second or third largest in the state.

### Grand Lodge F. and A.M.
### of the State of Indiana

| | |
|---|---|
| Junior Grand Deacon | 1939 |
| Senior Grand Deacon | 1940 - 41 |
| Junior Grand Warden | 1941 - 42 |
| Senior Grand Warden | 1942 - 43 |
| Deputy Grand Master | 1943 |

I was due to become the Grand Master of the State of Indiana in 1944. However, in 1943 I became Vice-President and General Counsel of the Transportation Association of America in Chicago. This made it impossible for me to take on the heavy duties of Grand Master, so I declined to be considered for that great honor. However, as former Deputy Grand Master I am a permanent officer of the Grand Lodge.

Scottish Rite
Scottish Rite Degrees
in the Valley of Fort Wayne

| | |
|---|---|
| 14° | April 12, 1921 |
| 16° | April 13, 1921 |
| 18° | April 13, 1921 |
| 32° | April 14, 1921 |

I was elected president of my class. Transferred to Valley of South Bend on January 10, 1927.

Crowned a 33° Honorary Member at Boston, Mass., September 27, 1939. I was notified of my nomination to the 33° while in Congress. During eight years in Washington I had been unable to participate in Masonic work. So I later asked Brother Geike of Fort Wayne, "Active" for Indiana, why I had been thus honored. He said, "Because of your defense of the Constitution of the United States in the Supreme Court Packing Bill fight."

Masonic Services Other Than Above

Speeches before Blue Lodges, Grand Lodges and Scottish Rite bodies in South Bend, Fort Wayne, Indianapolis, Chicago, Omaha, Columbus, Ohio, Milwaukee, Kalamazoo, Boston, New York City, Bloomington, Ill., Washington, D.C., Mount Vernon, etc.

Degree work in Scottish Rite, chiefly as Standard Bearer in the 32°, giving the Flag Speech.

Contributed six hundred dollars toward the cost of the Temple.

Especially Interesting Masonic Occasions
Where I Spoke

Grand Masters' Meeting in Washington, D.C. General Marshall and Admiral King at head table.

Samuel B. Pettengill addresses gathering at Washington's Tomb, Mount Vernon, Virginia, on June 20, 1941.

Washington's Tomb, Mount Vernon, June 20, 1941. A group of Masons from my old district, together with their wives and children, made a trip to Washington, D.C., and of course one of the places they visited was Mt. Vernon. The place where General Washington and his wife are buried is twenty or thirty rods from the mansion. They are in a catafalque behind an iron grille and the two tombs can be seen from the outside, but the iron gate is seldom unlocked. But this was a special occasion. The chief groundkeeper was no doubt a Mason himself for when I concluded my speech, he asked me if I would like to place the flower wreath on the casket. So I stepped inside and laid the wreath on Washington's tomb. I have seldom been so affected in all my life!

Boston Mass., 1939, the year I got the 33°. Josephine and Mrs. Shephard Crumpacker with other Masons' wives came for the occasion.

Council of Deliberation, Indianapolis, 1939, "The Liberty of Private Judgment," one of my more thoughtful talks, widely distributed.

On May 3, 1966, the Grand Lodge of Indiana presented me with the fifty-year gold button, through the medium of St. John Lodge #41, Springfield, Vt., presentation being made by F. Ray Adams. It is of interest that my great-great-grandfather, Col. John Barrett, was Master of the first Vermont Blue Lodge which was chartered at Boston on November 10, 1781, by St. Andrew's Grand Lodge of Massachusetts. The charter was signed by Paul Revere among others. Although the Vermont Lodge was chartered to meet in Springfield, Vt., it organized in Charlestown, N.H., because for a period of a few months at that time about thirty-five towns on the eastern side of the Connecticut River in southwestern New Hampshire annexed themselves to Vermont. However in February, 1782, this union was dissolved, but the Lodge continued to hold its meetings in Charlestown until 1788 or 1789. The original charter is still in existence and I believe in the possession of the Vermont Lodge at Windsor.

On April 29, 1973, I was awarded the Caleb B. Smith Medal of Honor, the highest decoration awarded by the Grand Lodge of Indiana. The award was made "in recognition of distinguished service to the Craft." At the time I was Indiana's only Past Deputy Grand Master in a century. On May 27, 1973, John H. Jena, P.G.M., Grand Master of the Grand Lodge of Indiana, came to my home in Grafton to make the formal presentation at a private ceremony. The citation and the beautiful bronze medal are hanging in my study at Robin Lawn.

# XVII

# PROFESSOR

My experience in teaching has been very limited. The first winter I was in South Bend I lived at the Y.M.C.A. for a time and helped earn my room rent by teaching the English language to employees at Studebaker's and Oliver's.

A number of years later I taught at Notre Dame Law School two hours a day for a year. My subject was Conflict of Laws. At the end of the year I received a check for three hundred dollars together with a note from the president of the University, Father Cavanaugh, that this little slip of blue paper could not possibly express their appreciation of my devoted services which had made the past year at the Law School such a distinguished success. This Irish blarney made the check look bigger.

About 1945 I was really tempted to become a college professor. Richard Lloyd Jones of Tulsa, Okla., editor of their leading paper, had become interested in setting up a chair of what you might call Americanism at some university. His idea was that the chair should be filled by someone who had had experience in public life, knew something about American history, and had a proven record of devotion to our free institutions, political and economic. The course would be purely voluntary on the part of the students, and no credits would be given. His thought about this was that the young men, and women if co-educational, would think it was more fun than work if it were on this basis.

The idea was that the professor would have a home on or near the campus, with a big living room and a fireplace, to which the students might come at any time of the day or evening when convenient; that coffee and doughnuts would be served and the professor and the students would sit around the fire and chew the fat in perfectly informal fashion and with complete freedom of discussion. There would be no required reading. But hopefully, as the students became interested, they would ask what to read on some subject of American history or economics that interested them and thus the course would just grow, like Topsy. It would be as informal as the schools in ancient Greece.

It was Mr. Jones' hope that such a chair established on some campus would attract national attention and that the idea might spread from campus to campus. And if so, the different professors of Americanism might form an association with the hope of developing the idea further, even into the high schools. These teachers of Americanism would be free to lecture to the outside public and write and thus become a counter force against the avalanche of left wing literature that was pouring over the country.

Mr. Jones was a graduate of the University of Wisconsin and tried to get them interested but without success. His suggestion for the post at Wisconsin was Edwin Markham, author of "The Man with the Hoe," and one of the most noted names in American literature. However, Wisconsin wouldn't have him because he was not a Ph.D. Jones was all burned up over the Ph.D. grip on college faculties which he felt practically barred students from access to men of great accomplishment simply because they were not Ph.D. bookworms.

Jones then developed the idea with the president and trustees of Knox College in Illinois. They were agreeable if the right man could be found. Jones thought that Knox would be an ideal place to get this thing started in American colleges because it was where one of the famous Lincoln-Douglas debates took place and was located in the grass roots of America.

Having gotten this far, Jones wrote me a long letter asking me to come to Knox, personally guaranteeing my salary for, as

I recall, three years, and said that he was certain that he could get some of his rich friends in Oklahoma to endow the chair on Americanism at Knox so its permanence would be assured.

The whole idea appealed to me tremendously, but I was then in New York writing my newspaper column, which was going into a million or two homes twice a week and I just couldn't see my way to give up access to this number of people for the infinitely smaller audience that would be provided by the boys and girls at Knox.

If, however, I had been ten years older at the time, I believe I would have accepted and in that case would have wound up as a college professor. The idea appeared to me to be very sound and with possibilities of spreading widely over the campuses of the country. In addition, the thought of three months vacation every summer up in Vermont had great appeal.

If someone else was found or what has happened at Knox since then, I do not know. However within the last two years chairs on Americanism have been established at Harvard, Cornell and Southern Methodist in Dallas, Texas. Strangely enough, Frank Gannett, a trustee of Cornell, wanted me to consider the Cornell post, which had been founded by Mrs. Senior, although he knew nothing of the Jones plan. The Dallas post, in very much the same pattern that Mr. Jones had in mind, has been filled by an old friend of mine, former Congressman Hatton Sumners.

# XVIII

## CONGRESS

I was elected to Congress for my first term in November, 1930, the first Democrat from my district since 1918. This was for the 72nd Congress and mine was the 13th Congressional District, composed of Elkhart, St. Joseph, LaPorte, Starke, Marshall, Fulton and Kosciusko counties. My opponent on the Republican ticket was Andrew J. Hickey, a lawyer in LaPorte. Mr. Hickey had already served twelve years, having succeeded Mr. Henry A. Barnhart of Rochester, Indiana. Mr. Hickey was considered unbeatable, as he had won year after year by very substantial majorities.

The immediate thing that took me into the Congressional race was the issue of prohibition. President Hoover had appointed the Wickersham Committee to report on what should be done about better enforcement of the prohibition laws and the 18th Amendment. I had no interest in the liquor business whatever, but as a states rights Democrat felt that prohibition should be left to the states and local communities under local option laws. Newton D. Baker, of Cleveland, Ohio, former Secretary of War, was a member of the Commission. Just before it was to make its report in February, 1930, I wrote a letter to Mr. Baker telling him that I considered federal prohibition to be a clear violation of the underlying principles which led to the formation of the Union, a violation from which enormous harm has and must come, and urged him to make a clear-cut statement on the prohibition question. I gave a copy of this letter to the South Bend Tribune, which published it in full and it immediately became a news item throughout Indiana, which was considered to be one of the dryest states in the nation. Because of this letter and the fact that I was not identified with the liquor interests, the "wets" in my district thought I would make a good candidate for Congress. What was needed was a man who could get the wet vote of St. Joseph County and of the Michigan City area, while holding the dry vote of the rest of the district. Since I was personally dry I seemed to fit this situation. I had never had any connection whatever with the liquor interests, not even as an attorney for breweries, distillers or saloons.

I had long since made my political peace with the Democratic leaders of St. Joseph county, particularly Chester Montgomery with whom I had tangled while I was on the Board of Education in connection with the purchase of coal for the school buildings. I had also campaigned for W. R. Hinkle, the Democratic party's candidate for mayor of South Bend in 1929. So under urging from Montgomery and other leaders of the party, I filed for the Democratic primary for Congress in March, 1930. I had to first win the primary on May 6th from J. Harry Browning of Elkhart county who had strong American Legion support. After twenty years of practicing law I did not have any real hope of winning but entered the race chiefly as a means of getting the question of prohibition before the public. Browning's appeal was chiefly to the dry voters and he carried five counties and I carried only two, but these were the populous ones and I won, receiving 12,671 votes and Browning 9,076, and I became the Democratic nominee.

Because I was practically unknown outside of my own county, I was anxious in my first campaign to become known in the other counties and so arranged with the Prairie Farmer radio station in Chicago to speak once a week for four weeks. The Prairie Farmer station had a large following among the farmers, most of whom were antagonistic to my stand on repeal. I had to speak from their station at six-thirty in the morning. I was told this was a good time to reach the farmers as they had already fed their cattle and were then eating breakfast listening to market reports and other items of farm interest. In order to speak in Chicago at six-thirty those October mornings I had to come up from South Bend the previous night, get up at five in the morning and get out to the station.

Thus I reached the farmers who were generally considered very dry and supposedly hostile to a "big city lawyer" from South Bend. However, I got a very favorable reaction from the farmers. The word went around the district, "By gum, there is a city fellow who can get up in the morning."

An interesting anecdote of my first campaign was my meeting with General Gignilliat, a West Pointer, who was head of Culver Military Academy. Since he was the leading citizen of Starke County, a friend of his, Colonel Stogsdall, drove me down to meet the General on a Saturday afternoon during the spring primary. Culver was playing another team on the baseball field where we were told we could find the General. As soon as the game was over, Col. Stogsdall brought me up to the General and said, "This is Sam Pettengill, who hopes to be the Democratic nominee for Congress." The General had gimlet eyes and without stopping to say he was glad to meet me, he demanded "Are you wet or dry?" Talk about a man living his life in a second, I was certainly on the spot. I felt certain that the head of this fine boys' school was sure to be against liquor, but for some reason which I never understood, I looked back into those gimlet eyes and said, "General, I am at the top of the W.C.T.U.'s black list." He grabbed my hand and said, "By God, I am for you!" He became one of the best friends I had and did all he could for me even after his county was no longer in my district. If I had flinched a tenth of a second he would have marked me down as the kind of politician he had learned to despise.

Andrew J. Hickey, who had served six terms, was my Republican opponent. As I was the only candidate for Congress in Indiana who had declared for the repeal of the 18th Amendment, the campaign attracted some attention nationwide. An organization which supported repeal spent about one thousand dollars on my behalf during the campaign, but as far as I knew this was the only wet money spent during the campaign. In November I defeated Hickey by about three thousand votes and I ran against him in my next three races. In three of these four campaigns I also had a primary contest.

*Sam Pettengill at the time of his election to Congress in 1930.*

During the first term of my being in office the legislature redistricted the state and my district became the 3rd Congressional District, with Starke, Fulton and Kosciusko counties assigned to other districts. In 1932 the Roosevelt landslide swept over the nation and as I recall I carried every county in my district. In my second term I voted against the Soldiers' Bonus Bill at Mr. Roosevelt's urging and the veterans' organizations made a strong effort to defeat me. Nevertheless I won by a small margin. In 1936, Landon's year, I won easily. In my four races I carried St. Joseph, my home county, every time; Elkhart County three times out of four; LaPorte County and LaPorte City where Mr. Hickey lived, two times out of four. Except in 1932, I never carried any of the other counties.

During my first term I was a member of the House Committee on Military Affairs. This committee was of no particular interest to the people of my district, but being a freshman I took what I could get. However, it was by a combination of this committee assignment and the fact that I let it be known that I stood for a free economy and for reasonable thrift in government spending that I first attracted the attention of the press staff on the hill. I was attending a hearing on the bill to create the Tennessee Valley Authority, in the big caucus room in the House Office Building at which a large number of reporters were present. It was in the daytime; the sunlight was streaming through the windows and yet, in the huge chandelier and other lighting fixtures, hundreds of electric bulbs were going full blast. I left my seat, hunted up the janitor and suggested that he turn the juice off. The reporters picked this up, regarding it as real news that a Congressman wanted to save money. Newspapers all over the country printed articles about the incident, with some favorable editorial comment.

When I was first elected in 1930, the depression had not yet become widely visible. At least it was not an issue in that campaign. But it came on fast. Banks and factories began to close, and only those who lived through those years can feel their despair. In South Bend, the Studebaker factory closed its doors and its president killed himself. In the 1932 election President Hoover carried only six states.

Mr. Roosevelt took office on March 3, 1933. By then the Great Depression was on. He immediately closed for five days all the banks that were still open and sent to the Congress bill after bill designed to restore the confidence of the people. At that time I was enthusiastic about him and supported him in every way I could, even to the reduction of the salaries of members of Congress, taking a cut of about a thousand dollars, which was ten percent of my salary. Later the old salary was restored.

It was then that Dr. Irving Fisher, professor of economics at Yale University, came to Washington to promote a bill designed to temporarily restore buying power which had been nearly wiped out by the closing of banks all over the country. The bill was to put stamp scrip money in circulation until the panic was over. As an emergency measure there was nothing wrong with it except inconvenience. It had been used successfully in many European cities to supply a medium of exchange when gold and silver money had disappeared. A number of cities and towns in the United States were already engaged in issuing stamp scrip as a medium of exchange.

Dr. Fisher got Senator Bankhead of Alabama, who was the brother of the Speaker of the House and the father of Tallulah Bankhead, the actress, to introduce a bill to authorize the President and the Secretary of the Treasury to put stamp scrip money in operation until the panic was over. He asked me to introduce the bill in the House. I did, and it became known as the Bankhead-Pettengill bill. I made a speech in its favor before the House as an emergency measure. However, it never got any farther as confidence soon returned to the banks of the nation.

Soon after Roosevelt came in, Tugwell began to pour millions of dollars into various so-called "Tugwell towns" building houses and factories in order to provide shelter and jobs for the unemployed. One of these projects was known as "Arthurdale" in West Virginia. Congressman Louis Ludlow of Indianapolis and I drove up there one weekend and found houses then averaging about sixteen thousand dollars each, which would certainly be equivalent to fifty thousand dollar homes at today's prices, occupied by coal miners. A factory was to be built and being remote from raw materials and markets it would certainly be an economic flop. Ludlow and I led the fight in the House against further appropriations for this project. It carried and was the first defeat the Roosevelt administration suffered.

During the 1932 campaign, I attracted considerable attention by urging that the prohibition question be removed as an issue in that election. Earlier I had proposed that Congress adopt a resolution for the repeal or amendment of the 18th Amendment and provide for ratification or rejection by state conventions chosen by the people. I felt this would provide a virtual referendum on the question. This suggestion was eventually adopted and prohibition came to an end.

During my second term I was responsible for the removal of the words "laughter" and "applause" that were liberally sprinkled in many speeches of Congressmen which appeared in great volume in the Congressional Record, although they had never been delivered. On May 3, 1934, I got up on the floor of the House and inquired of Speaker Rainey how there could be laughter and applause called out by a speech no one had ever heard. This was a poser.

The members of Congress who "deliver" these undelivered speeches prepare the copy for the government printer and revise the matter in proof, improving the opportunity to make parenthetical notations of laughter and applause at points where they believe there would be such things if the speeches were really made. Until I raised the point everybody seemed to have regarded it as all right. The congressmen get armfuls of extra copies of the Record containing their imaginary addresses and mail them postage free to constituents back home.

Speaker Rainey ordered that there was to be no more laughter and applause of the ghost audiences that the congressmen so favored, and for quite a while the newsmen called me "the ghost silencer."

I supported many of Roosevelt's measures during his first term, and voted against the Patman veterans' bonus bill, even though some of the politicos in my district back in Indiana feared the entire ticket might suffer in the 1934 elections. But this did not happen. In the 1934 campaign, Andrew Hickey, who was my Republican opponent in all four of my campaigns, placed considerable emphasis on the bonus bill and my part in its defeat. I spoke in South Bend to an audience of the American Legion and the Veterans of Foreign Wars, and explained why I had opposed the bonus. They were obviously hostile, but nevertheless I felt I had made a good impression and perhaps even gained some votes.

I had supported Roosevelt in many of his proposals to get the country back on its feet by helping to draft measures that seemed necessary. Such were the Security Exchange Act, the bills to regulate the stock exchanges and public utilities, and I was in charge of the Motor Carrier Act when it passed the House. However, I could not stomach the repudiation of the gold clause in U.S. Government bonds. When it came to the vote in the House in January, 1934, I was one of the few who voted against it. This was the first important measure of the Roosevelt administration that I opposed.

From that day on my confidence in Mr. Roosevelt was shaken, and when in 1937 the Supreme Court Packing bill was handed to Congress, I knew we had come to the parting of the ways. I made the first speech against it. And during the months the bill was before Congress I spoke in fifteen cities and made five nationwide radio broadcasts against it. In addition, I with a few others, organized anti-court packing Democrats in secret conferences in order to make an effective fight against the bill if it passed the Senate. In this fight, and later in the Purge fight, I had the subterranean support of men like

John Garner and Jim Farley, who wanted the bear killed but didn't want to get any of the blood on their hands where it would show. I welcomed their encouragement nevertheless.

Two big fights I engaged in during my eight years in Congress were to prevent the passage of the Supreme Court Packing bill and to defeat the Reorganization bill in 1938. In these fights I was in opposition to the administration.

Among the constructive things I helped accomplish I would put as number one the assistance rendered in forming the first Interstate Oil Compact, which was signed in Dallas, Texas, on February 16, 1935, and consented to by Congress August 27, 1935. I was a member of the sub-committee on Petroleum of the House Committee on Interstate and Foreign Commerce from 1932 through 1938.

Partly as a result of the depression in the early thirties, the petroleum industry was in great distress. Two major solutions were proposed. The New Dealers, led by Secretary of the Interior, Harold L. Ickes, proposed to run the industry from Washington as a public utility. Their proposal, incorporated in the Margold bill, went so far as to give the Federal Government the power to decide when and where wells should be drilled and who could own or operate a service station, and where and under what terms. Under this bill a man would have to get a federal permit before he could drill a well or put up a service station anywhere.

This solution was very repugnant to me as it did not differ much from the way Hitler controlled business in Germany or Mussolini in Italy.

Some common control over the flood of oil that was driving prices down to ruinous levels was necessary. An oil producing state, acting by itself, could scarcely ask its producers to limit their production if producers in other states could continue to produce without limit, and thus invade or take away the markets of the producers in the state that was attempting to limit or prorate production. So if any common solution for a nation-wide problem was to be worked out it would either be by turning the whole thing over to the Federal Government as the New Dealers wanted, or to permit oil producing states to enter into a compact among themselves to limit production according to the best engineering principles, and thus conserve this natural resource by preventing wasteful practices.

The framers of the Constitution must have foreseen situations of this sort where states would need to cooperate on a problem common to them without sending the whole problem to Washington, D.C. Hence the provision in the Constitution authorizing interstate compacts. I have discussed this on page 158 in my book "Jefferson, the Forgotten Man." To put it here briefly, an interstate compact is a treaty between states in their sovereign capacities to accomplish matters over which no state separately has effective power. It helps to span the twilight zone between state and federal authority. It demonstrates that the men who wrote the Constitution of the United States way back in 1787 were not so short sighted as some of their modern critics pretend.

Most of the states have authorized or entered into compacts or treaties among themselves with respect to different matters, including such subjects as the growing and marketing of tobacco, hour and wage legislation, child labor, etc. In 1938 the Supreme Court of the United States upheld the binding effect of an interstate compact entered into between Colorado and New Mexico in 1923, with respect to the use of the water of the La Plata River. Boulder Dam is the result of an interstate compact among seven states. The Port of New York Authority is the result of a compact between the states of New York and New Jersey and not an act of Congress.

I, and other members of our sub-committee, strongly favored the interstate compact in place of federal control. As to the importance of the struggle for an interstate compact, I quote the following from "Conservation of Gas and Oil" by B. M. Murphy, published by The Section of Mineral Law of the American Bar Association, page 556:

> "In the battle between the proponents of federalized control of the petroleum industry and those favoring the control of natural resources by the states, an historic point of reference was reached with the adoption of the compact principle in Dallas, February 16, 1935. Indeed there are many who feel that the fight fought in those years and the victory there won prevented further excursions into federal centralized planning for other industrial facets of the United States."

The first important meeting to promote the compact idea was held at the home of Governor-elect Marland at Ponca City, Oklahoma, December 5, 1934. This meeting was attended by the governors of Oklahoma, Kansas and Texas, together with William F. Cole, Jr., E. A. Kelly, Charles A. Wolverton and myself of the subcommittee. Marland had served with me in Congress.

On January 3, 1935, our committee filed a report, "We strongly urge upon the oil producing states the adoption of interstate compacts to deal with the problems of production of petroleum with which industrial states are powerless to cope." This pressure from our committee helped push dissenters into line with the result that the Compact was finally agreed to at Dallas. Twenty oil and gas producing states finally became members of the Compact by 1948.

The Compact, however, had to be implemented by legislation in each participating state to prevent wasteful practices. One thing necessary was to prohibit the production of oil and gas in excess of the "allowable" fixed from time to time by state conservation committees. Oil produced in violation of an "allowable" was known as "hot oil." As the states had no power over interstate commerce it was necessary, in addition to approval of the Interstate Compact, for Congress to prohibit the movement in interstate commerce of "hot oil." This led to the Hot Oil Act sponsored by Senator Connally of Texas and enacted February 22, 1935.

This also had my strong approval. Looking back these many years later it is plain that the Interstate Compact and the Hot Oil Act saved one of America's greatest industries from being taken over by the Federal Government.

In 1936 when I ran for my fourth term in Congress I was re-elected by the largest majority ever given to a Democratic congressional candidate from my district. By then I had begun to have serious doubts about Roosevelt and his policies and when in February, 1937, he sent his Court Packing bill to Congress and his Re-organization bill in 1938, I became so disgusted with his abandonment of the principles he had stood for in his first election that I knew I could not in good conscience continue to pretend to be for him. Consequently in the spring of 1938 I announced that I would not be a candidate for re-election.

I had previously been advised by Senator James Byrnes of South Carolina and by others not to stay too long in Congress. One, Speaker Sam Rayburn, said he regretted not to be able to take his own advice. He said he felt he had gotten to be a "political whore." By this he meant that if a man stays in Congress too long, he has lost his law practice if he's a lawyer, and if he is in business he has lost his business contacts. The job in Congress then becomes of prime importance; it becomes your bread and butter. From then on you will start to sacrifice your convictions just to hold on to the job.

Because this was only two years after Roosevelt had been re-elected by the largest majority in history, having carried all of the states but Vermont and Maine, my break with the party chief aroused a good deal of comment. The Republicans especially urged me to change my mind and Senator Vandenberg told me that if I would do so he would come to South Bend, get the Republican leaders of the district together and urge them to put no candidate in the field against me. In addition he said he would make speeches in my behalf. As he was the Republican leader in Congress at the time, it seems likely that I would have been re-elected, either on the Democratic ticket or as an Independent. It was in 1938 that Roosevelt attempted to purge Democratic senators and congressmen who had opposed him, for example, Senator George of Georgia. His purge campaign was almost a complete failure due to the fact that the voters resented his attempt to dictate who their congressmen and senators should be and is an additional reason for my thinking that I would have won.

However, I held to my decision and wrote a series of articles on "The Purge Comes to America" which were syndicated and published all over the country and no doubt helped re-elect the men Roosevelt wanted to drive out of public life. The gist of these syndicated articles appears in "Jefferson, the Forgotten Man" which I wrote as my political valedictory. In brief I told of the new doctrine that was in the making and what its consequences would be. The doctrine was that members of the executive branch of the federal government may use the vast powers of their offices to nominate, elect or defeat candidates for federal, state and local governments. This is a breach of constitutional morality and is based on contempt for the people. Behind whatever mask, it predicates the view that the people in the states are incapable of self-government, or that Washington does not want their self-government. It is a species of treason toward the very heart of democracy, a knife in the back of the American Constitution. It will have the inevitable effect of destroying the independence of Congress and the independence of the states. In fact it will destroy the states as such. The state can exist only through its elections. If it cannot control its own elections it cannot exist as a state. Federal control of its ballot box will destroy it as a government, as surely as would an armed force sent out from Washington.

The following chapter was given as an interview to a Washington newspaper man at that time and tells in detail about my break with Roosevelt.

## XIX

## MY BREAK WITH ROOSEVELT

Few die, and none resign. So goes an old political saying. Congressmen who retire voluntarily are as rare as oysters in a church stew. Nevertheless, half a dozen members of the 75th Congress have left Washington voluntarily. I am one. Most of them, if not all, could easily have been re-elected, even those who might have been marked for the Purge, as results indicate their constituents would have backed them up.

My service in Washington antedated the Roosevelt regime. I was elected in 1930, before the New Deal was invented. I did not ride into Congress on anybody's coattails. When Mr. Roosevelt became the Democratic nominee I supported him. In fact I was an F.R.B.C. Democrat, or "For Roosevelt Before Chicago." I had read his sound and sensible speeches made in 1928, 1929 and 1930. In 1931 I declared for him in a public statement, the only Hoosier holding a major office to do so.

In 1932 he seemed the answer to the nation's prayer. The platform on which he stood was built on the doctrines of Jefferson, the Party's founder. In Mr. Roosevelt's early years in the White House I was his loyal supporter. I stood with him on the so-called coffin-nail votes, such as the bonus and the economy acts. Many who now beat their breasts in his praise left him then. I do not question their sincerity; I mention my support only to show that I stayed with the President when the going was tough.

I supported him again in 1936. Along with millions of others, I thought he would use his second term to smooth the rough corners from the first; to adjust reform measures to ac-

*Sam Pettengill, then a member of Congress, at the time of his break with President Franklin D. Roosevelt in 1937.*

tual needs as shown by experience; to emphasize administration, not legislation. First term, Reform; second term, Recovery. That's what I thought and hoped.

I was mistaken.

The United States was ready to go to town when Mr. Roosevelt was re-elected. Immediately after the election Mr. James Farley issued his "No Reprisals" statement and Mr. Roosevelt left for South America on a good-will tour. In the next three months business had the greatest boom of his administration. But by February the country had been steered off the highway to prosperity and into the second depression.

However, had I dreamed in 1936 that Mr. Roosevelt was secretly nursing any such idea as his Supreme Court packing program, I would not have supported him. I could not have been a candidate on the same ticket and kept silent. I should have regarded myself as party to the perpetration of a fraud on the American people.

My faith in Mr. Roosevelt's fitness to lead the party of Jefferson had been jarred by the Roosevelt readiness to advocate extreme laws in the last half of his first term. I did not relish, for instance, the death sentence in the holding company act, the Huey Long soak-the-rich tax bill, and other measures. But I realized that much of this legislation had been rushed to stave off disaster. We had a giant depression with us for which he certainly was not to blame. There had been little time to split hairs.

Many laws had been passed purely to meet the emergency. They were neither requested by the President nor enacted by Congress as permanent legislation. The President had committed himself to trial and error and had created a belief that he would correct proven mistakes. Congress and the country gave him all he asked. Later we had to learn that Mr. Roosevelt was unwilling to admit error in anything he did, or move for its correction.

Democratic by a record majority, the 75th Congress convened January 3, 1937. Nine days later the President asked for enactment of a law ostensibly to enable him to reorganize the executive branch of government. With his request he submitted to Congress the Brownlow committee report detailing the reorganization program.

That's what it was called. In reality it was a grab for powers such as no other President ever had exercised in peacetime or should exercise under our democratic government. He sought more power than a good man should want or a bad man should have. Congress was asked to abdicate authority over the public purse and governmental machinery. Mr. Roosevelt sought blanket power to abolish or transfer federal agencies without restraint, and to create new agencies and prescribe their functions.

In effect, he asked for power to repeal laws or write new ones. It meant government by executive decree. They have that kind in Europe. Some people may like it; I don't.

The powers he sought were not to expire at any fixed time. They could pass on to his successor, whoever he might be. Once granted, they could not be recalled by Congress or the people against the will of the Executive except by a two-thirds vote in both House and Senate. A President with thirty-three yes-men to do his bidding in the Senate, for instance, could keep them forever.

Capacity for harm was almost infinite under the power sought. For example, the President could abolish the Federal Trade Commission, turn the Interstate Commerce Commission into an appendage of the Labor Board, place the tax bureau under the Labor Department, put the public health service and radio control under the Postmaster General, wipe out the local government of the District of Columbia and abolish the Civil Service. Money for one purpose could be spent, as much or as little as the President might wish, for any other purpose. In effect the President could effect wholesale changes repugnant to democratic government but highly regarded by contemporaneous European dictators.

Such, in its far-flung consequences, was the legislative bagatelle the President requested.

Soon thereafter a bill to make the proposal effective appeared on Capitol Hill. It came from some outside source, but that was not unusual; for four years bills had been coming up to be passed by Congress without change "to meet the emergency." This bill came secretly to a small group. It was submitted, I was told, to one trusted leader in the House and another in the Senate who had been chosen to give it their names and attend to its passage.

But it didn't work out that way. The bill was so fragrant that neither trusted leader wanted it around. They declined, I was told, with emphasis if not profanity, to lend their names to it. The outstanding copies were then recalled, except for a few held out by perverse members, and a slightly milder measure was substituted.

Before that came to debate in Congress it was overshadowed completely by another request from the President. On February 5, the court-packing proposal exploded like a bomb on Capitol Hill. Its submission carried me, a F.R.B.C. Democrat, to the Rubicon. I crossed it. I couldn't go along with the President.

I got a copy of the bill that night. It was a Friday, the 5th of February, and by Monday I had made up my mind what I was going to do. I sent a letter to all of the newspapers in my district saying that if it was the last thing I did as a congressman, I was going to prevent the packing of the Supreme Court. Not that I agreed with all of its opinions, but I was against the idea of having a lot of king's men appointed to the Supreme Court, as Roosevelt had attempted to do with the independent administrative commissions. I also said, "I cannot think of anything more likely to chill confidence and the upsurge of business."

I had come to my decision after a prolonged bout of serious thinking over the weekend. We had come to the third great crisis in American history. The first had been the Revolution, the second the Civil War and the third, now at hand, presented the issue whether the nation should endure as a republic.

Since the World War, seventeen constitutional governments had disappeared. Were we to be the eighteenth? The way they had gone we now were invited to tread. It was to start with putting the Executive over Congress and the courts and it was to end with the supremacy of the Executive over everything. Congress was asked to leave our children the heritage of a one-man government.

I couldn't become a party to that. I had shown my loyalty to the President. I had gone far along with him; certainly I had not been against his policies. Mentally I called the roll of major laws for which he had asked and for which I had voted. I had helped write the Securities Act of 1933, the Stock Exchange Act of 1934, and the Holding Company law of 1935, although I opposed its death sentence as a brake on prosperity, as it has proved to be. I had sponsored the truck and bus bill and had been author of the long-and-short-haul bill designed to permit the railroads to meet competitors on equal terms.

In addition, I had voted for guaranteeing bank deposits; for the H.O.L.C.; farm credit; the social security law and for relief. I had supported enthusiastically the move to revive our foreign trade through reciprocal agreements. On these and other measures I had stood by the President.

But I could not stand by him now. What had happened? Had I changed? Or had the President changed? I went to my bookshelf and turned to Mr. Roosevelt's campaign speeches for answer. Here I found what Mr. Roosevelt had said in Kansas in 1932:

"When the futility of maintaining prices of wheat and cotton through so-called stabilization became apparent, President Hoover's Farm Board, of which the Secretary of Agriculture was a member, invented the cruel joke of advising farmers to allow twenty percent of their wheat lands to lie idle, to plow up every third row of cotton and to shoot every tenth dairy cow."

The proposal had been a "cruel joke" to Candidate Roosevelt in 1932; what was its appeal to President Roosevelt in 1937? Hoover's Secretary of Agriculture was charged with inventing it in 1932; whose Secretary of Agriculture had revived and enlarged it now? Yet it was to validate this "cruel joke" that the Supreme Court in the later words of Senator Carter Glass, was to be packed with judges "speaking the ventriloquisms of the White House."

Here is an excerpt from another speech made by Mr. Roosevelt in 1932 which I read that night:

"For three long years I have been going up and down this country preaching that government costs too much . . . For three long years the federal government has been on the road towards bankruptcy . . .

"The (Hoover) spending, my friends, is the most reckless and extravagant that I have been able to discover in the fiscal record of any peacetime government anywhere, any time. Taxes are paid in the sweat of every man who labors. If those taxes are excessive they are reflected in idle factories and tax-sold farms and in hordes of hungry people tramping the streets and seeking jobs in vain. They pay in deductions from wages, in increased cost of what they buy or in broad unemployment throughout the land.

"Let us have the courage to stop borrowing to meet continuing deficits. Stop the deficits!"

How hollow those brave words of 1932 rang in my thoughts in February, 1937. I had not left the President; he had left me and millions of other Americans. I am still a Roosevelt Democrat — the Roosevelt of 1930-32.

The long range issue presented by the third crisis was whether democratic government in the United States was to endure. The immediate issue was whether the budding business revival was to be checked in millions more rendered idle. The material welfare of a hundred and thirty million Americans bulked large. I quote from my book, "Jefferson, The Forgotten Man:"

> There are some forty-four million savings bank accounts with deposits of twenty-four billion dollars; ten million members of building and loan associations with deposits of eight billion dollars . . . some sixty-four million persons whose lives are insured for about one hundred and eight billion dollars.
>
> Since 1776, America has produced three times as much wealth as existed in the entire world at that time. Today, with seven percent of the world's population, it has forty-five percent of the world's wealth. In the seventy-five years preceding 1922 our population increased five times, our wealth fifty times, or ten times as fast . . . I have never been able to understand how we accomplished this by doing everything wrong.

Yet, with that background the nation was struggling in 1937 — Mr. Roosevelt himself had said so — to attain a degree of prosperity equal to that we had known from the beginning of 1923 to the end of 1925.

Our national income had averaged seventy-nine billion dollars a year then; since then our population had increased fourteen per cent. On a man-to-man basis, our 1937 national income should equal seventy-nine billions plus fourteen per cent, or ninety billions. To that should be added ten billion dollars accruing through normal advances of science and technology, bringing our 1937 income to around one hundred billion dollars.

What were we going to get? The best 1937 estimates ranged between sixty and sixty-five billion dollars. Man for man and family for family, we were only two-thirds as prosperous as we had been twelve to fourteen years before.

Why?

Not because credit was lacking; it was almost inexhaustible. Not because the banks were shaky; they were free from failure, their deposits guaranteed. Not because industry needed no more machinery; obsolete plants dotted the land. Not because we had a plethora of housing; the greatest shortage in our history had developed. Not because the railroads needed no more equipment; their needs were monumental. Not because of a glut of skilled workmen; in many lines there was a shortage.

Why then?

I could find but one logical answer — too many experiments; too much reform; too much uncertainty. THAT was the brake on prosperity.

Business did not know what wages the government would compel it to pay. It did not know what the government would take from it in taxes. It did not know whether government ownership or the sit-down strike would leave it in possession of its own property. It did not know when, where, or how government would compete with it and destroy it. Business was in a fog of uncertainty, not knowing from one day to another what government would do to it next.

And now the President proposed to make the courts subservient to a regime whose experiments and waste had brought business to its unhappy plight. Jefferson's doctrines and the accumulated wisdom of one hundred eighty years had been junked. A Just-as-Good-or-Better kind of government promoted by Roosevelt was knocking at the door. As a congressman I had to choose between Jefferson and Roosevelt. I chose Jefferson, and in choosing him I chose Lincoln too, for Lincoln had been a follower of Jefferson.

I knew what Jefferson and Lincoln had advocated and how it had worked, whereas nobody could any longer know what Roosevelt would advocate or how it would work. He stood for unpredictable government, and prosperity can't be built on unpredictables.

So I arrived at my decision. When it was reached I and the other followers of Jefferson in Congress faced a great defensive battle against the court-packing bill. How that battle raged in the Senate has been told by others; this is the FIRST STORY of the fight in the House where it raged no less violently, although without publicity. Senate opponents of the bill were the shock troops in the front line trenches; we in the House brought up the munitions of war.

The program was sent to Congress on a Friday. The next Tuesday night I sat with nine Democratic colleagues to plan our campaign in the House. They were Eugene E. Cox and Hugh Peterson of Georgia; Andrew J. May and Virgil Chapman of Kentucky; Joseph J. Mansfield of Texas; Herron Pearson of Tennessee; A. Willis Robertson, Patrick Drewry and Howard W. Smith of Jefferson's own native Virginia. All were veterans. Mansfield with twenty years' service, was Chairman of the Rivers and Harbors Committee. Cox, who had served twelve years, was a member of the Rules Committee, as was Smith. Both were marked later for the Purge and both survived it with flying colors.

Drewry was ranking Democrat on the Naval Affairs Committee. Also he was Chairman of the Democratic National Congressional Committee, close to James Farley in directing party campaigns. We made Drewry chairman of the House group — a magnificent leader. May soon was to become Chairman of the Military Affairs Committee. Peterson was a member of the Public Lands Committee and Robertson of the Ways and Means Committee. Pearson, Chapman and myself were members of the Interstate Commerce Committee.

Such was the original steering committee in the House. Later it was expanded to fifteen members. We discussed whether the fight should open in the House or Senate and unanimously agreed on the Senate. Members of the group talked with Speaker Bankhead and Majority Leader Sam Rayburn. What we needed most was time to organize opposition in the House; lacking it there would be danger that the

House might be stampeded by administration pressure into passing the bill. We knew that the Senate could debate it longer than the rigid rules of the House would permit.

Senate leaders of the opposition discussed this with us and agreed to our suggestion. From that day, House and Senate groups worked as one. We were virtually a joint committee, self-appointed, although the Senate group bore the brunt of the actual battle.

The fate of the measure in the Senate was uncertain from the start. For weeks it appeared that the President would win. Thus it was imperative that we should make sure of stopping the bill in the House in the event of Senate passage. The general public, its eyes fastened on the stirring contest in the Senate, seemed to give the House little thought. The consensus was that if it passed the Senate it would pass the House. The public apparently did not think it possible to stop it in the House, but we did think it possible.

Our Senate colleagues agreed to use all the time possible and so our steering committee went to work. And I mean work. Every man in our group devoted long hours daily to seeking converts in the House. We observed no forty-hour week as we sought to pledge our friends, welcomed like-minded colleagues and put them to work, and tried to prevent uncommitted members from joining the administration forces.

Every legitimate publicity method was called into play as means to our end. Dove-tailing our efforts with those of our Senate colleagues, we unloosed a publicity drumfire which we heightened as the fight progressed. Whenever an advocate of the bill issued a press statement or made a speech or delivered a radio talk, our group matched it in kind within forty-eight hours.

We were taking our political lives in our hands and we knew it. Talk about keeping secrets on Capitol Hill — why, the administration's numerous agents there knew every move we made as soon as we made it. They fought back vigorously, politely as a rule, but savagely, with whatever weapons were handiest. I recall, for instance, that Harry Hopkins in a radio speech asked even the poor devils on relief to bombard us with letters.

It was no cream-puff party. The administration forces, backed by the whole power of the government, won converts too. Time and again members of our group were told privately by colleagues that they would have to vote for the bill on roll call against their personal inclinations because they didn't dare stick their necks out.

Nevertheless, we made headway. Daily reports from our Senate group also told of headway gained. Their fight at that stage was mainly for time. The lengthy public hearings helped, as did the long deliberation of the Senate Judiciary Committee after the hearings ended. The country was given time to understand the issues involved.

Our first big break came with the Senate committee's adverse report on the bill. The vote was ten to eight, but up to the moment of the poll the result was uncertain. Jubilation was unrestrained and in some cases, I heard, unrefined, when the vote was announced. We had won the first great skirmish. The bill's supporters were no longer on the offensive; it was their turn to fight defensively. Only those engaged in titanic contests know how such a change strengthens morale.

Then came a day, however, when the whole House group was unable to gain a single vote. At that state Capitol Hill buzzed with a report that the attack might be shifted from the Verdun line in the Senate to the House floor. Over the grapevine the rumor sped that in a flanking move the administration would force a House roll call before the Senate could act.

At that critical moment we lacked the votes to stop it in the House! A master stroke was needed. That fine patriot, Hatton

W. Sumners of Texas delivered it. He was Chairman of the House Judiciary Committee, the committee that would have been in charge of the bill had the administration pointed its artillery our way. I had talked with him an hour after the court packing message was first read in Congress. That had been in February. Months had passed; it was now summer, and while Judge Sumners had not announced his position, I had felt from the first that he would be with us.

One day when the shifting of the battlefield from Senate to House seemed imminent, the word went around that Sumners would speak. House office buildings disgorged their workers as members swarmed to the floor and their secretaries and clerks made for the crowded galleries. Hearing the report, the Senate strolled over to the House, senators temporarily deserting their own debate to hear ours.

Upon the crowded chamber and the packed galleries a hush fell as the veteran Texan rose. He stood in the well of the House and made his first public utterance on the bill. It was a ringing denunciation, logical, eloquent and shot through with the effective force of moderation in word and gesture. It was the most telling blow delivered against the bill on our side of the Capitol. Its timing was exquisite.

The roar of applause that greeted his courageous act thundered upon his slight figure from every nook and cranny of the House chamber and rolled through the cloakrooms and corridors. It was overpowering, tumultous. The galleries joined in the din and for once in their noisy history were unrebuked.

We did not grasp it fully then, but when Sumners took his seat the bill was dead.

It was drama that made pulses sing, but the historic day was not for drama alone. Tragedy shared the spotlight, for that night Joe Robinson died.

Joe Robinson was Majority Leader of the Senate and when he passed on, Roosevelt lost a brave and loyal soldier from the ranks. He had given his all in devotion and service to his chief. And I have wondered often if there were not a link between Sumners' great speech with the tumult it evoked, and the stilled heart of Joe Robinson as he lay alone in the solitude of his apartment that night.

Could he have known in his last moments that Sumners' speech had doomed the bill in the House, even should it pass the Senate? Could he have guessed that his loyal fight had been in vain? I wonder. He died for a cause lost on the last day of his distinguished career.

The Sumners' speech spelled the end of our fight. We in the House won our needed converts. Our tally sheet showed victory. We felt sure of a margin of ten votes, out of a House membership of four hundred and thirty-five.

Not long thereafter the bill came to a vote in the Senate where it met its doom. Our fight was over. I had participated in the greatest congressional struggle since the Webster-Hayne debates a century ago. I made the first public speech against the measure by a congressman. It was in Indianapolis and that same day Senator Burton Wheeler spoke against it in West Virginia. In the course of the battle to defeat it I toured the United States, making a total of fifteen speeches in as many cities and I also made five nationwide radio addresses.

When the session ended I announced my decision not to run for re-election. Even after almost eight years in Congress, I felt I could still go back to my law practice before I became a prisoner of politics. On August 23, 1937, I wrote a letter to Orlo Deahl, Democratic Chairman of the Third Congressional District, saying I would not enter the 1938 primary. There was only one more big fight ahead, to defeat the so-called Reorganization bill. In the dying hours of the session the House had passed minor parts of the program. But the heart of the

*In 1938, after serving four terms in Congress, Sam Pettengill decided not to seek reelection. This photo is taken from an article about him that appeared in* The Saturday Evening Post.

proposal still lived and it was carried into battle on the Senate floor when Congress reconvened in January, 1938.

Our House group bent again to the task, following the familiar pattern of our work against the court packing bill. We renewed the alliance with our Senate colleagues and again matched publicity for the reorganization bill with publicity against it. Once more we went to the press and radio and the speakers' platform.

A personal appearance I recall vividly was at New York's Town Hall of the Air, in January, to debate the program with James Roosevelt, the President's son and secretary, before a large audience and over a nationwide radio network.

The audience included, among others of the family, the President's mother who occupied a seat near the platform. Everybody in the hall knew of her presence. I could sense the sympathy for her. It was high drama. There she sat in the dignity of life's evening, a picture of gentleness and charm, while on the platform her grandson spoke for a measure dear to her distinguished son's heart. And who was I to mar such a pleasant scene?

Overwhelmingly I realized that I was the fly in the ointment. I had been assigned the role of villain and the audience telegraphed across the footlights that it realized my miserable status. I sensed the sickening certainty that the crowd doted on the visible Roosevelts. Something had to be done quickly to dissipate that emotion if Sam Pettengill were not to leave through the keyhole when the debate ended.

James Roosevelt made a good talk but I didn't enjoy it much. Nor did I get inspiration for my reply until he closed his argument and I rose to open mine. Then, with sudden thought of Mark Antony's great oration on Ceasar's death, it came to me. "Ladies and gentlemen" I began, "if you have tears prepare to shed them now. You have been given a sugar-coated pill and you are now at the point where the sugar coating leaves off and the pill begins."

Applause broke over the house. From that opening I handled the subject without kid gloves and the crowd, I felt, was with me.

Our lines failed to hold in the Senate as they had held against the court packing bill. The reorganization measure passed by a three vote margin and went to the House. We were ready for it. Our tally sheet forecast its defeat by nine votes. On a motion to recommit, the bill was defeated in the House by a vote of two hundred and ~~fifty~~ five to one hundred and ninety-six. Our nine votes held.

We are done, I hope, with rubber stamp congressmen. The result of Roosevelt's attempted purge is the most hopeful thing that has happened in America, in the entire world, for many months. It shows that the American people understand what is at stake.

Congress has but one reason for its existence. It is to exercise its own judgment on public questions as the Constitution intended. It is the town meeting of by-gone years grown to national dimensions. So long as Congress speaks its own unmortgaged thoughts, democracy in the United States will live. When it speaks for an alien force, whether that force be a popular president, a benevolent despot, or an American Hitler, democracy in the United States goes with the wind.

The independence of Congress must be preserved and the task of preserving it is the most important one before the American people today. For one thing, blank check appropriations must end. The use of public funds as a whip to lash members of Congress and their constituents into obedience to the dictates of political party leaders must be forever barred.

In private life I shall continue to fight for free enterprise as against federal socialism. And I shall continue the struggle in which it was my privilege to share at Washington for the integrity and independence of Congress. A courageous Congress is the bulwark against tides that would destroy the rights of free men. It is the protector of the public purse, of the independent commissions whose functions include the administration of justice in industry. In a war-crazed world its independence is the last protection Americans possess against secret decisions that might involve them in war.

And an independent Congress alone can protect the independence of the courts. But a servile and dependent Congress is the protector of no thing or person, not even of itself.

# XX

## A MOST IMPORTANT DECISION

As stated in the foregoing chapter, as soon as I had made up my mind as to what I should do, I wrote a letter to all the newspapers in my district telling them that I was going to do everything in my power as a congressman to prevent the passage of the court packing bill. Almost immediately I received from the Legislature of Indiana a copy of a concurrent resolution memorializing the senators and members of Congress from the State of Indiana to support the recommendations of the President, including those respecting the Supreme Court of the United States.

Since my reply of February 16, 1937, details the reasons for a decision which was one of the most important in my life, I include it here.

The Senate and the House of Representatives
80th General Assembly
State House
Indianapolis, Indiana

Dear Mr. President, Mr. Speaker and Gentlemen:

I beg to acknowledge copy of a concurrent resolution memorializing the senators and members of Congress of the National Legislature from the State of Indiana to support the recommendations of the President including those respecting the Supreme Court of the United States.

I appreciate your communication as it is always my desire to have the benefit of the views of men in whose judgment and patriotism I have such confidence, in coming to a decision on matters of great importance.

I have considered carefully all that you have said and upon full reflection I regret sincerely that I am unable to agree that the public interest would be served by following the course you urge.

Permit me to set forth the reasons which impel me to come to an opposite conclusion.

First, let me say that I am not opposed to constitutional change by act of the people. I have voted for two constitutional amendments which are now the supreme law of the land. Further, I have disagreed more often than most lawyers with the judgments of the Supreme Court of the United States. As examples, I refer particularly to the decisions in the New York minimum wage act and the railroad pension act.

Let me say also that I thoroughly approve most of the President's recommendations with reference to procedure in the Federal courts and am prepared to vote them into law.

The recommendation I do not approve is that the President be granted power to name at once six new judges to the Supreme Court. In effect this is a request *to create a new court*. No such grant of power has ever been given to any president in the life of this Republic.

It is more power than a good man should want or a bad man should have.

A court so constituted could and probably will redefine the interstate commerce, general welfare, and other clauses of the Constitution so as to destroy this "indissoluble union of indestructible states" and place the most minute affairs of each of them at the mercy of a distant legislature in which they have only fourteen votes out of five hundred and thirty-one.

Do the people want this done? If so, they have the power to accomplish it. And I am a good enough American to carefully consider any specific proposal along this line for the people to vote upon and will cheerfully abide the result.

But before voting to change the Constitution I want to know what I am changing.

The surface reasons for the proposal have already been answered by the official report of the Attorney General. There is no congestion or delay in the Supreme Court.

I am glad that this is not a party question. The Constitution is the property of the whole people. They alone can change it. It is not the property of a party. Congressional majorities have no right to so change the court as to change the Constitution. To do so is an act of usurpation.

I hold no such mandate from the people I represent. I was

elected upon a platform which pledged me if necessary to submit "clarifying amendments" to the people for their approval. Beyond that, in conscience, I cannot go.

Beyond that, in wisdom also, we ought not to go. I would oppose this matter by whomsoever or whatever party advanced, whether President Roosevelt and Attorney General Cummings, or another Harding and another Attorney General Dougherty, or another Huey Long. It is precisely because this supreme power once exercised by a good man would be claimed by a bad successor that you and I, who think in terms of our boys and girls, should consider long and carefully before embarking on such a course.

What a progressive president would do, a tory or fascist president, by the same means, would do again.

Those who now favor the proposal would denounce it from the house tops if it came from another president, for example, Harding. This demonstrates that the proposal cannot stand on its own legs.

It is for this reason that acknowledged liberals like Borah, Johnson, Wheeler, Clark, Van Nuys, Raymond Moley and many others are as much opposed to this course as the ultra-conservatives. It is not sound from any standpoint. I regret more than I can express that the President in his anxiety to serve the people has been persuaded to such a course.

We are about to celebrate the birthday of the man who is "first in the hearts of his countrymen." In his Farewell Address to the people he loved and whom he had served without stint for twenty-five arduous years, George Washington said:

> "If in the *opinion of the people* (not of Congress or the President) the distribution or modification of the constitutional power be in any particular wrong, let it be corrected by an amendment in the way which the Constitution designates.
>
> "But *let there be no change by usurpation;* for though this in one instance may be the instrument of good, it is the *customary weapon by which free governments* are destroyed. The precedent must always greatly overbalance in *permanent evil* any *partial or transient* benefit which the use can at any time yield."

These words were penned in 1796. They have been accepted as the highest political wisdom by the people to whom they were addressed and by their children. I stand on them. We should test the impulses of the moment by the ripened wisdom of fourteen decades of time.

The Supreme Court has made mistakes. It will, no doubt, make more. But since it first assembled one hundred and forty-eight years ago it has made fewer mistakes and held the confidence of five generations of Americans more surely than either presidents or Congress.

I would prefer an occasional mistake to a perpetual mistrust.

The Supreme Court has neither a purse nor a sword. But it does have power — the power that is yielded by all mankind to integrity, courage, learning, independence and unbought justice. Its authority is a moral one only. Its commands are based on confidence and respect alone. As such it is the final city of refuge to which you and I and our children may go.

I am not wise enough to read the future but I am certain that this is a solemn hour in the destiny of America.

I can only express my profound belief that a packed jury, a packed court and a stacked deck of cards are all on the same moral plane.

I do not believe we can rebuild America upon such foundations.

I am, gentlemen, with great respect,

                Faithfully yours,

      Samuel B. Pettengill, M. C.

## XXI

## IN THE ENEMY'S CAMP

If a thing can be fantastic and somewhat logical at the same time, my experience in the enemy's camp in 1942 is a good example.

When I decided to leave Congress in 1938 after eight years, to return to the practice of the law, I had the urge to write a sort of political valedictory, and that fall "Jefferson, the Forgotten Man" came off the press. Two chapters of that book were circularized under the heading "The Purge Comes to America" and were widely re-printed throughout the country, and especially in states in which Roosevelt was attempting to designate who should be congressmen or United States senators.

In 1940 the third term issue came up. There was strong objection to it on the part of thousands of Democrats who sponsored public meetings in a number of states. I spoke in Illinois, Oklahoma and Texas. At the Texas meeting, Irvin Cobb, of Paducah, a life-long Democrat, spoke with me. It was the only time in my life that I met him. He had a wonderful capacity for being mighty solemn one moment, and then sending the crowds roaring with laughter the next moment with one of his whimsies. I have always considered his the most effective political speech I ever heard. However, it did not influence Texas.

I was pleased when a few years later the Constitution was amended to forbid a third term for a president. Thus I played a part in the adoption of another Amendment to the Constitution.

I opposed the United States getting into World War II and spoke with Colonel Lindbergh at a huge mass meeting in

Chicago of the America First Committee, headed by General Robert E. Wood, president of the Sears-Roebuck Company. I also spoke at other meetings with Mrs. Robert Taft, Senator Burton K. Wheeler, Senator Mundt of North Dakota, former Senator Robertson of Indiana and others. Of course as soon as we got into the war, the America First organization died. Later on it was revived by a lot of crackpots with whom we had nothing to do.

With my fingers completely crossed, because I had made up my mind long before November that Wendell Willkie was a faker, I nevertheless voted for him in the election of 1940, this being my first vote for a Republican candidate for President in my life. But my conscience would not let me vote for Roosevelt.

Of course it was a withering defeat for the Republicans and after it the GOP was one of the most pathetic organizations in American history. By the time 1942 rolled around, the secretarial help in the Washington headquarters often went for weeks unpaid on account of lack of funds. Joe Martin, who was National Chairman, had to go around like a beggar with a tin cup to get a few ten, twenty or fifty dollar bills here and there to prevent closing the office. It was to this sad state that the mighty GOP had fallen. Defeatism was as thick as fog in Republican circles everywhere. Willkie had made a complete fool of himself with his "campaign oratory" remark, as the final witness for the Land-Lease bill, and nobody believed in anybody any more.

It was at such a time that a voice reached me via long distance in my South Bend office. The man introduced himself as John R. Todd. I didn't know Todd from Adam's ox, but he insisted that I come to New York at once for something very important. So I went. Todd was an old man and the head of a firm of engineers and contractors who had helped to build Rockefeller Plaza, and Todd had been a money collector for the GOP. He told me there had been a conference of Republican leaders and they had decided to ask me to be National Finance Chairman of the Republican Party.

This was the most fantastic proposal I have ever received. Generally the Chairman is a man who not only could make large contributions himself, but he is in contact with large givers, none of whom I knew, and with respect to many of whom and their business interests I had fought in legislation in Congress.

The proposal could only be explained by the saying, "A drowning man grasps at straws." I was not enough of a fool not to realize that the offer of becoming Finance Chairman had probably been made to several dozen people, all of whom had declined. The sheer deviltry of the proposition somehow appealed to me. As I had already broken with Roosevelt, I decided to enter the enemy's camp although it was thoroughly understood that I was still a Democrat. Joe Martin rushed up from Washington to urge me to take the job, and also Bud Kelland of Arizona, the short story writer.

*Sam Pettengill at the time he served as chairman of the Republican National Finance Committee.*

Todd himself refused to serve on the committee. But when our letterhead finally appeared, it bore the names of myself, Colby Chester of General Foods; Stanley Resor of J. Walter Thompson, the advertising agency; Edgar Queeny of the Monsanto Chemical Company of St. Louis; Richard Harte of Parkersburg, West Virginia; Silas Strawn of Chicago; Marrs McLean of San Antonio, Texas; Herbert Clark of San Francisco and J. W. Farley of Boston.

We engaged a suite of offices in the Barclay Hotel in New York City, with a staff of fifteen or twenty, and went to work. We sent out tens of thousands of letters appealing for funds. We raised less than three hundred thousand dollars as I recall, which was a very small total. But we parceled it out in states and districts where the chance seemed best that the GOP candidate for the House or Senate might win. My contribution to the cause, such as it was, was to put some zip into the campaign, and I spoke at closed meetings in St. Louis, Chicago, Detroit, New York, Boston, Wilmington, Washington and many other cities.

Stranger that I was at these meetings of GOP's with their tails between their legs, the remarkable thing was that nobody seemed to consider me a spy in the camp. My good faith was taken for granted. The Washington meeting was attended by practically all the Republican senators and congressmen. Joe Martin introduced me. He said, "Sam is a Democrat, but don't we need some Democratic votes?" There was a roar of "yeses" around the dining hall. It was the only meeting in my life where I got three standing ovations; once when I was referred to in a preliminary way; second, when I was introduced, and third when I concluded.

The result of the campaign however, which surprised everyone, was that we increased the Republican vote in the House by forty-two and added three or four senators.

I conclude this quixotic chapter with perhaps its most astonishing paragraph.

When I first met Mr. Todd in his office in New York, he had on his desk a little print of my WHEN LINCOLN WAS A BOY. Todd was very gruff, although a good soul at heart. He said, "Did you write this?" I said, "Yes." He said, "Well, a man who feels this way about his country is the kind of man we need." It had never happened before and I feel it will never happen again that the offer of becoming Finance Chairman of a great political party was made to a man without considering the money bags at his command. Which in my case were nonexistent. But because I had written about Lincoln as a boy and the primeval forest of Indiana, Mr. Todd thought I was the man for the job. This was certainly the smallest pebble that ever changed the current of my life.

**When Lincoln Was A Boy**

Have you ever been alone at night in primeval wilderness? There are not many places now where virgin timber stands untouched by axe or saw.

One such place is Turkey Run State Park in Indiana. I was there one September. It told me something about Lincoln. I pass it on to you.

Toward midnight I went in the woods alone far from sight or sound of the nearest human being. A huge harvest moon in a cloudless sky sent long pencils of light down through the foliage of the forest. The gigantic tulip trees and sycamores stood in a hush of attention as if listening for the remotest whisper from earth or sky. They reached almost as high as an eight-story building before sending off their lowest branches. The massive trunks, glistening in the moonlight, seemed like the columns of some temple of the Egyptians where men worshipped forty centuries ago.

A curious sensation came over me. I felt my utter insignificance — the merest speck in space, and yet, with that feeling of littleness, another quite different. It seemed that I could reach up past that leafy ceiling to the quiet stars; that I could reach down through the cool earth to the roots of those Titans of the forest as they sought and found the sap of their sustenance.

The patience of the stars, the calmness of the sleeping earth, the massive strength of those mighty trees, the clean tang of the midnight air — all these entered through some window I did not know I had. I hope you have felt these things, if only once in a lifetime.

And then as I stood there, I thought of Lincoln when he was a little boy in Indiana seven score years ago. It occurred to me, with a significance I had never realized, that when he was a lad it was primeval forest everywhere, not at Turkey Run alone; that every night when he was a little boy and everywhere when he was alone in the woods, he must have sensed those same impalpable presences; that what was to me an unforgettable hour was to him the constant companionship of all his impressionable years.

The friendliness of trees! We have lost something in this age of brick and steel and concrete. Not so in 1816. Trees made the flat boat that gave safe passage across the Ohio to little Abe and his sister Sarah, to his father and Nancy Hanks. Trees made the "half-faced" cabin — open on one side to the bleak weather — where they spent their first Indiana winter. Trees fed the fire that gave them warmth, and lighted the pages of the Bible. Trees made for them their bed of leaves. Trees gave them the sugar of the maples, the brown nuts of autumn. Trees drove out the mosquitoes with their pungent log-fire smoke. Trees drove back the wolf and the panther with their glowing pine knots. Yes, and trees made for them crude chairs, tables, beds, axe-helves, ox-yokes, cradles, coffins. Little Abe with a whipsaw helped fashion one of these pioneer coffins. In its embrace a pioneer woman went "over Jordan."

Trees were friendly things.

"Such were a few of the many, many things the moon might have told little Abe Lincoln, going on eight, on a winter night on Little Pigeon Creek, in the Buckhorn Valley in Southern Indiana — a high quarter-moon with a white shine of thin frost on the long open spaces of the sky." You will find this in Carl Sandburg's "Prairie Years."

And then I thought of how little schooling the world has said Lincoln had — little Abe and sister Sally tramping hand in hand over rough trails to school — four miles and back — eight miles a day. Not much schooling there for two little children.

But suddenly I felt less sorry for Abraham Lincoln. Everywhere he went were the trees of the primeval forest — tulips, sycamores, oaks, maples, elms, beeches, walnuts. Everywhere that sense of peace, that feeling of being close to God. And I knew then that the statement in the books that Lincoln had little schooling was false, that he was at school many and many an hour when the boy of today is teacherless, learning the patience and the strength and the toughness and tenderness of trees, a lesson from the great Book of Life that never needs revision.

I understood better then the saying of the pioneers, "The cowards never started and the weak never arrived." I understood the "railsplitter" better and America better in the big timber at Turkey Run.

The following is the statement I made and sent all over the country upon accepting the chairmanship of the Republican National Finance Committee.

> I have accepted the chairmanship of the Republican National Committee because I believe that the only political instrument through which the constitutional freedoms of the Republic can now be restored and maintained is in the Republican party.
>
> If principles mean anything the Democratic party no longer exists as a national organization. It has been strangled by the New Deal party. This party has abandoned every Jeffersonian principle. It is the party of collectivism, national socialism, complete government control over the lives of men.
>
> The Republican party recognizes its duty in time of war and will perform it. It stands for victory at the earliest possible date and with the least possible loss of life. It pledges one hundred percent effort to winning the war.
>
> But the New Deal party is postponing victory by taking time out to play fourth term politics and by the extreme reluctance of its fuzzy-minded theorists to stand aside and let capable men run the war. The longer the war needlessly lasts, the more men must needlessly die.
>
> The New Deal party still caters to the "gimmies" in refusing to strip for action by cutting out every dime of non-essential spending. It thus wastes the sinews of war.
>
> The American people are not behind the Administration; they are way ahead of it. They know this is Valley Forge, but without the spirit of General Washington. Every poll of public opinion shows that the people want great leadership and a call to universal sacrifice. To win the war they are anxious to work, go without, buy bonds, and be taxed. They are ready to accept any needed sacrifice. They know we will pay a fearful price for victory unless we concentrate on the war and stop using the war to promote alien philosophies of government.
>
> Thoughtful people at home and abroad are asking these questions even as they redouble their effort to win the war. When peace comes, are we going to get our liberties back? Will disastrous inflation wipe out the savings of a lifetime of toil and

destroy the thrifty, middle-class American? Are we going to have a one-party State? We know that a strong two-party system is the indispensable bulwark of free government. It is the most effective tool ever invented by the most ingenious people in the world to preserve freedom and prevent the abuse of power. One-party government means fascism, whatever perfume of sweet-smelling syllables you pour over it. If there had been a strong two-party system in Germany, Italy and Japan, there would be peace in the world today — not war.

New Dealers openly avow their plans to keep and even extend the war controls when peace comes. They would reduce you to impotence. You would become powerless to resist them because they would have made you dependent upon the State for your very bread.

This is the New Deal program. It is hidden by the smokescreen of war. It is moving toward the same economic controls that Hitler fastened upon Europe and the Japanese upon Asia. It is American fascism. The "planned economy" we now have for the war will become permanent if we do not create a rubber stamp shortage on Capitol Hill in Washington, D.C. We had better install some Congressional brakes to be used when the time comes. Meantime this war will move faster if we have an alert opposition that will continue to expose New Deal bungling and spur it to action as has finally been done in the appointments of Messrs. Nelson, Baruch and Jeffers.

If the New Deal party is to be fought at all, it must be fought effectively and not futilely. The Republican party is the only established political group now at hand to preserve the principles of Washington, Jefferson and Lincoln for post-war America. The issue is Americanism or collectivism, whether of the right or left, whether Brown Shirts or Red. We must not lose liberty at home while we fight tyranny abroad.

Mr. Roosevelt in 1932 appealed for the votes of Republicans "willing to leave the household of a betrayed faith." Jeffersonian Democrats should now leave the new household of a betrayed faith. For if the New Deal party, by smear, pap or purge increases its grip on Congress in November, will we ever have another chance to go forward along the American Way? The anti-New Deal votes in Congress must be increased, not to obstruct the war effort but to accelerate it, and in the end, to save the Republic. A rubber stamp Congress, if continued longer in office, will inevitably become an American Reichstag. God forbid! I am glad to see signs everywhere that the people are getting wise to the New Deal program.

We must have a stronger Congress, an American Congress,

one that will perform its constitutional duties as the great board of directors of the American people, elected by them alone and responsible to them alone.

To this end we must have a realignment in America. We must be patriotic enough to forget past differences and return to those fundamentals upon which we can all unite. We have done so before.

Lincoln was a political first cousin of Jefferson. He said in 1859, "Soberly, it is now no child's play to save the principles of Thomas Jefferson from total overthrow in this nation." Those words mean far more today than when he spoke them, here and throughout the world.

In 1856, the Republican party in its first platform, pledged itself to "restore the federal government to the principles of Washington and Jefferson." The common principles of these two great men are a platform sturdy enough to support and be supported by every real American, North, South, East, West.

Lincoln Republicans and Jeffersonian Democrats are far closer to each other now than either of them are to New Deal collectivism. They must march together to preserve the "last, best hope of earth." We must remind Wall Street that it is only a narrow alley off Main Street; tell Washington, D.C., that it is not our master; return to the Constitution as men return to the North Star, and rededicate ourselves to the service of the thrifty, steadfast Americans who stand between the plow handles or at factory lathes, and knuckle to no man on earth.

My influence will be exerted to that end.

## XXII

## MY BOOKS

In the six years in which I was a member of the Sub-committee on Petroleum of the House Committee on Interstate and Foreign Commerce, the main question was whether the petroleum industry should be nationalized or at least made a public utility subject to complete control by the federal government, right down to the service station. Or should the industry be permitted to function as part of our free enterprise economy with the necessary controls and regulations in the hands of the states rather than in the federal government. A bill, known as the Thomas Disney bill, was favored by the New Dealers and by some people in the industry. This would have given the Secretary of the Interior control over the industry even down to deciding how many filling stations there should be, where located and so forth.

As a member of the Committee, I favored state regulation which later took the form of the Interstate Oil Compact, which was worked out in a meeting which I attended at the home of Governor Marland of Oklahoma.

To make state regulation of the production of petroleum more effective, Congress with my support, passed the Connelly or "Hot Oil" Act, which forbade the shipment in interstate commerce of oil produced in violation of state law.

After this big question had been debated during 1933, 1934 and 1935, I asked Axtell Byles, President of the American Oil Institute, whether he thought a book might be welcomed by the industry which gave the pros and cons of the argument. He not only approved the idea, but said that he would try to promote the sale of the book when it was published.

So after Congress adjourned in the summer of 1936, I loaded my Ford car with all of the books, government reports, papers and hearings on the subject I could find in Washington, and drove up to the Adirondacks, where I rented a little cabin all to myself, but near a summer hotel where I could get my meals. I was there one month, and during that time didn't talk over the telephone to anyone nor saw anyone I knew, nor received any letters except from my wife. I fully recommend this method for writing a book. The book was at least half a scissors and paste job with copious quotes from testimony given before our committee. Every day or so I sent to my secretary in South Bend a few pages of hand-written manuscript. At the end of the month the job was done and when I got back to South Bend the book was typed. Few changes were necessary.

I called it HOT OIL, a name which had attention value, but was not entirely descriptive of the text, as I covered many more matters than oil sent across state lines in violation of state law. It was the kind of book for which there would normally be little sale in the book stores. Mr. Byles however, fulfilled his promise and induced oil companies to buy the book in quantity lots, with the result that eight or ten thousand copies were distributed, which yielded me about a thousand dollars. While I was glad to get this money, the greater satisfaction was in the book itself.

In 1938, after I had decided to leave Congress to return to the practice of law, I felt that I wanted to write a political valedictory. This became JEFFERSON, THE FORGOTTEN MAN. I wrote this in an isolated office on the top floor of the House Office Building, but I had been gathering material for it during a period of six months or a year. By the time Congress adjourned in the summer of 1938, the proofs were coming off the press, a few sheets a day, and I read them in a cottage which I took on Skyline Drive, some eighty miles from Washington. This book was published by America's Future, Inc., a subsidiary of the Committee for Constitutional Government. I had become acquainted with this organization as a result of the fight against the packing of the Supreme Court. A revised edition was brought out two years later, in 1940, with forty or fifty additional pages, including one on the third term, which had become a big national issue. I consider JEFFERSON, THE FORGOTTEN MAN as my best book because, more than the others, it tells of the enduring principles of government rather than matters soon dated. About seventy-five thousand copies of the Jefferson book were put out. Financially it was not very profitable, as the Committee for Constitutional Government was hard up and I had to forget much that was due me and accept payment in dribs and drabs over a long period of time. I think it probably yielded me about two thousand dollars.

One of the thoughtful readers of HOT OIL was Henry M. Dawes, President of the Pure Oil Company of Chicago. In January, 1940, he asked me to come up to Chicago for a conference. He felt the time had come for a good article to appear in a magazine of national circulation about the petroleum industry as an example of free enterprise in action, and wanted me to write the article. I started to write it in South Bend, but soon felt that a defense of the free enterprise system required, instead of a magazine article, a short book in which petroleum would be one chapter. Mr. Dawes agreed, and undertook to find a publisher. He finally settled on Southern Publishers, Inc. of Kingsport, Tenn.

I boiled down hard on the manuscript and the book was in print by the middle of May. This was a couple of months before the national conventions met that year. And, to the astonishment of all of us, and because there was nothing else in the field, SMOKE SCREEN became a sort of campaign document by the Republicans and the Anti-Third Term Democrats. This was a favorable wind none of us had anticipated, but it resulted in SMOKE SCREEN becoming a best seller. In the "best seller" list of books printed in the New York Herald-Tribune, it was in fifth or sixth position in book store sales for a number of weeks — exceeded only by some popular novels. Everybody opposed to the New Deal bought the book in quantity and distributed it to their friends. One of Willkie's speeches that year was taken largely word for word from SMOKE SCREEN. Then the Committee for Constitutional Government made arrangements with Southern Publishers and got behind the promotion of the book. Altogether some three hundred and seventy-five thousand copies got into readers' hands and it became the largest selling non-fiction book of the year. Its closest rival was John Flynn's COUNTRY SQUIRE IN THE WHITE HOUSE, which also became a political textbook.

Various chapters in the book were summarized and run serially in a good many newspapers. This book yielded me about ten thousand four hundred dollars and with this money I was encouraged to buy the farm in Grafton which we called "River Mowing."

In 1943 I was vice-president and general counsel of the Transportation Association of America, based in Chicago. By reason of the great interest taken in SMOKE SCREEN in 1940, I was prompted to undertake another book on political issues of the day in anticipation of the 1944 presidential campaign. So for this and other reasons, I resigned from the Transportation Association early in 1944. In March of 1944, and with the collaboration of Professor Paul Bartholomew of Notre Dame University, who did a great deal of research for me, I wrote FOR AMERICANS ONLY. This was also published by America's Future, Inc., but they were heavily in debt and skimped on the book in every way. No copies were printed in boards; all of them were in cheap paper covers and the use of poor paper and print made the manuscript more a pamphlet than a book. I was always dissatisfied with the way it was done. It never got into the bookstores at all as far as I know. Nevertheless, a large number were bought in bulk and distributed to people interested in political and economic questions that year. It nowhere approached SMOKE SCREEN's popularity, due in great part, I think, to the down-at-the-heels appearance of the paper bound copy. The Committee for Constitutional Government, of which America's Future was a subsidiary, was broke as usual and heavily in debt, so the result was that my work on the book was largely pro bono publico. I had to write off all but about one thousand five hundred dollars to which I was entitled. Actually I think my associate, Paul Bartholomew, was paid more than I was. Despite the rather sad way the book was put together the book had a lot of material which nobody else had taken the pains to gather, and was very widely quoted all over the country, particularly the quotes from various New Dealers in the chapter "The Prophets of the New Order" which showed how far people in the federal government were prepared to go to impose upon the country a form of government not much different from Hitler's Nazism and Mussolini's Fascism. Probably one reason why FOR AMERICANS ONLY was not as enthusiastically read as SMOKE SCREEN had been, was that in 1940 the third term issue was very hot. Jim Farley, Carter Glass and many other leading Democrats had broken from Roosevelt on it and there was considerable hope that Willkie might win with this issue. Whereas in 1944, when FOR AMERICANS ONLY appeared, Thomas Dewey was the candidate and there was no such burning issue. Dewey limited his appeal practically to promising that he would manage the New Deal better. The war was on also, and the old slogan about not changing horses in midstream was powerful. Besides, nobody really expected that Dewey would win.

At this point I want to mention the fact that a couple of years after we were married, my dear wife Helen had these four books beautifully bound in tooled leather and gave them to me as a Christmas gift. I was delighted and touched, as can be imagined.

> *Editor's Note:* In 1971, long after the foregoing chapter had been written, a fifth book by Sam Pettengill was published. It was entirely different from his other books. Having moved permanently to Vermont in 1956, Sam had become a trustee of the Vermont Historical Society, and in 1962 was one of the founders of the Grafton Historical Society and its president for the next ten years. He was intensely interested in how the early settlers had lived and in doing some research discovered many things in their lives that they took so much for granted they were seldom mentioned and today are almost unknown. For instance, when the pioneers first came to the wilderness that is

*Working in the study at Robin Lawn, his home in Grafton, Sam Pettengill wrote "The Yankee Pioneers, A Saga of Courage."*

now Vermont, there was no grass. He read about this in an old diary and he was amazed until he walked through the woods near his home and found — no grass. He then wondered what else happened that we do not know about today and the idea of the book was born. He decided to gather all the bits and pieces of information he could find and put them together to make a picture of how our pioneer ancestors lived when they first came to Vermont and New Hampshire. It took him seven years, until THE YANKEE PIONEERS — A SAGA OF COURAGE was published in 1971. According to librarians it is the first book to concentrate on the first few years of the settlers' lives, before there was any such thing as a community, or even neighbors. As one reviewer put it: "This superb little volume puts verbal flesh and blood upon the usual sterile bones of early American history." Published by the Charles E. Tuttle, Co. of Rutland, Vt., it has already gone through two printings.

Three years after Sam's death, an abridged edition of THE YANKEE PIONEERS — A SAGA OF COURAGE was published by the Regional Center for Educational Training at Hanover, N.H. Sam had been consulted about the possibility of having an abridged edition made of his book for use in grade schools, so that children would understand what their ancestors had done to give them a good country to live in. He approved of the idea, hoping that realization of the toil, privation and sorrow it took to tame the wilderness, would make present and future generations take pride in their heritage and work to preserve it.

It is too bad Sam did not live to see the abridged edition. It took time to raise the money for its publication, which was finally accomplished as a Bicentennial project. The book is now being used in many schools.

## XXIII

## HOW ROBIN LAWN BECAME OUR HOME

Miss Ella Dwinell was born in Grafton on September 18, 1855 and died on December 23, 1947 at a nursing home in Saxtons River, having lived over ninety-two years. She was born in the family homestead at the top of Middletown hill about half a mile from our old farm. When I was a boy the old Dwinell place had been sold to a man named Lamphier. It is now owned by R. R. Barrett, Jr., no relation, however, to the old Grafton Barrett family or to me. It is a beautiful brick house, very similar in appearance to the brick house my great-grandfather Peter built further north on the same road in 1820. The brick in it came from the Pettengill kiln as did the brick in other structures on the hill. Miss Dwinell was always proud of the fact that the stone wall in front of her birthplace had been laid by her father some years before she was born, and was still in good condition, showing fine workmanship. Her father was Major John Goodridge Dwinell, born in Grafton in 1805, died in 1893. His father, Benjamin Dwinell, built the brick homestead about 1815.

After the death of his first wife, Major Dwinell married Lavinia Miller, and they had two daughters, Juliet and Ella. The latter was five years old when in 1860 her father bought the house now known as Robin Lawn, and moved down the hill to it. At some time previous to his purchase, it was supposed to have been used as a Congregational parsonage, perhaps around the time the new brick meeting house was built in 1833. As far as I have been able to ascertain from town records, the land on which the house stands was bought in 1815 for forty dollars, and in 1816 there was another transaction for two hundred fifty dollars. This led me to believe that the house must have been built at that time to account for this increase in price, as in those days local deeds did not mention any buildings on property, but only boundary details. Over the next thirty years or so there were several changes in ownership for approximately the same price. However, when Major Dwinell bought it on April 5, 1860, he paid one thousand and fifty dollars for it.

Major John Dwinell was a deacon in the Congregational church. His mother was Mehitable Goodridge, a descendant of William Goodridge, who was born in England in 1605 and settled in Watertown, Mass. One of his grand-daughters was Hannah Goodridge who married Nathaniel Pettengill of Newbury in 1703. Nathaniel was the fourth son of my ancestors, Richard and Joanna Ingersoll Pettengill. Richard was born in England in 1620 and settled in Salem, Mass., sometime before 1640, as the records show him to have been a freeman of the colony at that time. His wife, Joanna, was the daughter of Richard Ingersoll, who came originally from Bedfordshire, England, arrived in Salem, Mass., on June 29, 1629. He is supposed to have built the famous House of the Seven Gables.

So through the marriage of Nathaniel Pettengill and Hannah Goodridge, Miss Dwinell and I were related, and even though it was a very distant relationship, the fact pleased both of us very much. In 1936, after Congress adjourned, I drove to Grafton, and as Miss Dwinell had never seen her ancestral home in Topsfield, near Salem, Mass., I drove her there and helped her locate a few distant relatives. Then we went on to Salem where we went through the House of the Seven Gables.

Miss Dwinell's grandfather, Benjamin Dwinell, and my great-grandfather, Peter Pettengill, probably came to Grafton at about the same time. Great-grandfather Pettengill came from Salem, N.H., in 1787, driving one of the teams of oxen belonging to Rev. William Hall, Grafton's first minister, who was installed the following year. The first Congregational church, which Peter helped to build in 1792, was located up on the hill on land that later was part of our old farm. When this old church was dismantled in 1858, Deacon Dwinell acquired the huge stone steps and later put them in front of the kitchen porch at Robin Lawn where they have been to this day. The stone is of a lighter shade than the other stones in front of the house, so can be easily identified.

When she was only fifteen years old, Miss Dwinell became a school teacher at a salary of two dollars a week. Her first school was over near the Burgess Cemetery. She taught school for many years, finally becoming a governess to the son and grandson of Thomas A. Edison in New Jersey. When she was about twenty-five, my father and mother came to Grafton on a visit and Miss Dwinell vividly remembered a tea my mother gave to some young women of the church on the lawn of the old farm and could even recall some of the things my mother said on that occasion. When I was a little boy, Miss Dwinell was one of my Sunday school teachers, and a happy memory of those days was when I occasionally dropped in at Robin Lawn, the name she had given to her home because it was a favorite nesting place for robins. She always had on hand some caraway seed cookies and they have been my favorites ever since.

I was always very fond of her. She symbolized the best of the old New England. We corresponded from time to time during the years when I was away at college, at South Bend, and in Congress. After we bought the farm in 1940 we saw each other more frequently. And when she needed any legal advice I was always glad to help her.

Miss Dwinell loved her peaceful home and it became a dread to her that it might fall into the hand of those who would neglect it like so many of the old homes which had fallen on evil days. She of course had no children, nor was she very fond of her sister's three children. Besides they were all grown up and far away and she was sure they would sell her home to strangers if they inherited it.

Her first thought was to leave it in trust for a number of years, with the right of four or five of her friends, including me (this was before I bought the farm), to occupy it in rotation, year by year, during the summer months. She abandoned this idea as not practical.

Her next thought was to deed it to me, retaining a life estate. But I declined, knowing that her nephews would not like it, nor her, for doing so, and it might cause trouble.

The end result, which I did not know about until after her death in 1947, was that in her will she gave me the option of buying Robin Lawn from her estate for about half of what it was worth. The rest of her property, in securities and cash, amounting to some twenty-five thousand dollars, she left to her nephew and niece, with a few small gifts to other relatives and old friends. She bequeathed an old mirror in a gilt frame to me and it now hangs in one of our bedrooms at Robin Lawn.

I executed the option but her nephews filed suit to break the will. The jury found against them and I received an executor's deed to the property.

When Helen and I were married in 1949, we decided that the farm with its two hundred and fifty acres of land was more responsibility than we wanted and was too far from the village, so we sold it after we had modernized Robin Lawn, putting in plumbing and electricity and converting the old barn and hayloft into a big library and study. We also added a garage.

The estate had a sale of Miss Dwinell's household goods in the fall of 1948, and I bought a few items, among them a fine old Governor Winthrop desk which badly needed refinishing. This was done and it is now one of our treasures. I also bought a very large grand piano more than a hundred years old. We kept it in the house until we moved permanently to Grafton in 1956 and then gave it to Fred Prouty, a fine local pianist who was also the contractor who worked on our house. We had a smaller piano which we preferred.

*Robin Lawn, the home of Sam and Helen Pettengill in Grafton, Vermont.*

Sam Pettengill on the bridge at Robin Lawn.

Left: The brook at Robin Lawn. Right: Helen and Sam Pettengill mark the high snow at Robin Lawn. These photos were taken in the spring of 1958.

The work of remodeling was nearly completed by the fall of 1951 and we moved in what furniture we wanted from the farm on October 5, spending nine days in our new home before returning to Evanston for the winter. The Whitney Snowmans, old friends, were our first guests, and we spent our vacations at Robin Lawn until I retired.

We have since acquired two small adjoining pieces of land from the Sue Daniels estate which had been part of the property when John Dwinell bought it in 1860. He had sold the land to her father some years later and we were pleased that we were able to restore the property to its original size.

We also acquired from her estate a burial lot in the cemetery across the road from our house. The heirs wanted to straighten out the boundaries of their land by giving a strip adjoining the cemetery to the town and we were very glad to be offered the chance to obtain part of it. In the summer of 1953 we moved Josephine's casket from the Saxtons River cemetery and reinterred it in our lot in Grafton.

About the same time we bought the old Bathric place across the brook on Hinckley Brook Road. Helen completely renovated the house, drawing up the plans herself, as she had done for Robin Lawn. A large wing was added, and part of the barn converted into a studio. It was sold to Miss Helen Evans, who for about fifteen years held art exhibitions there every summer, bringing many interesting people to Grafton and making it quite a cultural center.

## XXIV

## MORE MEMORIES

by
Helen M. Pettengill

Sam's recollections of the past, as set down in his gift to me, ended with his chapter on Robin Lawn, the home he dearly loved. But added to these memories should be others that meant much to him. I learned a good deal in our almost twenty-five years of marriage, and fortunately Sam kept voluminous files so that places, names and dates have been available to me.

However, in a life so full that volumes could be written about his accomplishments, I shall only touch on some of the highlights and leave it to scholars to do justice to a man who always had the courage of his convictions, and was recognized nationally as a constitutional lawyer, economist, author and outstanding speaker. His papers have been given to the University of Oregon Library and are available for research and I hope some day the complete story of his life will be told.

Sam loved a good story. And telling one well, as he always did, usually prefaced a speech and from then on, the audience was his. I heard him speak many times, and it was always the same. Voices quieted down, chairs stopped creaking, and with the exception of applause now and then, there was never a sound except his voice until he finished. I used to marvel at his sense of timing. When he spoke to a live audience, and at the same time was having his speech broadcast, he would wrap it all up and say the last, right word just as the red light went off.

Another strange thing always happened when I was present when Sam was making a speech. He was a tall, erect and handsome man and when he stood up on a platform to speak, it seemed that with each word he grew larger and taller. At first I thought my imagination was playing tricks because I admired and loved him so much, but one day Sumner Gerard, brother of former Ambassador to Germany, James W. Gerard, said to me, "every time I see Sam make a speech, he seems to grow a foot taller." So others felt the same way. He was truly a great orator. No gestures, no flowery phrases, his strong, expressive voice and well chosen words going to the heart of his subject, held his listeners spellbound. It is unfortunate that during his heyday there were no small portable tape recorders such as exist nowadays to preserve for posterity his voice when making some of his more famous speeches.

Fortunately, however, three speeches he made during the late fifties were recorded professionally at that time. Also a number of years ago a friend who owned a tape recorder asked Sam to record some of his favorite writings and he chose "The Song of the Capitol Dome," "When Lincoln Was a Boy," and "The Widow's Clearing." We had phonograph records made from the tape and gave many of them to family and friends. Although by then his voice had lost some of its strength, I am thankful that we have it even to this small degree, and for safe-keeping the tapes of the three speeches and one of the records have been given to the University of Oregon together with his papers and many of his books. I am sure the University will give them the care needed to preserve his voice indefinitely.

One reason why all of this memorabilia has been given to the University of Oregon is that Sam was born in that state and his mother is buried there, so he had a sentimental attachment. But there is a more important reason. Of all the universities and libraries that contacted Sam about giving them his papers, the University of Oregon seemed to be the most thorough in its efforts to set up a Special Collections Department that would house various viewpoints within the conservative political spectrum, making its library one of the major centers of conservative history in the country. All his political life Sam had argued for constitutional government and against the concentration of all political and financial power in Washington. He knew how the leftist establishment works and he did not want his papers buried, or as he put it, viewed with ideological disdain. The middle-of-the-road policies of the University of Oregon appealed to him. Also he knew their library had already received some important collections, a number from Sam's former colleagues. Therefore, beginning in 1965, Sam sent large quantities of his accumulated books and papers to the University of Oregon Library and the balance has been sent since his death. They have everything to do with his public life, with two exceptions. The bound volumes of his columns written under the heading "The Gentleman from Indiana" and his radio broadcasts for two years were given to the Guy W. Bailey Library of the University of Vermont when we first came to Vermont to make it our permanent home. This was long before Sam had made any decisions as to the disposition of his papers, and he thought it possible that he might eventually give them to the University of Vermont. Later however, he decided on the University of Oregon.

An incident that always amused Sam occurred while he was in Congress. Using his own words, "A few days after Congress adjourned one year, I was standing outside of the House Office Building on the sidewalk when a couple of women, obviously tourists, came up and stopped. One of them pointed to the House Office Building and said "Is that the zoo?" I answered, "No, Madam, the zoo is four or five miles over in that direction." She said, "Then what is that building?" and I said, "That is the House Office Building." And she said, "Oh, I thought it was the zoo."

"For many years now," Sam would conclude, "I have thought about this and have not yet made up my mind whether somebody had been kidding her, whether she was kidding me, or whether she had a far deeper insight into human nature than I gave her credit for."

Sam was well aware of the general feeling people have come to have about Congress and he remembered that in the last week of the Reorganization Bill fight, he was speaking at the Hippodrome in New York City with another congressman, who having just said something in his speech about Congress and congressmen, came to a pause, and somebody in the crowd of three or four thousand people, hollered out, "Are they feeble-minded?"

So when Sam was introduced, he referred to the incident and true to form, said it reminded him of the story of the politician who was visiting a lunatic asylum. Since the politician had expressed a great deal of interest in the inmates, the superintendent asked him if he would speak to them. The politician had just one speech in his system, and at a certain point asked the question. "Why are we here?" He got to this point, said "Why are we here?", and before he could continue, a lunatic in the rear of the room got up and said, "Mister, we're here because we're not all there."

Sam never regretted leaving Congress, but because of his reasons for so doing, Democrats who were firm believers in Roosevelt never forgave him. In South Bend, one political club turned his picture to the wall and his name was removed from the club's roster. This probably happened elsewhere, as well as a lot of nasty editorials. But it didn't bother Sam. He said James Farley had always been fair to him, and John Garner, Sam Rayburn and William Bankhead stood by him, as did many other old friends in the Democratic party. When he made his announcement in 1942 about becoming Chairman of the Republican National Finance Committee, there were shrill screams from some of the Democratic papers in the country. Yet later, the South Bend Tribune and some other newspapers wrote editorials urging him to run for President!

In 1939, Frank Gannett, the newspaper publisher, asked Sam to write a newspaper column commenting on national issues. He had hoped to do something of this sort after leaving Congress, so for ten years thereafter his twice-a-week column was syndicated to over a hundred newspapers all over the country, under the heading, "The Gentleman from Indiana."

During the campaign of 1940, Sam made many speeches and wrote articles against a third term for Roosevelt. He lost that fight but was vindicated later when a constitutional amendment was approved limiting a president to two terms in office.

In 1940 there were so many interventionist pressure groups in the country, it was felt that there should be a national non-interventionist organization to combat their powerful appeals for mass support. The America First Committee was formed with many prominent persons listed as members of the executive board and national committee, and with General Robert E. Wood as Chairman. Leaders in and out of Congress, while not on the policy making committee were consulted for advice. Sam was among them and also made many speeches. The one he remembered best was when he spoke to an audience of over ten thousand in Chicago in April, 1941. In addition to those inside the auditorium there were several thousand outside listening to the speeches through the loud speaker. General Wood introduced Sam, who spoke first, and then introduced Col. Charles Lindbergh. All the speeches were enthusiastically received. Afterwards, Col. Lindbergh and Sam drove home with General Wood to spend the night with him in Lake Forest.

However, in spite of all the efforts to keep the United States out of the war, when Pearl Harbor was attacked we got into it and America First was immediately disbanded with the statement that it gave its support to the war effort and pledged its aid to the President as Commander-in-Chief of the armed forces of the United States.

Although an America First Party was formed in 1943 and undoubtedly obtained some support from former followers of the America First Committee, it never had any connection with the Committee. Sam never had anything to do with this organization.

From January, 1943, to May, 1944, Sam was vice-president and general counsel for the Transportation Association of America. He then resigned in order to give more time to his law practice and other activities.

Beginning in May, 1946, he was a radio commentator for the American Broadcasting Company, being heard nationwide every Sunday afternoon for the next two years.

He was also writing many articles and made countless speeches on politics and economics in forty-four states of the Union. One short piece that he considered his best and which became one of his most famous was written at the request of the Indiana Legislature. It is reproduced on the facing page.

This resolution was commented upon and reproduced throughout the United States after it had been adopted by the Indiana House on January 13, 1947, and by the Senate on January 22, 1947.

Almost eight years later, on December 29, 1954, the Chicago Daily Tribune published an editorial entitled "Indiana Shows the Way" and quoted Sam's article word for word, with the following comment:

> "Indiana is winding up its fourth successive year of having as little to do with federal handouts and "matching funds" as it can. It is estimated that the state has passed up twenty-five million dollars in federal handouts since 1951. During the last year it declined federal money for hospital construction, blocked the building of an armory that wasn't needed, and killed off a federal housing program.
>
> "This policy began with an historic declaration of the Indiana general assembly in 1945. "Indiana needs no guardian . . .
>
> "This is a simple truth, but one that states and people seem to find it difficult to comprehend. The federal government produces nothing and can "give" nothing which it has not first wrung from the taxpayers.

## 85th General Assembly

## STATE OF INDIANA

### House Concurrent Resolution No. 2

Indiana needs no guardian and intends to have none. We Hoosiers — like the people of our sister states — were fooled for quite a spell with the magician's trick that a dollar taxed out of our pockets and sent to Washington, will be bigger when it comes back to us. We have taken a good look at said dollar. We find that it lost weight on its journey to Washington and back. The political brokerage of the bureaucrats has been deducted. We have decided that there is no such thing as "federal" aid. We know that there is no wealth to tax that is not already within the boundaries of the 48 states.

So we propose henceforward to tax ourselves and take care of ourselves. We are fed up with subsidies, doles and paternalism. We are no one's stepchild. We have grown up. We serve notice that we will resist Washington, D.C. adopting us.

Be it resolved, by the House of Representatives of the General Assembly of the State of Indiana, the Senate concurring: That we respectfully petition and urge Indiana's Congressmen and Senators to vote to fetch our county court house and city halls back from Pennsylvania Avenue. We want government to come home. Resolved, further, that we call upon the legislatures of our sister states and on good citizens everywhere who believe in the basic principles of Lincoln and Jefferson to join with us, and we with them to restore the American Republic and our 48 states to the foundations built by our fathers.

*This drawing was done in 1948 when Samuel Pettengill was a weekly radio commentator.*

"What Indiana has had the wit to perceive is that dollars rebounding from the states to Washington come back diminished in value and with strings attached. The government keeps a part of all of them. It also directs the states to spend them according to prescribed federal patterns. Local control and self-government are undermined and the people of the states become enslaved to those who hold the purse strings in Washington.

"We hope that more states will see the light and adopt Indiana's course."

Five colleges gave Sam honorary degrees — Harding, Franklin, Marietta, Middlebury and Norwich University. He was a trustee of Middlebury from 1936 to 1939 when he felt he should not continue on account of the press of other duties. On June 14, 1941, the Associated Alumni of Middlebury awarded Sam a handsome pewter plaque for "meritorious service" to his Alma Mater. He was very proud of this and hung it in his study.

Twice he was awarded the bronze George Washington Honor Medal by Freedoms Foundation of Valley Forge, and in 1953 he received a patriotic service award from the Illinois Society of the Sons of the American Revolution, to which he belonged, having had twelve ancestors who fought in the Revolution.

It was in 1932, the worst year of the depression, that he wrote "The Dome of the Capitol." He would walk from home to the Capitol in the morning and see the dome in the bright sunlight, and he remembered that Lincoln insisted on its building being continued even in the midst of the Civil War. He asked himself what the dome could say to the United States during the crisis everyone was going through during those hard times, and he said it took him a year until he found his answer.

### The Dome Of The Capitol
"Architecture is frozen music"
                              Goethe

I have not yet found the cadence
Of the song of the Capitol Dome.

It is a long slow measure;
The swing of the decades is in it
And its beat is the timing of generations.
It is a long slow cadence
That poets have not found.

And I know they never shall find it.
They shall not travel far enough
They shall not live long enough
To come to the end of that measure.

It is somewhere beyond the gamut of voices,
Beyond the notation of music,
Beyond the octameter's roll.

The patience of Lincoln is in it,
The gravity of judges deciding great causes,
The thunder of Webster is in it
Speaking to senates,
And the wisdom of Washington
Speaking to nations.

It is a long slow measure,
Slow as the plodding feet of oxen
As they bend their great shoulders
To the weight and the freight
Of covered wagons moving westward
Toward the setting of the sun.

The Atlantic, the Pacific
Are in it,
Deep calling to deep.
The Rockies are in it
Echoing gravely and surely
Over measureless prairies
The Alleghenies' antiphonal chorus.

The rhythm of paddles is in it,
Paddling canoes
Up the St. Joseph,
Down the Ohio,
Up the Missouri,
The long strong sweep of the paddles of pioneer men.

The tempo of axe-strokes is in it
Cutting rafters for cabins,
And firewood for hearthstones,
And rockers for cradles,
The axe making room for the plow,
The axes of pioneer men.

It is a long slow cadence,
Slow as seedtime and a lingering harvest,
Slow as the growing of oak trees,
Slow as the movement of centuries.
Sometimes it seems like the soft lullaby
Of a mother as her babe falls asleep.

Sometimes I hear in it
The roll of the Oregon,
The roar of Niagara,
The winds of the Yukon,
The hush of the forests,
The silence of stars,
The taciturn march of the stars.

And again it brings to my ears
The long overtones of the past
Echoing far into the future,
    — When in the course of human events —
    — We, the people of the United States —
    — The Union, it must and shall be preserved —
    — A just and lasting peace among ourselves
    — And with all nations —
    — Nor take from the mouth of labor
    — the bread that it has earned —
Words —
Sharper than swords,
Greater than greed,
Words for the writing of judgments,
Words for the healing of nations,
Forged on the anvil of God.

And when I hear all these voices,
This multitudinous music
Of acorns and oak trees,
Of lovers and roof trees,

> Of millions of women and men
> Joining the centuries' chorus,
> I know that the voice of each singer
> Will sometime stop singing,
> But that song with a measureless measure
> Will go on.
> On past spring time and seed time,
> On past war time and peace time,
> On with a swelling crescendo,
> On to a grand diapason,
> On,
> I know that song will go on.

In 1935 the poem was set to music by Siegfried Scharbau, leader of the United States Marine Band. A fine baritone sang the words to the accompaniment of the band seated on a barge in the Potomac at the Watergate. Among the thousands who sat on the bank that night was Mrs. Franklin D. Roosevelt. Later the band repeated the performance at the Marine Band's Hall. For some years it was produced as a patriotic pageant by the schools in Pasadena, Calif.

The poem introduced to us Beth Landis, eminent musician and author, when she wrote and asked permission to include it in her notable collection of music, literature and visual arts entitled "Exploring Music." It is a series of eight volumes, plus teachers' manuals, that are used in many of the junior and senior high schools in the United States and abroad, and are designed to acquaint young people with the joys of music and its origins and ramifications. With the words inscribed, "This book is dedicated to Samuel B. Pettengill, whose 'Song of the Capitol Dome' has been an inspiration and blessing to me for twenty-five years," she handed us Volume VIII which concluded the series, and on pages 244 and 245 appeared the poem. Beth Landis has remained a close and beloved friend ever since that day when she visited us in 1970.

On March 7, 1971, the Washington Sunday Star devoted a whole page to the poem, stating that it seemed to provide an unusual commentary out of the past on a troubling contemporary event, the sad bombing of the Capitol which had just taken place.

The poem was brought to the editor's attention by Sam's daughter, Mrs. Thomas B. Douglas, who lives in Washington. Later as a gift to us, she had the newspaper page handsomely framed, and it now hangs in my husband's study with other memorabilia of his life.

While still in Congress Sam had an interesting experience. He was interviewed by reporters and photographers from Life and Time magazines for their forthcoming radio and newsreel presentation of the crisis between the Capitol and the White House. As an outstanding fighter in both the Supreme Court and Reorganization crusades, Sam was chosen as the "Man of the Year" and he spent a whole day posing before sound cameras while going through the routine of what a member of Congress does from day to day. The presentation went all over the United States on their "March of Time," a famous newsreel in those days. As far as I know, this was the only time Sam was ever a motion picture star!

*In 1938, Sam Pettengill was a "motion picture star." He appeared in "Man of the Year," on the March of Time newsreel.*

On July 18, 1938, Sam was the principal speaker at the convention of the Commercial Law League of America at the Grand Hotel on Mackinac Island, Michigan. He was introduced by Mr. Thad M. Talcott, Treasurer and Past President of the League with the words, "Mr. Pettengill is not just another congressman. He is one of the outstanding members of that great body. He has a distinguished record over a period of years and his influence has been felt on all important issues. He is a man who has the courage of his convictions and can call his soul his own. His service as a speaker is in demand from all parts of the country."

Sam's speech that night was entitled "A New Order of the Ages" and he always considered it one of his best. It is reprinted in full at the end of this book.

A happy memory for Sam was when he gave the address during the celebration of the one hundredth anniversary of the building of the Brick Meeting House in his old home town of Grafton, Vt.

Except for driving through Grafton in 1929 from Saxtons River to Manchester, Vt., when he took his cousin, Helen Pettengill, and his old Vermont Academy teacher, Miss Julia Goodwin, on a short trip, he had not been back since he was graduated from Yale Law School in 1911. Having left the village as a poor boy with his way to make in the world, it must have given him much satisfaction and happiness to come back in 1933 as a member of the Congress of the United States. An old friend of his family, Hon. John Barrett, former Ambassador to Argentina and Director-General of the Pan-American Union, extended the invitation. His grandfather had helped finance the building of the meeting house, which was once described by the great architect, Stanford White, as the finest example of post-Revolutionary church architecture in New England. Among those present to do Sam honor were Senator Warren R. Austin of Vermont, later U.S. Representative to the Security Council of the United Nations, Congressman Ernest Gibson of Brattleboro, and the president of Middlebury Col-

Sam Pettengill and Thad Talcott, treasurer and past president of the Commercial Law League of America, at the Grand Hotel, Mackinac Island, Michigan, where he delivered the speech, "A New Order of the Ages," in July, 1938.

lege, Paul Dwight Moody. Sam was the fourth generation of his family to worship in this church and he always retained his membership. Using much of the material assembled by his father in writing the history of the church in 1906, Sam gave the main historical facts and then paid tribute to the part the churches had played in the building of America, because they "built men."

*The Brick Meeting House in Grafton.*

In Rockingham, about fourteen miles from Grafton, stands another old church, the beautiful Rockingham Meeting House, erected in 1787. It is built on an eminence in almost the exact center of the township, adjoining a peaceful graveyard, and overlooks the valleys of the Williams and Connecticut rivers. Over the years, after its regular use as a church and town hall was discontinued in the mid-1800's, it fell into disrepair, but in 1907 public spirited citizens raised a fund to renovate it. Once more it became as it had been originally, with its high pulpit, sounding board and square box pews. Hundreds of people from all over the United States visit it each year and since its re-dedication in 1907, so-called pilgrimages take place annually to this shrine, erected the same year our Constitution was adopted. The day is usually the first Sunday in August, and in 1937, on the one hundred and fiftieth anniversary of the building of the church, Sam was invited to give the address. Again in 1941 and in 1960 Sam was the speaker, the only person to date who has addressed the pilgrimage three times.

In 1941, on the hundred and fiftieth anniversary of Vermont's joining the Union, Sam was invited to address a joint session of both houses of the Vermont Legislature.

Sam was always an advocate of sound money and in 1951 he wrote an article entitled "Inflation Concerns Everyone." It was published by Readers' Digest in its October issue and so many letters were received commenting on it, that he was asked to follow it up with another article. This was published in March, 1952, and was called "Why Put Counterfeiters in Jail?" After the first article appeared, Sam was asked to debate the issue on a televised program of Theodore Granik's "American Forum of the Air" with Leon H. Keyserling, then Chairman of the President's Council of Economic Advisers. Sam bore down hard on the fact that inflation was reducing the value of all life insurance policies, industrial pensions, bonds, bank accounts — the savings of all Americans. He said it was up to these millions of people to see to it that government policies in the future would not further exhaust their savings, and they could do so by supporting strong men in Congress who would restore integrity to the American dollar. He quoted Jefferson who said, "We must cease being residents and become citizens." Unfortunately Sam's continuous fight over many years against the government's taxing power and excessive spending seems to have been a lost cause.

In 1947 Sam was spending so much time in New York City he decided to buy a house in Irvington-on-Hudson that his wife liked. It was only about twenty miles north of the city and it seemed preferable to paying rent. But in June, 1948, Josephine became ill with what was thought to be a gall bladder attack and entered the hospital in nearby Tarrytown. She seemed to be recovering, but on the morning of June 26, while eating breakfast and conversing with her nurse, she leaned back on her pillow and quietly passed away. They had been married thirty-six years on June 1. A few days later, Sam and Susan brought her back to Vermont and she is buried in the Grafton Village Cemetery.

*The home of Sam and Josephine Pettengill at Irvington-on-Hudson, New York.*

By the end of 1948, Sam decided that he had had enough of public life. He had resigned from his law firm in South Bend of which he was a partner, a year or two before, as his columns, weekly broadcasts and the speeches he was making all over the country, interfered with his active practice of the law. His old friend, Henry M. Dawes, brother of Charles G. Dawes, Vice-President under Calvin Coolidge, had for some time been urging him to take life a little easier, and suggested that he come to Chicago as Assistant to the President of the Pure Oil Company, and also to be available as consultant to the company's legal department. Sam had never liked living in New York and so on January 1, 1949, with his last column written after producing it for ten years under the heading "The Gentleman from Indiana," he moved to Chicago and took up residence in the Chicago Club. His daughter Susan was already living in Florida and the Irvington house was on the market.

In March, 1949, Sam attended a company meeting at the Rod and Gun Club at Everglades, Florida, and invited me to come down to the last night's dinner from Sarasota, Florida, where I was spending the winter. We had known each other for some time and I had always had great admiration for him. But at the Everglades we admitted that there was more than friendship in our feelings for one another and we became engaged. Mr. Leon Wescoat, President of Pure Oil, always said he had played the part of Cupid in this affair, as he had arranged the meeting at the club and was host at the dinner party. A few months later, on July 16, 1949, Sam and I were married in New York City, his daughter acting as my maid of honor and my younger son as Sam's best man. (I had been a widow for twelve years.) The following November we attended Susan's wedding to Thomas B. Douglas, in Washington, D.C.

As mentioned earlier, one of Sam's five honorary degrees, that of Doctor of Laws, was conferred on him by Middlebury College in June, 1949, shortly before our marriage. We drove up from New York together, as he had come on from Chicago to close the sale of the Irvington house and he was to give the Commencement address at Middlebury, and of course I

*Helen and Sam Pettengill,". . .our favorite photos of one another."*

wanted to be there. When we got to the Field House where the ceremonies were to take place, I was seated next to Mrs. Warren R. Austin, wife of the senator who was present in 1933 when Sam was the speaker at the one hundredth anniversary of the building of the Brick Meeting House in Grafton. Sam was a completely un-selfconscious man, and after his hood had been adjusted and the citation read, he turned towards the audience, caught my eye, and in front of hundreds of people, threw me a kiss! Mrs. Austin patted my hand and said, "My husband would never do a thing like that. I envy you." I was thrilled, as can be imagined. Incidentally her husband was also awarded an honorary degree a few minutes later and she was right! The speech Sam made that day was called "The Responsibility of College Graduates as Citizens." He put it in the same category as the one he had made at the lawyers' convention at Mackinac Island in 1938 — "one of my best." It is quoted in full in the appendix of this book.

Sam remained with the Pure Oil Company in Chicago until he retired at the end of June, 1956. We had been living in

Evanston since our marriage, and spending the summer vacations in Grafton, where we had done much work on Robin Lawn, getting it ready to be our permanent home. While with Pure, Sam had been editor-in-chief of Volume II of the history of the company, writing a good part of it himself. After moving to Grafton he worked on the third volume. In April, 1964, the Fiftieth Anniversary issue of the Pure Oil News appeared, with a twenty-page article by Sam entitled "The First 50 Years." A critic said it was "one of the best company backgrounds I've ever seen," and another remarked that the way the history of the company was interwoven with the happenings in the country and the world over the fifty year period, made what could have been dry, dull reading, most interesting.

After he retired, one of Sam's activities that he most enjoyed was being Director of the Coe Foundation's American Studies program, which pioneered Summer Refresher courses in American History for high school teachers. He arranged for colleges all over the country to have the courses held on their campuses, did a lot of traveling, made many speeches and enjoyed being with the teachers and young people and they enjoyed being with him.

I went with him on a number of these trips, and one very happy time which we long remembered was when, after visiting a few of the western colleges where the courses were being given, we rented a car in Laramie, Wyoming, and drove to the Grand Tetons where we spent a week at Jackson Lake Lodge. We leisurely explored the country for miles around, drove up to the top of Signal Mountain with its awe-inspiring views, and took boat trips on the lake. When we were ready to start for home we drove up to Yellowstone Park which we had saved for last, and stayed overnight. We watched Old Faithful erupt on schedule, saw the fantastic hot springs and geysers, the Upper and Lower Falls of the Yellowstone and everything else we were supposed to see, including thirteen bears. It gave us a thrill knowing that it was Sam's Uncle Will who made all these marvels available to the public forever by the introduction of his bill in Congress establishing Yellowstone as the first national park. Clagett Butte in the northwestern part of Yellowstone is named for him.

We started for home by driving north and east over Beartooth Pass, a magnificent but terrifying experience. We kept going up and up no matter how many times we thought we'd reached the top, and when we finally got there, almost eleven thousand feet and above the timber line, with glaciers all around us in the middle of July, it began to rain. The temperature kept dropping and we were afraid of skidding on the breathtaking switchbacks, but Sam was a careful driver and at last we reached the bottom. Sam had a nasty headache from the strain — he said the first he had ever had — and I had to take over after giving him some aspirin and drive about sixty miles to Billings, Mont., where we had reservations to fly home the next day.

Sam was a 1904 graduate of Vermont Academy in Saxtons River, and on May 24, 1957, he was honored by being made a member of the Cum Laude Society. Only those in the graduating class who have maintained an over ninety average during the four preceding years are eligible, so only a few are named each year. Knowing this, in his speech to the students, entitled "The Blessing of Struggle" Sam congratulated those who did not win as well as the winners, for they both had had the struggle. A friend sent a copy of this address to Vital Speeches magazine. Human Events reprinted it, and Scouting, and many other magazines and newspapers in the United States and even some foreign countries. With the exception of his articles on inflation which appeared in the Readers' Digest and its foreign editions, "The Blessing of Struggle" has been read by more people than any other speech or article he ever wrote. It is of interest that Sam made this address before the Russians put "Sputnik," the world's first man-made satellite, into the sky on October 4, 1957. That event revolutionized education in all its dimensions.

*Sam Pettengill at Robin Lawn in 1957, when he was 71 years old and when he wrote "The Blessing of Struggle."*

I quote it here as Sam gave it that night and received a rising ovation from the boys.

## The Blessing of Struggle
### May 24, 1957

When I got through Vermont Academy, college and law school, I played a good deal of chess while waiting for clients who were bold enough to let me practice on them!

Chess, as some of you know, is the most difficult of all games. The combinations and permutations on the chess board run into the octillions and no man has, or ever will, completely master it.

Chess "masters" are relative only to other players. Nevertheless they are remarkable men. One of several I got to know was Emmanuel Lasker of Berlin, Germany, who had been world's champion for twenty-four years. He was not a mental freak. He had a Ph.D. in mathematics and wrote a profound book on philosophy. In addition he was a kind and gentle man, then in his sixties.

We got him to come to my home town of South Bend to put on an exhibition match with some thirty players. At supper that night, we asked this grand master why he had given so much of his life to chess.

He said, "The chessboard is a symbol of life, of all life. The essence of life is struggle. Take struggle out of chess, or out of life, and what is left? In chess I have found happiness."

That was thirty-five years ago. I have never forgotten his words and have often said to young parents, "Don't take struggle out of your children's lives."

The instinct of parents is to do just that — to make "life easier for my boy than it was for me." It is interesting to note that youth is sounder in this matter than age. Youth revels in competitive sport, whether to do something better than his fellows, or to beat some previous record.

Even small children, when they invent games of their own, always put struggle into them. Struggle is a blessing to be sought for, not an evil to be avoided.

We have met tonight to honor those who have won the honor of a Cum Laude student. But honors are silly toys, unimportant in themselves, important only as evidence of something well done. Those of you who did not win had the struggle as well as the winners, which is the thing that counts.

So I congratulate both the winners and those who tried but did not win. You are going to get the big rewards of life.

In recent years, society has gone "nuts" on the pusillanimous cult of "security," guaranteed by government; in short, a nation of parasites. The illusion of the age is that people can vote themselves rich. It is a superstition that "social security" depends on the promises of politicians, not on the character, competence and courage of men. It is a fable and a fraud that the out-put of society can be greater than the in-put of individuals.

It is a universal complaint that nobody *wants* to work any more, or only enough to "get by." Employers are frantic for dependable employees. Labor unions have the laudable desire to improve the position of their members, but they over-play this hand when they say "Stretch it out. Take it easy. Do no more than enough to stay on the payroll."

When young people apply for their first job, they ask "When will I begin to draw a pension? How many coffee breaks in a day? How many holidays? How long and frequent are the paid vacations? If I work more than forty hours in a week, do I get time-and-a-half?"

The young men who ask none of these questions are sure to get and hold a job. In fact, this sort of young men have a golden age ahead of them. They will have less competition than that kind of men have ever had, and greater rewards.

When I was at Vermont Academy, Theodore Roosevelt was President. He attracted national attention when he said, "I wish to preach not the doctrine of ignoble ease, but the doctrine of the strenuous life." He said of himself, "let me wear out, not rust out." He told young men to hit the hard line. He told women not to shirk their prime function to bear children. He said this at a time when any woman who had more than two children was considered sub-human, if not a little indecent.

Theodore Roosevelt dreamed nobly of his country, and by the fire of his example, he lit other fires in millions of homes. It was said that Washington founded the nation, Lincoln saved it, and T.R. revitalized it. He appealed to the *strong side* of men as is done now chiefly by marine sergeants and the coaches of athletes like Knute Rockne.

"Rock" had no use for "lounge lizards" or "tea hounds" on a college campus. Youth liked that. They flocked to Notre Dame to play under Rockne, and when his players were behind at the end of the first half, they proceeded to pull the game out of the fire because "we can't let Rock down."

A century ago, Italy was under foreign rule. It was then that Mazzini, or was it his fellow patriot, Garibaldi, appealed to the strong side of men with these words, "Young men of Italy, I offer you nothing but the water of the streams as your drink. I offer you nothing but black bread as your food, and nothing but the blue canopy of heaven and the lights of the eternal stars as your covering at night. But if you follow me, young men of Italy, you and I will be free!"

They followed, and Italy became a republic.

Today the general appeal is to the soft side of men — envy, self-pity, covetousness, class hatred. Our elections have become auctions in which rival politicians out-bid each other by opening the door of the treasury in exchange for votes.

"Come and get it" is the slogan as people become the vandals of their own country and "bread and circuses" the formula for political advancement.

In the educational field, men have tried to eliminate struggle from the class room. No required subjects! No examinations! They develop inferiority complexes, rather than the challenge to do better. Never punish a child. Children should be wholly free. And so forth. With the result that employers despair because "Johnny can't read and Mabel can't spell."

So we have cities with few citizens, but many who wish to share the blessings of liberty, but shirk its burdens.

This is not the spirit of 1776, nor of the great chess master, nor of Theodore Roosevelt. America needs a rebirth of the "strenuous life" and I know I am talking to young men who will take their part in it.

It was said of those who crossed the Appalachians down into the valleys of the Ohio, the Mississippi and the Missouri and pushed the frontiers of freedom to the Pacific shore that "the cowards never started and the weak never arrived." With no capital save courage and no resource except resourcefulness they built the American empire.

Here are the hundreds of miles of stone walls of Vermont, every stone dug from the ground and moved to where it now lies, by ox-power and human muscle alone. We think of the pyramids of Egypt, and the tens of thousands of slaves who dragged the huge stones across the desert under the whips of their masters. It is my guess that the stone walls of Vermont represent more toil than the pyramids. But the walls were laid by the free choice of free men. "They scorned delights and lived laborious days."

It is good to have a school like this in sight of those stone walls!

Avoid struggle, and life becomes sterile, vapid and meaningless. Our mental hospitals are being filled with thousands of neurotics, many of whom feel inadequate to meet life because they were protected from taking the bumps in childhood.

No man was ever greater than the difficulties he overcame. Great difficulties, great men. Small difficulties, small men. From struggle comes strength, and physical and mental health.

It is only struggle that calls forth hidden powers we do not know we have. The great psychologist, William James, said that the average person does not put forth more than ten percent of his potential.

Let me tell you a story of my great-grandfather Peter Pettengill who came to Vermont in 1787. One day his hired man was chopping down trees in the virgin forest and did not come to the house at noon for lunch. My great-grandfather went to see what was wrong. He found that a tree had fallen on the hired man and killed him. With nothing but the strength of his own powerful body, Peter lifted the tree off the dead man and carried him to the house.

Whence came his strength to do that? From the challenge before him. That tree was never cut into timber or fire wood. It lay where it fell. Other strong men from miles around came and tried to lift the tree. They could not. Why? Because they did not have the incentive that Peter had. Nor could Peter himself ever lift the tree again. The incentive was gone.

You have all seen athletes at times "play over their heads." Why? Because of the challenge and its acceptance.

It is men who have counted challenge as a blessing who get the big rewards in life. As Emerson said, God keeps an honest account with men.

The hard surgical cases, where life hangs on a heart beat, do not go to the dilettante surgeon. The tough engineering problem, like building a bridge across a mighty river, does not go to the engineer who has always looked for the easy jobs. And the same for lawyers and top executives in business.

If at times you feel that you did not have the same chance that others have, ask yourself what chance did Abraham Lincoln have? Remember that it is not so much the size of the dog in the fight that counts, but the size of the fight in the dog.

You young men face a time of struggle with an enemy of your country more dangerous than King George III in 1776 — the godless Caesars of atheistic communism. Face up to it. Lick it. Put it and all its teaching out of our schools, churches, public affairs and private life. What our fathers bequeathed us is still the last, best hope of earth. Save it for your boys and girls.

Remember robust Robert Browning: "I count life just a stuff to try the soul's strength on, educe the man."

Remember Tennyson's Ulysses and the old Greeks "who ever with a frolic welcome took the thunder and the sunshine" — the hard hours with the same zest as the pleasant ones.

Remember the poem of the frontier:
"I dream no dream of a nursemaid state,
That spoons me out my food.
No, the stout heart sings in its strife with fate
For the toil and the sweat are good."

In addition to being nationally known and esteemed as a constitutional lawyer, economist, author and speaker, Sam was a fine poet. It was while at Middlebury that he first became really interested in poetry through one of his professors, the head of the English department, Prof. C. B. Wright. From him he learned not only to love poetry but to write it, and from then until almost the end of his life, he wrote "verses" as he modestly called them, but some were very beautiful and can be found in a few anthologies. One in particular was his favorite, "The Widow's Clearing," which he wrote about an abandoned farm on Breadloaf Mountain, near Middlebury. It was also near Robert Frost's home.

# The Widow's Clearing

Beauty was there,
And peace,
And the strength of the hills.
So they came,
They came a long ways —
Came from across the Atlantic,
Up the Connecticut,
Up the White River,
Across the Divide,
Up to the clearing,
It took a long time —
Four generations.

The view was wonderful.
The grass tasted good to the oxen;
There were trout in the stream;
And deer on the mountain,
And the sugar maples were sweet in the spring.

They stayed a long time —
Four generations —
From Bunker Hill to the Klondike.
The axe and the scythe,
The plow and the cradle
Did their work.

Finally the tide moved on —
On to Michigan, Iowa, Oregon.
The boys went West,
And the girls married boys
Who went West.

There was work out there,
Out there in the West.
So they took the axe and the scythe,
The plow and the cradle.
Only the widow stayed.
Finally she went
West.

Scrub apples and thistles
And immortelles.
The clearing is smaller now,
Smaller.
The pines and the spruce and the hemlocks
Have resumed their march.

Only the hills are there,
And beauty,
And peace.

The magnificent statue in the Capitoline Museum in Rome inspired him to write:

### The Dying Gaul

When, in some far-off land, two thousand years ago,
Your strong right arm gave way, and the last red drops did flow,
What happened then, O soldier, to justify your pain?
Was there a Roman holiday to pomp a tyrant's reign?
Did a woman's tears fall bitterly on a peasant's lonely bed
As carrion vultures tore the flesh where she once laid her head?
The war you fought — has history writ down a single page
That proves your death in battle has made a better age?

Not one bleak line remains, nor does the record even show
The darkling plain you fought upon, and received your fatal
  blow.
A sculptor felt and carved your august pain, but he is not
Remembered. Victor, vanquished, battle, artist — all forgot.

Only the stone remembers, not futile deed nor name,
But the spirit that dares death — to that it lends sure fame.
So, as the ages pass, let this great word be said,
Courage eludes the clutch of death, and is inherited!

Rodin's sculpture, "The Kiss" was another that stirred his imagination.

### The Kiss

Their kiss will never end; no war's mad rage
Nor vain pursuit of fame will ever lift
His hand away; throughout an endless age
Her arm will hold his lips to her sweet gift.
Ah, happy they, more blessed than Keats' fair youth
And Grecian maid who could not have their bliss.
The rock-hewn lips proclaim the greater truth
That life must not withhold from love its kiss,
Else life has beauty lost. Let time stand still
While timeless love shall work its ageless will.

*The Dying Gaul.*

As a loving father, he wrote the following verses when his daughter was seven.

### To My Little Daughter At The Piano

Unbade, my daughter oft returns from romp
And play, and eager children's voices; comes
From all earth's radiant beauty, felt by her
Intensely, but felt without a thought of all
It means, and sits her down and plays. And when
Her fingers falter, sweetly then her voice
Joins in to aid them. All the while I sit
Enraptured as I feel her happy heart
Blend with this soul of mine. If tears come
She does not understand, she cannot guess how much
Her discords please me more than Chopin's perfect touch.

And could I ever forget the tender poems he wrote me before and during our marriage?

His sense of humor often asserted itself and one piece of doggerel he wrote for one of my grandchildren who owned a dachshund is as amusing today as it was years ago.

There was a dachshund once so long
He hadn't any notion
How long it took to notify
His tail of his emotion.
And so it happened, while his eyes
Were filled with woe and sadness,
His little tail went wagging on
Because of previous gladness.

And still another which he illustrated!

Two inches long, the centipede
Is propped with legs beyond his need;
Whereas the dachshund, caring little
Endures a sag about his middle!

In a small, privately printed volume "Stars Above Babel" are poems he wrote before 1925, some lovely, some exciting, and many amusing.

In a previous chapter entitled "Practicing Law" Sam briefly mentioned his paper "Poetry and the Poet's Mission" which he read at a meeting of the Round Table in 1929, and which was judged the best of the year. It is the finest analysis of what poetry is all about that I have ever read, and deserves to be given in full. It will be found at the end of this book with some of his outstanding speeches and writings.

In some of his serious writings Sam's sense of humor often evidenced itself to make a point. In a letter which he wrote to the editor of the Chicago Tribune he said the following article should be read against the background of today's crowded school rooms, filthy slums, broken homes, teen-age crimes, and so forth. It was published, and it is still applicable today.

> Those who tax and neglect our own poor to give alms to distant foreigners have a long ancestry.
>
> Charles Dickens, in "Bleak House" written over a hundred years ago, told us of Mrs. Jellyby, the founder, no doubt, of the American Jellybies. This estimable female devoted her life to "the subject of Africa, with a view to the general cultivation of the natives and a happy settlement on the banks of the African rivers of our superabundant population."
>
> "The African project at present employs my whole time," she said. "We hope next year to be educating the natives of Borrioboola-Gha on the left bank of the Niger. My work is never done."
>
> She had a large brood of children but she was too busy with Africa to give them any attention. When visitors called one day, one of the children fell down a whole flight of stairs making seven bumps on the way down. When the wounded child, having been patched up by the neighbors, exhibited himself to his mother, she said with the serene composure with which she said everything, "Go away, you naughty Peepy," and fixed her fine eyes on Africa again.
>
> Her visitors told her miserable, dissatisfied children stories about Puss-in-boots and I don't know what else while Mrs. Jellyby opened her correspondence with public bodies on the African subject until four envelopes fell into the gravy at once.
>
> Mrs. Pardiggle, a formidable style of lady with a loud voice and giving the effect of wanting a great deal of room, was a rival of Mrs. Jellyby in rapacious benevolence. Her children, too, were positively ferocious with discontent. She said, "My children are not frivolous; they expend the entire amount of their

allowances on subscriptions under my direction to the Superannuated Widows, the Tockohoopo Indians, and the Infant Bonds of Joy." The face of each child darkened balefully as each of the above were mentioned.

Mrs. Jellyby, meanwhile, drank black coffee and dictated to her eldest daughter regarding the African project all evening. Peepy scaled his crib, crept down in his bedgown and was so cold his teeth chattered. The room was not only untidy but dirty. But Africa was of momentous importance and all other places and things were of utter insignificance.

An accomplishment during his retirement which gave Sam great satisfaction was being one of the founders of the Grafton Historical Society in 1962, at which time he was elected its first president. He personally raised enough money to purchase the historic little post office built in 1855, and to have it renovated, and it opened as a museum on May 30, 1963 with a large collection of Grafton memorabilia. At that time he was able to announce that it was free and clear of debt, and from then on it became an outstanding success. From twenty charter members in 1962, Sam lived to see the membership grow to over four hundred, with almost a thousand people visiting the museum each summer. His presidency lasted for ten years until he resigned because of ill health.

It is unfortunate that he did not live long enough to know that his hope for expansion of the Museum, when it began to "burst at the seams," has finally been realized. In 1978, the Museum moved to an old house, just three doors away from the old post office on Main Street, which has been restored and converted into beautiful, large quarters. A room in the new museum has been dedicated to his memory and his portrait hangs over the fireplace.

The first home of the Grafton Historical Museum, formerly the old post office building, was erected in 1855. In 1978 it moved to larger quarters.

## XXV

## THE MAN HIMSELF

No account of a man's life can be complete without a description of the man himself — his appearance, disposition, character, the opinions of those who knew him.

A handsome man, Samuel Barrett Pettengill was just under six feet tall, with broad shoulders and an erect carriage which made him appear even taller. He had a beautifully shaped head and strong, regular features. His complexion was fair, his eyes deep-set and a very dark blue. As a boy his hair was blonde, becoming brown as he grew older and except at the temples, it did not turn gray until he was in his early seventies. At that time also he started growing a small, clipped mustache. He had a deep, resonant voice which commanded attention when he spoke. He had a phenomenal memory and could recite poems by the score. Even more important he could always produce an apt quotation when needed. He spoke to the point, used simple language and never talked down to anyone. Neither did he ever try to impress anyone with his knowledge or vocabulary.

As a politician he was an effective campaigner, with a warm personality. When he was campaigning in the countryside he would often excuse himself from the speakers' table and go back into the kitchen where volunteer cooks had prepared the meal. "Who made *that* pumpkin pie?" he would ask, thus picking up a kitchenful of votes. He really liked pie, and he really liked people, and people knew it and liked him.

His friendly manner drew all who knew him to him. Even the youngsters on the village streets in Grafton where in later

*Sam Pettengill at home in 1964 at age 78.*

years he took his daily walk, would call "Hi, Sam" and receive a smiling greeting in return.

He was unselfish, kind and generous, thoughtful of others and sensitive to their feelings. He accepted the sorrows and disappointments that came to him, as they do to all, calmly and without complaint. He had complete control over himself and in all the years of our marriage I never knew him to lose his temper, even when I knew he was angry. He was in all respects what he himself described as

### A Gentleman

> A gentleman is a man who faces life's hard hours with a sort of gay fortitude; meets rebuff without bitterness and triumph without boast; pities others but never himself; is kind to all animals as distant kinsmen; loves children with the happy heart of the boy he was; treats age and infirmity with tenderness; honors women as persons and not chattels; is incapable of the misuse of his strength or any cruelty, large or small; whose unfailing guidepost to conduct is to be kind. Such a man is a *gentle man*, whether he be a diplomat of the court or a rail splitter of the wilderness.

No more honorable man ever lived. His word once given, could be trusted. It was impossible for him to tell a lie. It was also impossible for him to do anything he knew was wrong. He had great courage, never flinching when following through on a decision he thought was right. When he first ran for Congress, a reporter asked him how he made his decisions. The answer was "I believe in an independent mind. But independence should follow thought. When I have made up my mind, then I am ready to abide by my convictions."

When he announced that he would not seek nomination for a fifth term in Congress, one newspaper editorial comment was "Samuel B. Pettengill has been no ordinary office holder. He has been literally a statesman. His diligence, courage and patriotism have impressed thoughtful citizens throughout this nation." Economic Forum, an important New York newspaper wrote, "Take the down-east conservatism of New England; the go-getting Americanism of the middle west; add the poetic vision that typifies the far west, and you have the attributes of the Hon. Samuel B. Pettengill, one of the most constructive, brilliant and hard-working all-American congressmen that Washington has seen in many a year." An editorial writer who was NOT a friend of Sam's and who over the preceding six or seven years had let hardly a week pass without taking a shot at him, wrote, "A diluted Democracy has driven from public life one of the most intelligent, discerning, wisest and truly patriotic and courageous statesmen of our time." Quite a reversal and a handsome apology.

Almost ten years later, in March, 1947, an interesting editorial appeared in a New York City newspaper entitled AN IDEAL CANDIDATE.

"These are momentous days for this Republic. The pattern of our life can well be determined by the decisions that are being made and will be made by the men and women we elect to office. In this connection it is paramount that we name as President in the election of 1948 a man who will guide us along the way that will preserve and make stronger the system of government that has made us a great nation.

"One man who is well qualified to do this is former Congressman from Indiana, Samuel B. Pettengill.

"We are not the first to mention Mr. Pettengill. Thousands of people who know him and the good work he is doing approve him and would like to see him named by both the major parties. In publicizing this fact we hope it will not lead to a misinterpretation of Mr. Pettengill's talks, for they are not tainted by self-seeking, but are the pure expressions of an American of sterling patriotism and are entirely divorced from all political ties.

"Mr. Pettengill is trained in law and law-making. He comes from the Middle West, an area that has produced so many outstanding Americans. He is a Jeffersonian Democrat, but above party allegiance he has always placed the welfare of our country. His philosophy of government, American to the core, is well known to millions of citizens who listen every Sunday to his inspiring radio addresses.

"With Mr. Pettengill as President our country would be sure to have a leader who would be a staunch advocate of sound

Americanism; a believer in the rights of the individual; a foe of degrading socialism, a man exceptionally qualified to direct us along the path that has made our country the greatest in the world."

After his death, at the Memorial Service held for him in Grafton on May 29, 1974, the Rev. Norman Vincent Peale, notable pastor of the Marble Collegiate Church in New York City, said, "Sam was first a thinker and second a philosopher. He was a towering, rugged man, a truly great man. He was born in Oregon, but his roots were in Vermont. Had he been less honest, he might have been President. But he was a man not interested in Sam Pettengill, but in his country."

I could quote from many others, all in the same vein, but these are enough to show what the world thought of him.

What I thought of him after almost twenty-five years of marriage was that he was a perfect husband; a delightful companion; a "cheerful spirit" as his father always advised him to be; a cordial host who enjoyed his many friends; a man who loved nature in all its aspects; a man who loved his home and the man who made me the happiest of women.

Sam enjoyed exceptionally good health for most of his life. Yet when it began to fail four years before he died, and he was hospitalized eight times, with five operations, the only time he complained was on our twenty-third wedding anniversary when he was in the hospital and he said to me, "This is a hell of a way for us to spend our anniversary." We were able to spend our twenty-fourth anniversary happily at home on July 16, 1973, for he was feeling quite well. But on January 21, 1974, two days after his eighty-eighth birthday, he had to return to the hospital. Suffering great pain before his death on March 20, 1974, not a word of complaint passed his lips. He held tightly to my hand and was a man to the end.

*"When shall we look upon his like again!"*

# SELECTIONS FROM THE MANY SPEECHES AND WRITINGS OF SAMUEL B. PETTENGILL

Although these speeches and articles were written between ten and forty years ago, they apply even more to today's conditions in the United States. Samuel B. Pettengill was a prophet, but his was "a voice crying in the wilderness." It would be well for the future of our country to listen to him now.

| | |
|---|---|
| Inflation Concerns Everyone | 288 |
| Why Put Counterfeiters In Jail? | 296 |
| A New Order of the Ages | 299 |
| The Responsibility of College Graduates as Citizens | 313 |
| Where Karl Marx Went Wrong | 324 |
| A Boundless Field of Power | 329 |
| False Balance Sheet | 335 |
| The World's Illusion | 340 |
| The Future of Free Enterprise | 342 |
| The Grand Strategy of Freedom | 358 |
| Not the Supreme Law of the Land | 364 |
| Poetry and the Poet's Mission | 367 |

# INFLATION CONCERNS EVERYONE

*Samuel B. Pettengill wrote this article on inflation for the* Reader's Digest *of October, 1951. It was circulated throughout the world and was translated into several languages but, unfortunately, public interest at the time was not strong enough to change the trend. Perhaps today the evils he prophesied will be better understood and the fight will begin. Reprinted with permission of Reader's Digest Association, Inc.*

The American dollar is now worth less than at any time since the Constitution was adopted, 162 years ago. Prices are on the way to becoming still higher; the dollar still cheaper.

The dollar is worth, roughly, only as much as a 50-cent piece was worth ten years ago. This rot in the dollar has confiscated billions of dollars of buying power which thrifty Americans thought they had saved against old age or a rainy day. If weather were rotting the timbers of your home as fast as inflation is rotting your savings, you'd take steps. But the average man does nothing effective about inflation because he thinks the subject is complicated. Yet the core of the matter is within the grasp of anyone who can balance a checkbook or play bridge.

Few things are more important to you or your country or more fascinating than money — sound money. More than your own savings is involved. This spreading rot in the dollar threatens the stability and security of the Government of the United States — and of our entire social and economic system. Lenin said that the surest way to overthrow a government is to debauch its currency.

*Only the people can stop inflation.* Politicians are the captives of voting pressure groups which they think they must continue to appease. The political leaders have not the courage to act effectively *without wide popular support.*

What is happening to your money? Who and what causes inflation? Who is hurt by it and how much? What must you do personally to stop it?

What is happening to the 80 million thrifty Americans who have loaned their savings to Uncle Sam? Do you own any kind of bond, or a life-insurance policy, a savings-bank account, a social-security card, an annuity, an industrial pension, or an interest in a civil-service retirement fund? If you have any claim to a fixed number of dollars payable to you, or your wife, or child, now or in the future, you are being hurt badly by inflation. Remember, too, that as you grow older your chance to reacquire a nest egg will be less.

There are 83 million persons who hold life insurance policies. Women are the chief beneficiaries. Inflation has punished them severely. Life insurance in force in 1932 was 101 billion dollars. In 1949 it was 214 billion dollars. This looks like a marvelous record. But is it? The 214 billions would actually buy no more groceries, coal, shoes, etc., than 123 billion dollars would in 1932. This shows how dollars are melting away.

There are 34 million more life-insurance policyholders than the total number of voters for President on all tickets in 1948. If they, and their wives, understood how the security painfully paid for during a lifetime is melting away, their demand for protection against inflation could be overwhelming.

Similar losses are being taken by the 100-odd million who hold social-security cards, the 38 million employes who hold industrial group life insurance or retirement pensions, the 50 million savings-bank and building-and-loan depositors, not to mention many smaller groups like schoolteachers, professors, clergymen, firemen, policemen, postmen, who are paying to various retirement or old-age-benefit funds.

As the average life-span is increasing, the total number, as well as the percent, of our people living past 65 is also rapidly increasing. They have more old age to insure against and inflation leaves them less to insure it with. If they cannot live out their lives on their own savings, the burden of supporting them by taxes levied against those who are still in their working years is likely to become intolerable. Inflation therefore concerns everyone from the time he gets his first job, both as an earner and as a taxpayer.

The Government itself is hurt by inflation as the price of all it buys rises as its own dollars become cheap. And the federal government is the biggest buyer in the world. The same is true of the price of everything bought by state and local governments. To equip a soldier with clothing for a year cost $122 in 1939. Today it costs $377. Mr. Bernard Baruch estimates that "in the last war inflation added 100 billion dollars to the cost of the conflict."

Inflation puts a false glow on the cheeks of its victims. More dollars of income make people feel that they are getting ahead. The profits of business companies in an inflationary period are also largely fictitious. New machines cost about twice what worn-out machines cost when new. Hence the depreciation reserve will pay only half the cost of the new machine. The balance must be taken out of "profits." Yet these inescapable expenditures are taxed as if they were true profits. Thus a business company can go broke at the same time that it appears to be making a profit. This is a point that labor leaders seldom explain as they point at "big profits." The profit and dividend dollar has shrunk equally with the wage dollar.

What is inflation? It is not high prices, the high cost of living. Price is a *result* of inflation. Unless that one fact is clearly understood by the millions who are being hurt, their efforts to stop inflation will be futile.

Few even among the economists will quarrel much with this definition: Inflation is an increase in the total supply of money which people *have and want to spend* that is greater than the supply of goods available for them to purchase. For short, let the word "goods" include all services, such as a railroad ride, a hairdo, or dental care.

The following figures show clearly how this has worked in the past ten years. Before looking at them, we must understand what is here included in the term "money." Money is coins and Government currency in the hands of the people, *and* checking accounts in our commercial banks. This is the active money that is involved in our problem of inflation. Of course, money in savings banks, Postal Savings, building-and-loan associations, or even Government bonds, may be used to buy goods. But this is generally inactive money — money people do not want to spend.

Now see what happened to each kind of money.

|  | Dec. 31, 1939 | April, 1951 | Percent of Increase |
|---|---|---|---|
| Pocketbook money (Billions) | $ 6.4 | $ 24.6 | 284% |
| Checkbook money (Billions) | 29.8 | 89.4 | 200% |
| Total money supply (Billions) | $ 36.2 | $114 | 215% |
| Money per Capita (Dollars) | $276 | $742 | 169% |

In these ten years, our industrial production of goods, measured by actual tons, bushels, barrels — not by price tags in dollars — increased only 99 percent. The volume of money increased more than twice as fast as the volume of goods. Hence the purchasing power of each dollar went down and prices went up. The wholesale price index of the Government tells the story: it went up from 77.1 to 183.5; it more than doubled. It took $183.50 to buy at wholesale in October 1950 what $77.10 bought in 1939.

To think that price controls stop inflation is to believe that you can cool a room or cure a fever by putting ice next to the thermometer. There is no case in history where price and wage controls have stopped inflation for any length of time. To quote Thomas B. Mc-

Cabe, former chairman of the Federal Reserve Board: "Price and wage controls conceal the source of the inflation. Therein lies a great danger. By covering up the source, they tend to weaken the popular will to deal with the causes of the disease." That is the danger today. It is like thinking that wet streets cause rain. A tied-down safety valve on a boiler won't hold the steam in check long if you keep shoveling in fuel.

Admitting all this, some folks say, "I don't like these high prices, but still I've never had it so good as now. So what?" This is no argument at all. Our advancing science, technology and invention are the main reasons for more and better things for more people. As we produce more, we have more. There would have been as much produced without inflation. The people would "have it just as good" today, and what they now save for old age would not lose its power to buy things for them later on.

The chief cause of inflation is that the federal government ever since 1930 has spent more than it has taken in. It has gone into debt during 18 of the past 21 years. That, and the *way* it has gone into debt. If I save money by useful work, producing goods which others have bought, and lend $1000 — my savings — to Uncle Sam, there has been no increase in the nation's money supply. Uncle Sam has $1000 more; I have $1000 less. But if the Government borrows $1000 from a commercial bank, the money supply of the nation has increased by that amount. The bank takes Uncle Sam's promissory note (a Government bond) and credits him with a $1000 deposit against which he draws checks to pay his bills. As the debt goes up, as more bonds are sold to the banks, the money supply goes up. And it stays up, moving from hand to hand and from bank to bank, until the Government pays what it has borrowed. This creates a continuing demand for goods and the demand presses prices upward.

Some people call this "manufacturing money out of thin air." But there is nothing wrong in the practice itself. It is done every day by farmers, merchants and manufacturers. A merchant borrows $1000 at the bank to carry his inventory of Christmas toys until December. However, between private borrowing and Government borrowing, as practiced for 20 years, there are great and vital distinctions. In the first place, money borrowed to produce and market Christmas toys not only expands the money supply, but also the supply of goods for which the money will be spent. But Government buying goes into things that cannot be bought in the stores. No one can eat a Government building, an airplane or a gun. The second distinction is that, when the Christmas season is over, the merchant pays off his loan at the bank. He got the money to do so from the pockets of his customers. The $1000 of new checkbook money he created by borrowing at the bank is canceled. It no longer circulates. There is no inflation.

But when the Government never pays its debt, the new money it created by borrowing at the banks continues to circulate year after year. As a result, more money than goods; each dollar loses value. We see here the danger of continually unbalanced national budgets. If Uncle Sam does not pay his debts, you pay them. You pay in the shrinkage of your savings as money becomes too plentiful and cheap.

The greatest inflationary factor at present is, of course, the defense program. It acts in two ways. First, every dollar the Government spends for planes, guns, uniforms, ships or any of the 10,000 other things it needs for war, goes straight into private pockets — mostly as wages. Thus the Government is creating purchasing power of consumers at a dizzying rate that soon will approach a billion dollars a week. At the same time, the Government not only fails to supply goods for people to buy with this money but sharply decreases the output of consumer's goods. It uses up steel and aluminum that otherwise might be made into cars or quick freezers or TV sets. Even more drastic in effect, it stops hundreds of thousands of men from making cars and sets them to making guns. It stops another 3,500,000 men from making *anything at all,* and puts them into uniform.

But there are many other practices the Government has engaged in to cause prices to rise and money to lose value.

The Government, let us say, buys $100,000,000 worth of potatoes to maintain the price — that is, to make them cost more to the customer. There's inflation for you. It then destroys the potatoes by painting them blue for the hogs to eat or letting them rot. You pay a higher price for potatoes. And you pay a second time in taxes to provide the Government with the $100,000,000 even if you don't eat potatoes. But the $100,000,000 which the Government paid for the potatoes it destroyed continues to circulate and creates a demand for other goods, causing them also to rise in price. This potato case could be multiplied a hundred times.

Whatever arguments are given for favoring sellers with price floors and buyers with price ceilings, it is certain that the practice builds up pressure blocs which produce a chain reaction on prices as each voting group tries to get an advantage over the others. For example, take the parity price floor for farm products. It is based on the cost to the farmer of the things he buys that are made in the city. As city wages go up, city goods go up, and then the farm parity price goes up again. This makes groceries cost still more in the city. The city worker then demands and gets more money to equalize his higher cost of living. This makes the farmer pay still more for city goods, and he demands another increase in his parity price.

The peculiar hazards of farming may justify some kind of national insurance against crop failures or crop gluts, but with the farmer taking some share of the risk, like the "$100 deductible" clause in automobile accident insurance. But this would be a far cry from the present inflationary political farm policy.

All wasteful and inefficient operation of Government departments — the "empire building" in Washington bureaus — adds to the fires of inflation. More dollars paid out for services, and competing for goods, cause prices to rise. The waste must be made good by taxes and practically every tax is added to the cost of living. Other forces pushing the inflationary spiral constantly upward are the increases in minimum wages, larger unemployment-compensation checks, and longer periods to enjoy them. More money but no more goods.

Stockpiling, however necessary, creates shortages of goods as they are locked up in Government warehouses. But the dollars paid for the goods continue to circulate.

Our aid programs to foreign countries may be necessary for many reasons, but they are definitely inflationary. We do not send billions of dollars abroad. That is a short cut of language. Foreigners can't eat money! We send billions of dollars' worth of goods abroad. The wheat, cotton, steel, eggs, etc., vanish overseas. But the money paid to American producers for these goods stays home and continues to circulate. More money at home and less goods. Prices rise.

All of these practices of the Government, and many more, adulterate all dollar savings. Inflation is a species of taxation and the cruelest of all. No one is exempted from it. The people pay thrice, in prices today, in taxes tomorrow, and in the loss of their savings the day after.

The national grab bag, once opened, is hard to close. Only an awakening of millions of voters whose savings are melting away under the impact of high taxes and inflation as it gathers momentum can turn the tide.

With the possible exception of the Swiss franc, the American dollar is still the best money in the world. We must keep it so. But new pressures are arising to depreciate it still further. Of especial importance at this time is the escalator clause in labor-union contracts, now recognized and implemented by Government officials. This clause raises wages as the cost of living goes up, regardless of whether the wage earner produces more goods. But as wages go up, prices must go up. And so on and on, in an ever-ascending wage-price spiral. The demand for an escalator clause in union contracts is apt to become universal. However helpful it may be to the individual employe and his wife for a few short months, it is self-defeating for the nation. How about escalators for the landlords, for stockholders, for Government-bond holders, for professional men, for merchants, for life-insurance policy holders, for everybody?

No, the escalator clause is no cure for inflation. We must go to the roots of inflation and stop the governmental practices that cheapen money and force the cost of living constantly higher.

There is no necessity for inflation, and it can be stopped if the problem is understood. America's tremendous capacity to produce is on the side of sound money. With our constantly better tools, our harnessing of energy, our science, invention and technology ready to work their miracles, we can produce such a flood of goods as to keep goods and money in balance. But no technology can produce goods as fast as a government can produce money.

The millions of thrifty Americans must demand that Government spending at all levels be limited to necessities and cut to the bone; insist on rigid economy and efficiency, including purchases for the armed services; demand balanced budgets from now on — pay-as-you-go taxes; stop politicians from creating artificial shortages of goods (not connected with stockpiling for national defense); make payments on the national debt whenever it can be done; and especially get Government bonds out of the commercial banks and into the hands of the people, where they are not inflationary.

You yourself can do very practical things to combat inflation. Here are some of them:

1. Write your Congressman. Yes, this is what you've been told so often! It is old advice. But to curb inflation it is still the best advice and far too few act on it. Remind your Congressman that you expect him to fight for economy; rebuke him when he yields to the pressure of some special group that wants exemption from controls or a special subsidy. Send him a word of appreciation when he stands up to be counted on the right side.

2. Whatever your walk in life, you can do your bit to keep prices down. You can give a good day's work for a day's pay; if everybody does that, we shall produce more goods at less cost. If you manufacture or sell goods, you can give good value and refrain from taking advantage of the fact that you *could* profiteer.

3. You can stop unnecessary spending. You can do without that TV set for awhile. Later on things are going to be more abundant and cheaper than they are now.

4. Economy begins at home. Watch your local governments — your town board, city council, park board, school board. This is no time for any but essential expenditures. Sure, a new bandstand in the park would be nice, and the town can afford it. But don't build it!

The sum of all such little unessential projects all over the land helps boost the price of materials and labor.

5. Discuss the problem of inflation with your neighbors, make it a topic in your clubs, get speakers who can present the problem effectively, try to see that the high school students are told the economic facts of life. In short, do your best to make sure that everyone in your neighborhood is aware of the menace and what can be done to combat it.

6. Above all, save! If it were possible to withhold part of our income from us, to be paid to us at a later date, that would be a most effective weapon against inflation. But since we cannot be forced to save, we must save voluntarily; that is, remove our little cupful of money from the flood. A cupful doesn't count? Wrong. The flood of money consists entirely of cupfuls.

7. One thing the Government can do and must do is to sop up as much of the increased money supply as possible by taxes. Your part in this is to pay without evasion. Better pay taxes now than have your widow cash in your life insurance some day for just enough to buy a meal — as actually happened in Germany.

The only hedge against inflation that is worth anything to the millions of people now being hurt is to understand the simple arithmetic of money and prices and make that understanding felt at the ballot box.

# Why Put Counterfeiters In Jail?

*This article by Samuel B. Pettengill was requested by the editors of the* Reader's Digest *as a followup to his previous article, "Inflation Concerns Everyone," and was published in the March, 1952, edition of* Reader's Digest. *Reprinted with permission of Reader's Digest Association, Inc.*

Remember the boy with warts which made him bashful with girls? One day he walked through a covered bridge and his warts disappeared. He has been recommending the bridge treatment ever since.

A great many people are dragging their feet in the fight against inflation because of the same kind of reasoning. We have inflation and we never had things so good. "Look — TV sets, vitamin pills, nylon undies, ball point pens." So it must be inflation that makes us prosperous.

Probably everyone has credited some good fortune in his life to a cause which had nothing whatever to do with it, including lucky stones and rabbits' feet. Such fables are harmless. But the belief that inflation and prosperity go hand in hand is dangerous. The people who think this are unconscious Greenbackers.

According to an official index, the consumer's dollar was worth one hundred cents at the stores in 1939. Today (1952) it is worth fifty-three cents, the lowest point in record. If the fifty-three cent dollar had made us prosperous, a twenty-five cent dollar should make us twice as prosperous, shouldn't it? And a five-cent dollar would be better still? But even Greenbackers won't follow their logic that far. There is plainly a catch in this notion that fifty-three cent dollars have cured our financial warts. But what is it?

Let us look not only at dollar comparisons but at other contrasts between 1939 and 1949. In 1949 we produced 405 million more bushels of wheat and 797 million more bushels of corn than in 1939. With more to eat, we are better off. In that ten-year period, 2,053,000 tractors were added to the productive capacity of our farms. Inflation grows no wheat. Tractors do.

In the same period the annual production of petroleum went up by 677 million barrels. Use of natural gas rose by 4,213 billion cubic feet.

There were similar advances in our great research laboratories, our mines, factories, transportation systems and sales outlets. But it is science, technology and power, not inflation, which have enabled us to make more and better things for more people.

We cannot be far wrong if we say that the material standard of living of a nation is its production divided by its population. Take India and pile all its food, clothing, churches, loincloths, elephants, automobiles, schools, household furnishings and medical supplies in one big heap. Do the same in America. Divide each heap by the number of people and you are pretty close to the average standard of living in each country. If on top of these vast heaps of goods you piled thick layers of thousand dollar bills, would they add anything to the standard of living? No. You can't eat money or patch a roof with it.

Behind the Greenback notion — the more money, the more prosperity — is the superstition that money is wealth. There was a time when money WAS wealth because things that had value in themselves — gold, silver, cattle, tobacco, furs and so on — were used as money. A gold coin weighing one ounce, even if minted by a forgotten monarch two thousand years ago, is worth thirty-five dollars (in 1952!) Beat it into a shapeless mass and it is still worth thirty-five dollars. And for more than a century every paper dollar could be exchanged, on demand, for precious metal. But it is now a criminal offense for an American citizen to possess gold dollars. Except for pocket coins, all our money today is paper NOT redeemable in gold. Yet the belief thousands of years old that money is wealth has been transferred to our paper currency.

If paper bills are wealth, then Germany should have been the most prosperous nation on the globe during the inflation of the 1920's, when the poverty-strocken Germans were rolling in paper money — which wouldn't buy anything. No, a paper dollar is only a ticket exchangeable for goods or services. And like anything that becomes too plentiful, dollars lose value when they increase faster than the production of goods. Dollars have multiplied as the national debt has increased, and this is the chief cause of the inflation that is destroying the value of our life insurance, social security cards and savings bonds.

Suppose a counterfeiter produces some perfect phony bank notes. He buys several suits and pays for them with his homemade bills. That makes a profit for the merchants and reduces his stock of goods. So the merchant sends an order to the factory and that makes the factory order more wool. Orders flow everywhere. Happy days are here again!

Now, this counterfeiter has performed the same economic function as a government that prints money to pay its bills. Why put him in jail?

The answer is that the counterfeiter has not added to, but subtracted from the community's stock of wealth, by obtaining goods for which he gave no real values in exchange. In short, he is a thief. Inflation is a thief. We should arrest both.

We know the Government is trying to stop counterfeiters.

WHAT is the Government doing to stop inflation?

# A NEW ORDER OF THE AGES

*A speech made at the 44th Annual Convention of the Commercial Law League of America, Mackinac Island, Michigan, on July 18, 1938.*

I am speaking under a very great disadvantage tonight because I know the general feeling that people have for members of Congress and federal officials.

At the meeting of the American Bar Association last fall, I was told that there was a lawyer who had apparently had a good year. The New Deal has been very good to lawyers, I am told. This lawyer, having had a good year and feeling very happy and hospitable and kind and charitable toward the world, was seen tossing five dollar bills from a window on the sixth floor of a hotel down to the crowd on the street below. Do you know what happened to him? He was arrested for impersonating a federal official!

I am very happy to be here tonight. Despite the fact that there has been so much discussion in the last year or two of the fundamental values that have affected our civilization, I feel that we might again discuss this new order of the ages, constitutional government.

I know that wherever I go there is a degree of hopelessness about the present situation in our country which I do not think is justified. Wherever I go I talk with people and they say, "Oh, what's the use? With fifteen million people getting checks from the federal treasury, what can you do about it?"

But I am here to say that as the result of what has taken place in the last eighteen months, I am beginning to put my money on the long-odds horse. When the Supreme Court Bill was proposed on the fifth of February in 1937, within three days I declared against it with a statement to the newspapers of the Third District saying that I would be against the bill.

I thought then, and the country did too, that it was a hopeless adventure to try to defeat that bill. We had the feeling that we were simply fighting a rear-guard action for a lost cause. But some of us had had fathers in the Civil War and ancestors in the American Revolution, and we had the feeling "For how can man die better than facing fearful odds, for the ashes of his fathers and the temples of his gods?"

And so we got into the fight. It looked desperately hopeless, but it seemed as if the lord of hosts himself was fighting on our side, because one event after the other followed in significant sequence until finally the bill was defeated on the floor of the nation's senate.

And the Reorganization Bill was given to the country about the same time. That fight was postponed until the Supreme Court battle was over, but it was resumed when the 75th Congress, the third session, met last November and this past winter.

And again those of us who took the opposition on that bill thought it was a hopeless fight. As you know the bill carried in the Senate by three votes. Although they had defeated the Supreme Court Bill the opposition lost in the Senate, and the bill came over to the House and nobody thought we could win. Even the newspaper boys, after all concessions had been made to obtain votes, thought it would carry by twenty-five to fifty votes. Yet when the roll was called on the motion to re-commit it, it was defeated by 205 to 196.

In my own state recently we have seen that the attempt to purge from public life men of independent courage and spirit is meeting with opposition. I made a radio disc speech in favor of Fred Van Nuys that was sent to all of the radio stations in Indiana and put on electric transcription. It did not seem six weeks ago that Fred Van Nuys would be renominated. And yet he was.

So having been in the Supreme Court fight, in the Reorganization fight, and this lesser one in Indiana, I am beginning to place my money on the long-odds horse. It shows what a few bold, determined, resolute men can do in this twentieth century, backed as they have been by the lawyers of America, by many of the people in the editorial offices and pulpits of this country, and by thousands and millions of humble American citizens.

This battle to save constitutional democracy in America is not lost. It is not a hopeless struggle. We are making headway. We have met the enemy on two great occasions, and we have come from the field with its scalp. It is not a hopeless struggle. That is the first thing I wish to state to you, because I have noted this feeling of hopelessness wherever I go.

Why did our forefathers, when the first Congress met in 1789, after the Constitution had been adopted and after George Washington was sworn in as our first President, have a committee of Congress created to draw a coat of arms for the United States government?

They prepared a design, and that design, with a few changes, is in use today. I am happy to say that you will find it today on the back of the dollar bill that is in general circulation. The coat of arms of the United States is in two parts. One side represents the well-known emblem of the American Eagle. It is now used as part of the great seal of the United States impressed upon state papers. It pictures the American Eagle holding in his talons the arrows of war and the olive branch of peace, symbolical of the relationship of this country in foreign affairs with other nations. The eagle is holding in its beak the ribbon with the words "E pluribus unum," one republic from many republics, an indissoluble union of indestructible states, emblematical of the relationship of the federal and the forty-eight state governments.

For fifty years before the Civil War broke out, the great question before the Americans of that generation was whether this union of states would endure. That question was settled by the heroism at Gettysburg, and through the long contest of the Civil War, and it received its final answer at Appomattox where, with the point of the sword dipped in human blood, the Constitution of the United States was, in effect, amended to read that this is a partnership of states from which no partner may withdraw.

That part of the coat of arms of the nation is symbolical of the relationship between the central government and foreign governments and the forty-eight state governments.

The other side of the coat of arms of the United States, shown on the back of the dollar bill in general use, is symbolical not of the relationship of one government with another. It is symbolical of the relationship of the government with the individual. It shows the unfinished pyramid of government resting upon the broad base of popular sovereignty, symbolical of the aspirations and the hope of the men who drew that emblem and that symbol a long time ago, that America still has a great destiny. And over the pyramid the all-seeing eye of Divine Providence, and underneath the words "novus ordo seclorum" — a new order of the ages.

Why was it, my friends, that when this committee of Congress in 1789 sat down to prepare a coat of arms for the United States, they had reason to hope and to believe that they had created a new order of the ages? What was there new about this new government that was being set up on American soil, this government under the Constitution of the United States? There had been many other great charters in man's long progress upward from despotism and his escape toward liberty throughout the centuries that had preceded that time; there had been Magna Carta of 1215, the Bill of Rights, and Petition of Rights, in the centuries.

But there was something different between the Constitution of the United States and these other great milestones of human liberty. These other great milestones of human liberty had placed restrictions and limitations only upon the power of kings in whose elevation to the seats of power the people had no voice or vote.

But when the Constitution of the United States was written, for the first time in human history with respect to any large number of people and over any large expanse of territory, restrictions and limitations were placed upon the power not of kings, but on the power of the elected representatives of the people themselves, chosen by the people.

The Constitution of the United States is a power of attorney, and it contains limitations and restrictions upon the powers and the responsibilities and the duties of the agents of the people. That was something new in the history of the world. That had never been done before on any large scale anywhere in all of the many centuries that had preceded it.

Now, I find, as we discuss constitutional government, that people are apt to think of it in an abstract way. I think that has been one of the great failures, especially of those of us who have had the benefit of college and law school education, that we have not sufficiently explained constitutional government to our lay friends, to those whom we are called upon to address, not in terms of abstract rights and abstract duties, but with reference to its practical application, the happiness, the peace and the prosperity of a great people.

I want to discuss with you for a few moments the Constitution of the United States in these terms and not in the abstract. In order to live successfully we have to have formulae. Two plus two equal four. Two minus two equal nothing. It is a formula, but civilization would come to an end if the formula were not right, and if it did not prove to be right on all occasions. And the same is true of the Constitution of the United States.

Now, why do I say that? What is the practical effect of constitutional government that is under challenge today here and throughout the world? What has it meant to us, what has it meant to you, your father, your grandfather, your son, your daughter, and those who will carry your blood on far to the last generation? What has it meant? When did civilization begin? I will tell you when civilization began. I will tell you when, for the first time the law of the jungle, tooth against tooth and claw against claw, reached its peak and began to decline.

Civilization began when, in some distant dawn of some dim day, some man somewhere, at the cost of sacrifice to himself, lived up to some promise that he had made. That is when civilization began. Civilization is built on promises. Without faith in promises, civilization would go back to the jungle in twenty-four hours. Every contract is a promise. The yard, the bushel, the pound, the dollar are all promises. Every bill, every note, every check is a promise. A bank is a promise, the deposit book is a promise. A promissory note is a promise. A life insurance policy is a promise. Every law is a promise.

Marriage is a promise. The relationship between parenthood and childhood is a promise, because when the mother holds her babe in her arms for the first time with the proud father looking on happily, there is an implied promise that they will nurture and protect that little child until it can become a self-sufficient, economic unit.

And there is an implied promise on the part of the child that as long as it lives it will honor and respect and obey its parents and their name.

So civilization is based upon promises. Constitutional government is a promise. Without faith in promise, civilization stops. This vast scheme of government and business which is carried on by promissory notes, checks and so forth would immediately come to an end.

No long-time engagement of any sort to build a house or anything else could go on. International treaties are nothing but promises.

We have fortunately found throughout the ages here and there a ruler whose word was as good as his bond; a man who would say when he accepted a duty or a trust that he would do thus and so and would not go beyond certain limits. But those men are very rare.

So mankind, as a result of hard and bitter experience, has decided that written promises for the purpose of binding men who are elected to public office are important and necessary. And so the Constitution of the United States is the fundamental promise upon which the civilization of this country is based.

Let us discuss this Constitution of yours and mine in terms of trade and barter for a few minutes. The Constitution of the United States, as we all know, was written in a time of chaos. It was written at a time when seven of the thirteen colonies were printing paper money as a repudiation of all obligations; their own and the obligations of one citizen to the other. It was written at a time when debtors chased their creditors down the street to force into their pockets worthless money in nominal discharge of obligations. It was written at a time when judges were being hanged in effigy because they signed foreclosure decrees or tax sale warrants. It was a time of total collapse of public confidence, and the little money that was here in America in 1787 did not dare risk investment in the future of this country.

And so this written promise of the Constitution was put on paper, and it contained a pledge on the part of every state that joined in the ratification of that document, that no state would pass a law impairing the obligation of a contract; would not repudiate its own bond if it issued a bond, and would not permit a citizen by any act, or by its legislature to repudiate a contract.

It contained in the fifth amendment to the Constitution, a provision that Congress itself could not take from a man his property without due compensation. And there are at least twenty other promises contained in the Constitution of the United States that man can rely upon for business dealings alone.

As soon as the Constitution was signed, in a time of repudiation and chaos, when business was at an end, when nobody was making long-time plans or contracts or engagements into the future, within three years after the Constitution of the United States was signed, Alexander Hamilton, Secretary of the Treasury, borrowed from Holland three million florins upon better terms than any nation in the world could borrow money, with one single exception.

It was the Constitution of the United States that established the credit of the young republic, and to this land of limitless natural resources, to this land of indomitable men and women who had no capital, the capital of Europe, from the day the Constitution of the United States was signed, began to flow across the Atlantic to build our canals, our docks, our wharves, our railroads and our great industrial enterprise. This money put men to work. It was the beginning of our prosperity.

And then as we began to accumulate capital of our own, American investors felt safe in buying ten, twenty, thirty, forty and fifty year bonds of American industry, realizing that although they took the risk of the business, they were not taking the risk of legislative confiscation or executive usurpation of property, as has recently happened in Mexico with reference to the great petroleum industry down there, and has happened repeatedly throughout the ages.

There is the foundation for the prosperity of this nation.

If I were asked the three pillars of that prosperity I would say, first, the natural resources of this continent, the fertility of the soil, its deposits of coal and copper, and its timber and its falling water. These are the gifts of God.

And the second great thing that has made this a great country is the kind of people who have had the courage from Plymouth Rock down to brave the hazards of the North Atlantic crossing to dwell on this continent.

But the third reason that I would give, if I were asked what has made this a great country, is the Constitution of the United States. It is a limitation upon government itself; a limitation upon the power of elected public officials and the promises of public officials enforceable in independent courts.

We look over our long history of one hundred and fifty years, over this vast territory with many different kinds of people settling here — the Scandinavians of Minnesota and the northwest, the Irish in Boston, the Swedes in Delaware, and many other European peoples of fine blood who have settled here — and we say to ourselves, that with the exception of the Civil War, the seeds of which unfortunately were laid when the republic was born, we have never had serious trouble in this country following an election. There has never been armed revolt or rebellion despite the fact that we have had many desperately contested elections like the election of Hayes and Tilden in 1876.

It is a distinction from what happens in South America and in many other countries. We flatter ourselves and say, "Well, it is because we are good sports, because we accept the result and the minority yields to the majority." That is not the real reason. We would like to flatter ourselves to think it was that, but that is not the reason. The reason is that the great rights of Americans, property rights and personal rights, have never been at stake in a political campaign, not as long as we have an independent Supreme Court to see to it that government and government officials do not break their promises to the people.

The ideas of confiscating property, the repudiation of debts by act of Congress or state legislatures has never been at stake in a political campaign in this country under constitutional government.

People sometimes say, rather sneeringly, that you cannot eat the Constitution. I have heard that said a good many times by a good many different people. I am willing to grant that it is said in ignorance, but whether it is said in ignorance or said with malice, it can have only one effect, and that is to break down respect for constitutional government.

It is true that in a narrow sense of the word you cannot eat the Constitution. But there are many other things you cannot eat. You cannot eat the Ten Commandments, or the Sermon on the Mount, or the Lord's Prayer, or the Golden Rule, or the letters that are exchanged between young lovers, or the last letter an American mother may have received from her boy in France before he went over the top. Thank God there are still left in America some things you cannot eat!

But under the protection of the Constitution of the United States, more people have eaten more bread over a longer period of time, over a greater expanse of territory, than in any other government since time began.

You cannot tamper with constitutional government, break down faith in these promises and expect business to go on in this country. We have a depression today. Why do we have a depression today?

There are many reasons for it. I would not be so immodest as to say that the reason I shall assign is the only reason for this breakdown today, the most precipitous decline in the history of America from the time that it got well underway in 1937 down to the present.

There are many people who think that this depression began last August, or began last October. It did not begin then. We became aware of it then. We knew we were in a depression then, but that is not when it began. It began in February of 1937.

On the 5th of February, the day of the attack upon the Supreme Court of the United States, in the statement that I referred to that I sent to the papers of the Third Indiana District declaring my opposition to it, I said then, and it was published in the papers on February 9, 1937, that the calling of a constitutional convention to consider not a single amendment only, but an entire new Constitution could scarcely be more disturbing to American business than this attack upon and effort to create a new Supreme Court in the United States.

And I said that at a time when the public debt was rapidly approaching the forty billion mark, and we still had millions of men unemployed, I could not think of anything that was more designed to bring back the depression than that.

Well, events have proved it. That is one time that I guessed right, although it was a guess in the dark. The indices of the Federal Reserve Board show that industrial production began to go downhill in February of 1937 after it had had a long climb since the N.R.A. decision of May, 1935.

The figures of the New York Stock Exchange show that all stocks and all bonds reached their maximum value in February of 1937. The attack upon the Supreme Court which was an attack upon constitutional government chilled confidence. Businessmen no longer had reason to believe that they could consider the settled opinions and decisions of the Supreme Court with any confidence in the future. They began to draw in. It was like a ship at sea, seeing a storm, beginning to get close to shore. It reefs sails. It gets ready for whatever there may be in the future.

And this depression we have been suffering from, the most intense depression that a great nation ever suffered from, began with the attack on the Supreme Court in February of 1937. So I say that you cannot attack constitutional government, these promises on which civilization is built, if you want to put it purely on the bread-and-butter side. You cannot do it and expect business to go forward.

Businessmen today are struggling to go forward but they are not certain. Why aren't they certain? Because they have a feeling that this attack on the Supreme Court will be renewed if the Supreme Court again has the courage to hold unconstitutional some important act of Congress. They have that feeling today. That is part of it. I do not say it is all that is creating this feeling of uncertainty today, but it is part of it and it is a major, substantial part of the present depression.

Let me refer to the position taken by Mr. Justice Black last week in the case of Connecticut General Life Insurance Company vs. Johnson. Justice Black for the first time in fifty years held that the fourteenth amendment to the Constitution of the United States does not apply to corporations.

What does that mean? That means if you get four more men on the Supreme Court of the United States who agree with Justice Black, constitutional government under the Constitution of the United States has ended here in America with respect to all business carried on under corporate form. That is exactly what it means.

It means that if a state legislature or a state utility commission, were to fix a rate for a railroad, a telephone company, a pipeline, a truck or bus, gas, electricity, power, any of these public utilities, and the rate was one under which they could not live, under which no investor would put money into them, and that if Justice Black's dissenting opinion becomes the prevailing judgment of the Supreme Court of the United States, that corporation has no protection whatever under the Constitution of the United States. That is exactly what it means.

And not only the public utility corporations, but all corporations, will have no protection against the acts of legislatures, utility commissions, or any other public regulatory bodies.

And then would you expect people to go on putting money into the utilities, into the railroads? Why the railroads today are in the most critical position they have probably been in the history of this republic. They are facing all of these uncertainties that have been created with reference to faith in the promises of the Constitution of the United States.

So I say from a bread-and-butter standpoint, this attack on constitutional government in this country is a very serious matter. It is not that men do not have the right to criticize the opinions of the Supreme Court. Certainly they do, and have done so, and if as a result of criticism, the court in re-examining a question comes to a different conclusion, well and good. That is a part of the democratic process.

But this effort to overwhelm the Supreme Court by force to make it do the will of the majority, is the end of constitutional government.

The idea of our fathers was not government by mandate, not at all. They were very careful to see to it that we did not get incorporated into the life of America the idea of government by mandate, government by the prevailing majority elected to office as a result of a great depression; elected to office as a result of some religious situation, like the Klu Klux Klan, or anything else. They did not want such a majority to be supreme. So they provided in the Constitution that Congressmen should be elected for two years, a President for four years, the United States Senators for six years, and Federal Judges for life, no two of these groups of officials owing their election to the same group of people at the same election. That was for the purpose of preventing government by mandate, government by a temporary majority. They placed the great rights of Americans beyond the control of the mandate.

But we see this government of ours under attack today by people, some of whom have become fainthearted friends of democracy, and others who know exactly what they want. They want to seize government at the throat of its power and they know exactly what they are going to do with it if they do. Thank God that number is not great in this country, not so great but what we can meet the issue if it arises in the future, as it arose with respect to the Supreme Court and the government Reorganization bill. We can meet it if faith in these promises of the Constitution is still held strong in the hearts of Americans; if in their hearts a warm glow of love and affection for this great instrument still obtains, then I shall not fear for the future of this country against any man or any group of men.

But if we become indifferent about it, if we do not understand what constitutional government has meant to us, if we do not have any feeling for it and what it may mean to our children and grandchildren, why then the battle will be lost. Because it is indifference which is the only blind Samson that can tear down the pillars of government in this country — indifference on the part of the people who enjoy its benefits and privileges.

Oh, you see it going on all over the world. When the Constitution of the United States was written in 1787, Gouverneur Morris, as a member of that convention, said that all future ages would be affected by the proceedings of that convention. Never was human prophecy better justified by the passage of time, for from that day down to 1917, one hundred and thirty years, in the states of this Union, the Provinces of Canada, in South America, Australia, New Zealand, British South Africa, Switzerland and in the Scandinavian countries and elsewhere, in that period of one hundred and thirty years not less than four hundred written constitutions were put on paper by freedom-loving men and women. They were based in a large part on the basic concepts of our own great Magna Carta, of which I think the two greatest are first, the distribution rather than the concentration of power, and secondly, that the individual because he is a child of God created in His image, has dignities and rights as a human soul which are beyond the power of princes or the might of majorities.

But in 1917 the tide turned with the Russian Revolution, and from that time to this, with the exception of the short-lived German republic, there has not been a movement upon this planet that has not been a movement away from constitutional democracy and toward the doctrine that the state is supreme and the individual has no rights which government is bound to respect. The minorities have no rights, religious minorities, racial minorities or political or social minorities have no rights which government is bound to respect.

Mussolini tells the Catholics in Italy, "You must be Fascist members of the party before you are Catholic." We know what is happening to minority groups in Germany today.

This destruction of constitutional government abroad and here is advertised by its followers as a progressive movement!

We have a Federal Pure Food and Drug Act to see to it that the consumers of our foods in America are protected against false labels. We ought to have a similar law against advertising this movement of destroying constitutional government as a liberal and progressive movement. It is a deadly reactionary movement and it is carrying us, and it is carrying the world back to the same conditions from which our forefathers once crossed the stormy North Atlantic to escape.

Let me tell you a story. When George Washington was alive, Frederick the Great was King of Prussia. The story is told that outside of Berlin one hundred and fifty one years ago, where a beautiful stream flowed down a peaceful valley, a miller had his mill and the water furnished the power to turn the wheel that ground the grist.

One day Frederick the Great came along and he saw the lovely little valley that is now known as Sans Souci, so he said to the miller, "Miller, you will have to move your mill." The miller looked his sovereign in the eye and said, "Sire, there are judges in Berlin." He could not say that in Germany today. Today neither the miller, the butcher, the baker nor the candlestick maker has any rights that the state is bound to respect.

You are going back beyond Frederick the Great in European history today. You are going back to the dark ages. You are going back to medievalism. You are going back to serfdom. The German worker today is the new serf. The same in Russia; the same in Italy. Today no one living on a German farm, for the purpose of improving his condition in life for himself and his wife and his children, can move to a German city, or the reverse, unless he gets a permit from officialdom. No man who is a carpenter can become an automobile mechanic, or vice versa, unless he gets a permit from government.

Labor unions are abolished. Collective bargaining is at an end — all in the name of this pseudo-liberalism. Nobody has any rights the state is bound to respect.

And yet in the name of progressivism, in the name of liberalism, in the name of security if you choose, men are trying to destroy faith in the Constitution of the United States.

I spoke about this pyramid of government that is shown in the coat of arms resting upon the broad base of popular sovereignty with the powers separated and distributed among the states and to Congress and to the President and the courts. This distribution of power was done by our fathers to prevent the abuse of power when it became concentrated in the hands of one man.

But today, here and throughout the world, we are taking this pyramid which had been resting upon its base and tipping it over to rest upon its apex. One-man rule. And we call that progress in the name of security. But a pyramid resting upon its apex is not secure whether it is Mussolini or anybody else.

What is the constitution of Russia? It is the iron will of Stalin. And what is the constitution of Germany? It is the will of Hitler. What is the constitution of Italy? It is the ambition of Mussolini who wants to leave in this twentieth century a record and reputation and a name as the greatest Caesar of them all, and if to serve that ambition of his he sends five hundred thousand or a million Italian boys to die in Africa, well and good.

There have been many faults in our system of constitutional government and free enterprise. We have raised many ugly ducklings under that system. I am in favor of taking those ugly ducklings out and giving them a bath. I am in favor of necessary reform legislation. But I do protest against throwing out the baby with the dirty water.

We have that situation in America today. It becomes your problem and mine, and let me say that if there is any group in America which ought to hold on to constitutional government, it is the women of America or the women of any country. Constitutional government has meant more to women than it has to men since it was established one hundred and fifty years ago, here and abroad.

You go back to one-man rule, and the woman in that country goes back to the barn and the field and the kitchen and the factory, because whether she likes it or not, she does not have the economic importance of the man, of the soldier. This movement of the destruction of constitutional democracy, if it goes on in this country, will mean that the women are going to suffer more than the men. Under the Constitution a woman is a citizen. But men of blood and iron have never been kind to women.

Under this government the old disabilities that once encumbered woman in her rights, in her property, have been all swept away. She is now as much of a citizen as a man. Thank God for that. But she is in danger today.

The man on horseback has very little use for the rights of women. It is true now and it is true throughout history.

We are all so busy these days, whether we are in business, whether we are practicing law, whatever we are doing — it is one of the penalties we pay for this twentieth century civilization of ours — we are so busy that we do not feel sufficiently concerned with the great events that are taking place around us.

Recently I was speaking in New York City and just before I went to the meeting, I was in the office of a lawyer there. Upon his wall under glass was a page of the London Times containing the first news of the Battle of Waterloo. Down in the lower left hand corner, in a very small space in one column, it said, "Great battle fought. A number of British officers killed." That was about all that it said.

There was one of the great turning points of the world's history and it was being recorded in the London Times of that day below an advertisement of a man who had a horse for sale. The people who read the London Times of that day could not realize that there was taking place not more than a hundred and fifty miles from there, one of the great turning points in human history.

And I sometimes have the feeling today we are so busy that we do not realize that a great struggle is taking place which is going to mean more to us and to our children than the Battle of Waterloo multiplied ten or a dozen times. It is taking place and we hardly know about it. We read about the divorces and the murders and all the things that happen, in big box-car headlines in the newspapers, and somewhere on the editorial page, there will be a little discussion of this great struggle to preserve constitutional government in this country. We hardly know it is going on, and yet it is.

However the events that I took part in during the last year and a half lead me to believe that America is waking up, and that we are not going to let this fine heritage handed to us by our fathers go by default in this country.

And I close with this final thought. Your business is important to you if you are a lawyer, if you are a business man, a manufacturer, a farmer, or what not; it is important to you, but how much more important it is to save this system itself, under which in the brief space of one hundred and fifty years, this little seven percent of the world population had accumulated forty-five percent of the wealth of the entire world. No accident about that. That did not just happen.

That happened because behind the barrier of the Constitution of the United States against the abuse of concentrated power our people have been free people in a free land.

And so while your business is important to you, and my business is important to me, let us remember this bigger battle-field. I see American business spending millions of dollars to advertise cold cream and toothpaste and electric ear-muffs, and this, that and the other thing. Important as are automobiles and radios and everything else, for they all help to make employment and are extremely important to American business and industry, yet that business and industry will spend millions of dollars advertising the products of the American system of free enterprise under constitutional government while we have the greatest difficulty getting them to take part in saving the whole system itself under which their entire business and all their products are produced.

So let us remember that "he who saves his country saves all things, and all things saved shall bless him, but he who lets his country die, lets all things die, and all things dying, curse him."

# THE RESPONSIBILITY OF
# COLLEGE GRADUATES AS CITIZENS

*Commencement address made at Middlebury College, Middlebury, Vermont, in June, 1949.*

A great lawyer of the old South said, "He who saves his country saves all things, and all things saved shall bless him. But he who lets his country die, lets all things die, and all things dying, curse him." No one has a future outside of the future of his country. I shall, therefore, talk today on the responsibility of college graduates as citizens of their country and their community. This is a good day to discuss it. Tomorrow is Flag Day — a day of dedication to our Republic.

Buckle, the great English historian, says that the advance of civilization depends solely on the knowledge possessed by the ablest, and how far that knowledge pervades the whole society. Otherwise the uninformed and mediocre control the course of events.

This theme should be stressed on every campus and in words that bounce along the sidewalk. Our country is fast drifting into a condition of deep concern to all of us, but especially to young men and women. The government is rapidly passing out of the hands of the American people. A vast and arrogant bureaucracy, greedy for lifetime jobs on public payrolls, is fighting every effort to reduce their powers or prevent their waste of the people's money. This Frankenstein challenges Congress itself. It is the super-lobby of all history. The bureaucrats are becoming the "untouchables" of the Western World. Sober and patriotic men are given little or no support in their struggle to keep our country solvent, upon which depends the fortunes of every one of you. While workers in private industry are now being laid off daily, government spending and taxing goes on. The thoughtless mob follows the Pied Pipers of the "Social Welfare State."

Never before has there been such a desperate need for analytical, discriminating minds able to debunk the sloppy slogans of the crowd which never thinks, but only feels. The abdication of college men from their responsibility to give leadership in political affairs is almost universal. How many college graduates can you name who are mayors of a city?

For thousands of years mankind has been raised from childhood on stories of good fairies, the magic wand, the magic carpet, the magic key, the lucky stone, Jack-the-Giant-Killer, St. George and the Dragon, David and Goliath, the Medicine Men of the American red Indian or the voodoo of the African savage. Always some easy escape from difficulty, if one can but find the right magician or political party. These superstitions help to explain why we are returning today to the *divine right of the state* when our fathers once rejected the *divine right of kings*.

That the twelve year old mind believes the prevailing nonsense can be understood. But that college graduates promote the myth of the State, indicts our educational system. Yet certain "intellectuals" are more responsible than blacksmiths and farmers for the naive belief that the Federal Government has a magic cornucopia; that it can "aid" the states with funds which it first gets FROM the states to return to them LESS the political brokerage; that society can get something from nothing; that any social service is FREE; that if the government prints enough dollar signs on pieces of paper called money or bonds, it can make a nation rich. Printing-press money is the magic key today. The age of witchcraft has come back. John Law and the Mississippi Bubble have returned. Ponzi is here again.

The politicians, of course, thrive on these nursery tales. Their jobs depend on them.

But in their failure to expose this black magic, too many college men and women have defaulted as citizens. As The New York Times has pointed out, thousands graduate with little knowledge of American history; few have any grasp of the meaning of constitutional liberty. Thousands swallow political propaganda as if it were divine revelation. Thousands view politics as too sordid for the Phi Beta Kappa intellect, and wonder why a fine man like Charles Evans Hughes ever got into the dust and dirt of the political arena. They should remember Emerson's words, "The scholar loses no hour that the man lives." Sophistries which cannot stand the simple test of grade school arithmetic have become the abracadabra of the political medicine men. The experience of the ages and the convictions of great statesmen molded in the long struggle of men to be free are tossed recklessly aside. Shrill voices fill the air telling us that there is a magic substitute for work.

Because of this default of the educated mind, if you can call it educated, the tides of mass ignorance and class hatred are sweeping America into the maelstrom of discredited European systems which our fathers thought they were leaving behind forever. When I think of the high proportion of college graduates who did accept the responsibility of citizenship in writing the Declaration of Independence, the Federalist Papers, and the Constitution of the United

States, men who had pondered deeply all that history had taught of the blight of Caesarism, today's default of college men and women as citizens is tragic indeed.

Putting aside for the moment any sense of the obligations of patriotism, this belief in the magic of political medicine men is the direct personal concern of ambitious college men and women in three respects. One is in your capacity as the loyal alumni of alma mater. Big government is slowly throttling the privately endowed colleges. Second, big government is putting a ceiling on the attainment of those rightful ambitions which led you to spend four years on the campus. You are being ambushed in a cold war against success — against the thrifty middle class. And third, this concerns your responsibility toward the less fortunate, the uneducated.

At first blush you may say, "Well, aren't we doing all right under big government? Look at our prosperity." All right, let's look at it — closely. Is it solid, or do the magic mirrors of the medicine men make it look solid?

Consider the following. Today's prosperity is measured in fifty cent dollars. That makes it seem twice as big. It is based on the effort to catch up with the production of goods postponed by four years of war. It is the result largely of mortgaging, almost up to the hilt, the wealth and savings of four centuries of toil. A debt of a quarter of a trillion dollars is now called a great national asset! We are told that immense purchasing power is to be found in what we owe! No Svengali ever equalled such hypnotism as this. In large part, the recent boom is based on huge exports which will never be paid for and which, perhaps, will never cease this side of financial collapse. The break even point of business has risen which means that the cushion between good times and bad has grown thin. Due to artificial support given, however necessarily, to the price of government bonds, no one knows what they are actually worth — how solid our foundation is. Our books of account have been doctored. The billions paid in for Social Security have all been spent. Forty-three new spending programs have been proposed by the present Congress to be super-imposed on bigger spending under old programs.

Ninety percent mortgages of the public's money are being made on houses with payments strung out so that the first old age pension check may possibly be used to pay the last installment of the mortgage! Government having taken from the people their century old yardstick to measure the value of money — convertibility into gold — no one knows what the dollar or any foreign money is worth or will be worth. The brake which the people could once clamp down on profligate government spending by demanding gold for paper is gone. The Chinese maze of eighteen hundred government bureaus in Washington, all fighting like wildcats to perpetuate themselves, have reached a state of chaos, as the report of the Hoover commission shows.

Pompous plans are in the hands of little men. Their eager desire to manage the affairs of other men varies directly with their inability to manage their own. Our political leaders were completely taken in by the masters of the Kremlin. As a result the peace they promised the boys who died has been lost. After being grandiloquently told there would be no more balances of power, we now have the Atlantic Pact and are arming one-half the world against the other. We are now burdened with a weight of non-productive armament no free people ever were called upon to carry or can, perhaps, carry and remain free. We are threatened with the permanent militarization of our country, and the conscription of our youth, thus removing them during important years from contributing to the economic growth of the nation.

These are some of the FACTS behind the PROPAGANDA.

This is Santa Claus without his mask. Behind him comes the tax collector.

A large part of the economy of the nation rests on economic stilts and statistical falsehoods. Every country in the world, including our own, has repudiated its obligations in whole or in part, either outright or by devaluation of the currency. In order to cover up, the politicians and Socialists have seduced the masses with the superstition that government can create purchasing power by writing dollar signs on pieces of paper called money. If that were so, counterfeiters should be honored as public benefactors rather than be put in jail. As long as the counterfeiter's money is accepted, it certainly creates a market for goods and jobs producing them. But don't you see that the counterfeiter is a thief? He creates no wealth, yet obtains it from those who WORKED to create it, with the result that THEY have less. Every government that prints money to pay its bills is a moral counterfeiter. It pours water into milk. It dilutes every dollar. Like a thief in the night, it reaches its stealthy fingers into every purse, into every college endowment. It robs the poorest the most.

In the meantime the waste of the people's wealth goes on. Taxes are now above the point at which a free society can long survive if the fiscal history of centuries is worth anything. Taxes have already passed the point of diminishing returns.

A man from Vermont, Calvin Coolidge, once said in substance, "If you tax a man thirty percent of what he makes on Monday, forty percent on Tuesday, fifty percent on Wednesday, and sixty percent on Thursday, he won't show up for work the rest of the week." Taxes are destroying the incentive to work. Every tax tells someone not to do something. They discourage the enterpriser and tell the investor not to risk his capital. Last year only one dollar in twenty-five dollars which went into the expansion of business represented risk capital

— the lowest percent in history. Consequently the limitless promise of human happiness which the great multiplier of science, technology and power has made possible for mankind, is being curtailed.

If there is any group who should now accept the responsibility for exposing this evil spell, it is the young men and women because they have the longest to live and the most to lose. It is time for you to stick a harpoon into this political blubber.

I return now to my first point: that the privately supported colleges of America are in process of being liquidated. This should appeal to college graduates as graduates, and to all of us as citizens, because of the priceless spiritual and cultural contributions which these colleges have made to our country.

The endowments of private colleges made by public spirited men and women when taxes on their earnings were light made it possible for every student to obtain his education at less than cost. That has enabled hundreds of thousands of poor boys and girls, myself among them, to go to college when they otherwise could not. Every graduate of these colleges, and America itself, has been a beneficiary of the system that permitted the ambitious to succeed, and then to help build the colleges that help build our country.

But money spent on taxes can not be given to colleges. Did you ever buy groceries with a tax receipt? In the height of war prosperity, the per capita contribution to private charities was one-third less than in the worst year of the depression! Moreover, in order to borrow as cheaply as possible, our debt-ridden federal government forces down the interest rates on money. As a result college endowments earn less and less, while inflation adds to the cost of maintaining our colleges in the pay of every professor or janitor, and in the price of all equipment. So, as a result of the cheap money policies of the Pied Pipers of the Welfare State, colleges find their expenses going up and their income going down. Meantime, for the same reasons, their possible benefactors are being liquidated by income taxes and their estates being cut in two by inheritance taxes, which are a capital levy.

So, as in Germany under Hitler, colleges are to be subsidized by the State and their professors morally intimidated into silence or told outright to teach nothing critical of the politicians in charge. A Congressional committee might investigate them! Or reduce their appropriations. Educators who defend intellectual freedom and at the same time clamor for federal aid are political Babes in the Woods.

As Rudyard Kipling wrote:
"This is the law and the law shall run
Till the earth and its course is still
That he who eateth another's bread
Shall do that other's will."

As President Wriston of Brown University says, "Professors in endowed colleges no longer look to endowment . . . They have become dependent on Government funds . . . They are not likely to oppose the expansion of governmental activities."

As the difficulties created by the political medicine men increase, the needs of our colleges — of Middlebury — multiply. I hope there are men and women here who still believe in the philosophy of freedom — some unbuyable Americans. I hope they will give generously to the College on the Hill so that it will not be forced to become a beggar at Washington, D.C. We must not sell our colleges or country short! We must fight to preserve our island of freedom in this rising sea of world-wide slavery to the State. We should do for our children what our fathers did for us. I want to pay back the scholarship I received from others, together with interest, and more. I intend to do so.

The second plank of the Communist Manifesto of 1848 called for a heavy progressive income tax, and its third plank, for the abolition of the right of inheritance. These doctrines are moving to their logical end here as elsewhere. The power to tax is the power to destroy, and is being used to destroy, either blindly or DELIBERATELY! We spend billions to fight communism abroad and adopt its major planks here at home.

Spendthrift government is thus slowly strangling our free private colleges. It is of course, all being done under the banner of humanitarianism! But no dictator ever rose to power except on the claim that he was "a protector of the people."

Aside from the Communists, few advocates of the Welfare State are either smart enough to see or honest enough to tell what they are doing. An exception was President Peron of Argentina. He said frankly that the old American ideal of "equal justice under law" — words inscribed on the portal of our Supreme Court building in Washington, — must be thrown into the ash can. He said that the Welfare State exists for the *express purpose* of treating men unequally! In short, to tax the successful in order to provide bread and circuses for those who vote to keep the political humanitarians in power.

So naked power usurps the throne of the blindfolded goddess of justice. The cement of a free society — the old time faith that all men will be treated equally before the law — and by the law makers — crumbles away. The flag of fraternal union is torn in a cold war as pressure blocs struggle for the favors of the Welfare State, a war of all against all, the most deadly struggle known. Thus democracy goes to rot. The question in legislative halls is not — What is Right? — but Who has the Votes?

We have seen this alliance in Jersey City under Hague, in Kansas City under Pendergast, in New York under Tammany. Yet, for lack of leaders, millions are so naive as to believe this cancer will not — has not — spread into the heart of our Republic at Washington.

Two thousand years ago Plutarch wrote, "The real destroyer of the liberties of the people is he who spreads among them bounties, donations and benefits." Something for nothing. *Everything* for *nothing*. When the "gimmies" outnumber the taxpayers, a nation begins its decline. Sixteen million people now receive government checks. Many, of course, are honestly earned, but the number grows ominously.

The Constitution says that certain rights such as trial by jury and Habeas Corpus are beyond the power of government. But there is no limitation on its power to tax. History has not yet proved that any republic can long endure when the unlimited right to tax is coupled with the unlimited power to tax. You should support a Constitutional limitation on the peace time taxing powers of government. England's sun began to set when Lloyd George promised "nine pence for four pence" — something for nothing. The pressure blocs and crushing taxation have done to England what war alone could not achieve.

It is reported that in the State of Illinois forty-eight percent of those drawing unemployment compensation quit their jobs voluntarily! The professional loafer and job jumper is encouraged to take a vacation on public pay. You can find similar conditions everywhere. The pressure blocs, aided by the bleeding hearts, demand longer unemployment vacations at higher pay. Strikers demand to be supported by taxpayers while on strike. Many veterans who came back from war wholly unscathed demand huge bonuses and lifetime care for non-service disabilities at taxpayers' expense.

Members of Chambers of Commerce demand federal pork for local improvements. They want someone else to build their schools and dredge Mud Creek. Labor unions demand more for doing less. The Welfare State having promised to care for everyone from the cradle to the grave, the stampede to get on the gravy train gathers speed. The mayors of American cities have formed a lobby in Washington to get the easy money of the political medicine men.

Political charity beyond a certain point releases forces no democratic government can hold in check. It explains how the big city boss stays in power. He levies toll on the productive members of the community to distribute to his retainers. The latter wink at his personal graft so long as they get theirs. It is a sign of the times when high federal officials are voted huge expense allowances free both from taxes and all public accounting.

Yet after seeing enormous tolls collected from saloons, race tracks, red light districts, prize fighting, slot machines, road building and municipal supplies in one city after another, people who claim to be educated hanker and yearn to turn the control of ALL business, trade, farming, commerce and industry over to the bigger politicians on the Potomac who perpetuate themselves in office by similar methods, and with the same corrosion of public honor and private morality. Finally some super-gangster rides to power on the ruins of liberty. It is this evil course —camouflaged as the Welfare State — which colleges and college men and women should expose with the passionate intensity of the prophets of the Old Testament.

Such is the "degradation of the democratic dogma" to use the phrase of Henry Adams. Here is the rotting cancer of our free society — something for nothing.

Economics has been called the "dismal science." Nevertheless every sound book on that subject can be boiled down to a few words: There is no such thing as something for nothing; nothing is free; everything has its price and someone must pay for it.

If you shy away from economics, all that is necessary is to bring the moral sense to bear on these questions. The Bible says "In the sweat of *thy* face (not another man's face) shalt thou eat bread. . . . Thou shalt not steal . . . nor covet anything that is thy neighbor's."

I am amazed that so many men in the Christian ministry do not see the ultimate immorality of the Welfare State. It is finally and politically based on this question: "What is my fair share of what you have earned?" The pulpit condemns a candidate who gives his own money for a vote. That is bribery. But when the candidate asks for the vote of A on the ground that he will take money from B to give to A, he is acclaimed a great humanitarian. Thus the wants of rogues become the rights of man!

I make no defense of wealth acquired by monopoly, force or fraud. I am talking about the fruits of honest toil. Who has any legal claim to it superior to the man who *worked* for it? The thief and defrauder should be forced to make restitution to those they have despoiled. That *is* a function of government. But the political redistribution of honestly acquired wealth is a path no Christian nation should tread. It cannot survive the cancer of the soul of something for nothing. President Coolidge said that he was for economy in government not merely to save money but to save men.

Political charity gives the recipients the power, by their votes, to continue to live at public expense. Why work when you can compel others to work for you, or sell goods to you, or rent houses to you at less than the price stablished in a free market? As Lord Acton said of Machiavelli, "In the name of the public's good, he destroyed the conscience of the individual."

This brings us to the next point, your responsibility to the less fortunate — the uneducated — those at the base of the economic pyramid. "Would you let them starve?" is the question that is always asked as if it had no answer except to seize the power of government to rob Peter to pay Paul.

No, I would not let them starve. To care for the truly lame, the halt and the blind is an obligation of Christian civilization binding on every conscience. But how is that best done? That is the only question.

I submit that as political humanitarianism runs wild, the loafers and the cheaters will rob our storehouse of wealth so that we will be *less* able to care for those in genuine distress.

Let us reduce this problem to simple terms. In every society in every age — true among the pioneers in a wilderness cabin, or in a great city — it is the well who take care of the sick, the strong who take care of the weak, the able who take care of the disabled, the foresighted who care for the foolish, those in middle life who care for the little child or the aged. Who else *can* care for them, regardless of how it is done, whether within a family, or through a government bureau? Because this is true, we should not overtax the strong. We should give incentives to the ambitious, rewards to the industrious, security to thrift, honor to achievement, praise to success.

In 1928, Congress gave its highest honor, the Gold Medal, to Thomas Edison. In the official citation Congress placed a value of fifteen billion dollars as the worth of his brain to his country. At that time that was one-twentieth of the national wealth. Millions of jobs flowed from his workshop. If Edison made a few millions it was only because in a free market he gave more than he got. No one had to buy his inventions. They did so only because they were worth more to the buyers than the price they paid. Why should we take the heart out of such men, stifle them in the red tape of a politically planned economy, and tolerate the hissing against them by those with a foreign accent?

Your jobs depend on the freedom of creative minds. Your jobs depend on a dynamic economy which can only be tooled from private savings, not from public spending. High taxes are fencing you in.

We have had four hundred experiments with Socialism in America, such as the Plymouth Rock Colony, New Harmony and Brook Farm. They all failed. They failed because in time the industrious got tired of supporting the drones. So they quit. On a nation-wide scale, the result can only be the same.

Let the ambitious and the industrious continue to build up our country. That is the only way that the lame, the halt and the blind can hope for better conditions. The spendthrift supports no charities, no colleges. He steals from them.

The strong should help the weak, but you can not help the weak by weakening the strong. You can not make sick people well by making well people sick. You can not lift up the wage earner by pulling down the wage payer.

When the world's hard work could finally be done by machinery cheaper than the cost of keeping slaves alive, the emancipation of mankind from a life of hopeless, ceaseless drudgery began. Not until then did the weary and heavy laden have a chance. Life was once so hard and brutish that philosophers said no man could call himself fortunate while he lived. What has changed his condition so much for the better? It is the private property system, which the Social Welfare system would tax to destruction. It is the profit and loss system, with its incentives to succeed, when lightly taxed by government. It was not Karl Marx who took the women and children out of the coal mines in England a century ago. It was the steam engine and the power of machinery. Inventions and technology have done more to abolish slavery and child labor than the reformers. The laboratories do more for mankind than the legislatures. The plow that turns the sod under does more to feed the hungry than any act of Congress.

If some calamity forced us back to the same crude tools and horse and ox and man and woman power that we had when Franklin caught the lightning from the sky, our production of wealth would at once go down ninety percent, and wages would go down in proportion. Hours of toil would increase to the limit of human endurance, and nothing that government or the political medicine men could do would prevent it.

The economic progress of mankind is chiefly measured by the substitution of giant slaves of iron and steel for the puny strength of animals and human backs. Under the hood of a fifty horse power automobile is the strength of five hundred men. Yet it is this system, sparkplugged by the hope of economic rewards, which has lifted more burdens from the backs of more people than any other system the world has ever known, that is derided in many college lecture halls today.

How does all this concern you young men and women? You hope to climb the ladder of success. What do you hope to get for your effort? The satisfaction of achievement? Yes. Recognition? Yes. But you must have dollars to live. So let's look at these dollars.

The president of a great life insurance company said recently that the American people have taken out seventy billion dollars more of life insurance than they had in 1940, yet collectively are no better off.

Why? Because dollars have become cheap. And because taxes on dollars have gone up. If you bought a government bond ten years ago for seventy-five dollars, the hundred dollars you get for it today will buy less than the seventy-five dollars you paid. You have lost your interest and part of your principal. And you are ten years older. If you save one thousand dollars and put it in a savings bank, you get from ten to twenty dollars in interest as against forty dollars twenty years ago. So you have to work twice as many years as your father did, when he was your age, to provide the same income for old age. As the Welfare State goes up, individual security goes down. The cards are stacked against the independent, thrifty, hard working American. His chance to get ahead grows less.

Except for the action of Congress last year, taxes are going up everywhere, every year. In some cities a man pays three income taxes. If he has invested his savings in building up his country and gets dividends, he pays four income taxes. His savings earn less, they are taxed more, and what is left buys less. His pension or social security check buys less. Men old enough to retire are unable to do so. So they hold on to their jobs. This reduces the opportunities for young men and women.

This downhill course was speeded up by the cost and waste of war. But high taxes and cheap money were doing their deadly work before the war began, as any college president can testify.

Young ladies and gentlemen of the Class of 1949, I hope I make myself clear as to your responsibility to yourselves, your college and your country. A lot of folks want to be taken care of, and a lot of other people want the job of taking care of those who want to be taken care of. But it should be your ambition, as honest men and women, to stand on your own feet, make your own way, demand to be permitted to keep the fruits of your toil, and not have the job of providing a job for those who want to take care of you.

Your future depends not only on your education, but upon your taking an active part in public affairs, in promoting a public opinion in a free society that is friendly to honest success. Modern science, technology and power have placed in your hands searchlights to progress that make Aladdin's lamp seem dim. Don't let the medicine men take them from you.

I have one dream for my old college and my old state — that whatever is taught on other campuses or whatever is done in other states, that you will not bow the knee to the false gods of big government; that you will look shrewdly at the glib promisers who would strengthen *Society* by weakening the *Individual*. My dream for my old college and state is that they will continue to honor the sturdy virtues of those who laid your foundations in days long gone; that you will kindle a fire on these Green Mountains that will guide our country from darkness into light.

# WHERE KARL MARX WENT WRONG

*This was one of Samuel Pettengill's most famous columns.*

In view of the continuing Communist threat to our country, both at home and abroad, it seems a good time to again consider what is wrong with Marxism.

It was in 1848 when Marx and Engels wrote the Communist Manifesto which began with the words, "A specter is haunting Europe, the specter of Communism." This sounds like today's newspaper. That was one year before gold was discovered in California; before the covered wagon began to roll across the plains. Please keep this date in mind. It is significant to what I shall say.

A little later, Marx, in London, wrote Das Kapital, the bible of the Communists and Socialists. As a reporter, Marx was accurate. The conditions of the workers in England and Europe a century ago, as he points out, were very grim. Women pulled canal boats along the tow-path with ropes over their shoulders. Women were harnessed like beasts of burden to cars pulling coal out of British mines. In the textile mills children began to work when they were nine or ten years old, and worked twelve to fifteen hours a day. It was said that the beds in which they slept never got cold, as one shift took the place of the other. It was said that they were machines by day and beasts by night. Tuberculosis and other occupational diseases killed them off like flies.

Conditions were terrible. Not only Marx, but other warm-hearted men, such as Charles Dickens, Ruskin and Carlyle, poured out a literature of protest which was read around the world.

On his facts, Marx can scarcely be challenged. But his diagnosis was wrong and therefore the remedy he prescribed was wrong also.

Marx said these terrible conditions were due to greed, exploitation, the theft by the owners of the mines and mills of the "surplus value" produced by the workers. That was his diagnosis and therefore his remedy was to preach the gospel of hate, of the class struggle, of the redistribution of wealth, of the confiscation of property and its ownership by the state, which always means the politicians.

Now if that diagnosis and remedy were, and still are, in the main correct, we have no business fighting communism. It becomes mighty important to ask whether they were correct.

The diagnosis of Marx was in some small measure correct. "Man's inhumanity to man" has always been a factor in human affairs. Greed can never be defended whether in business or government. Sympathy for the underdog will always have its work to do. Always certainly in Communist Russia, with its forced labor camps and human slavery.

Greed and exploitation are not cured by socialism. The Kremlin bosses live like oriental potentates with state dinners that would make Nero and Caligula green with envy. All this, in the name of the down-trodden proletariat!

But greed was not the main reason for the conditions which Marx described. If all the wealth of the owners of the mines and mills had been redistributed to the workers, it would have relieved their condition but slightly and for but a little while.

So the class struggle as the remedy for these conditions was wrong. It diverted attention from the principal reason. Moreover the chief planks in the Communist creed had been written by Marx's predecessors, St. Simon and Fourier, a half century before his Manifesto, and before the industrial revolution.

What was wrong? What was the real trouble?

It was the low productivity of labor, and as labor can be paid only out of production, whether in England and Europe a century ago, or in Russia today, wages must be low and hours of work long when production is low.

Production was low because tools and equipment were poor; because human backs had to do what slaves of iron and steel do today here in America; because capital had not been accumulated to buy better tools; because freedom had so recently emerged from centuries of feudalism that the inventors and scientists and businessmen had not had a chance to dream and plan. They have had that chance here in America.

Before World War II began, it was estimated that electric power alone in this country was performing the work equal to the labor of half a billion men — five hundred million men — working eight hours a day. This was equal to nearly ten times the total human labor force employed in America and fifty times the number employed in manufacturing, and that leaves out steam power and gasoline power, with their tremendous contribution for increasing the productivity of workers and lifting burdens from human backs.

Is it any wonder that America outproduced the world in two world wars? That wages are higher here than anywhere in the world?

While Marx preached the gospel of hate and the class struggle, America gave the green light to the Edisons, the Whitneys, the Burbanks and the Fords.

James Watt, the inventor of the steam engine, which started to revolutionize the modern world, and those who followed him in the competitive struggle to make a better engine and sell it for less, did more to take women out of the coal mines and off the tow-paths of the canal boats, more to take children out of the factories, than all the Socialists and Communists and politicians of the world combined.

Yet Watt would be an unknown name today if one of those despised capitalists, a man named Mathew Boulton, had not risked a hundred and fifty thousand dollars on Watt's invention.

One measure of the progress of civilization is the mechanical horse-power and tools which supplement human labor. The steam engine did more to outlaw slavery, both in England and America, than all the political humanitarians put together. The laboratories do more for mankind than the legislatures.

Please understand me. Welfare regulation has its place. There must be laws to require safety appliances in coal mines, and they should be enforced, whether private owners or the government runs them. There must be laws to require fire escapes for factories and hotels. There must be laws to require the inspection of milk and meat. There must be laws for honest weights and measures. Otherwise some men would risk death to human beings to make a greater profit.

I do not disparage such legislation at all. I endorse it as part of the responsibility of modern government.

I simply point out that if modern America were to go back to the same tools and horse-power that we had when Benjamin Franklin was trying to capture lightning from the sky, our production of wealth would at once go down ninety percent, wages would go down in proportion, hours of labor would increase to the limit of human endurance, and nothing that government or humanitarians or labor unions or Karl Marx could do, would prevent it.

I mentioned the discovery of gold in California in connection with the Communist Manifesto of 1848.

With pick and shovel and the pan with which men washed gravel from gold, did not men work long hours for a meager return or none? Did not they sleep in filthy cabins, live on jerked meat and were covered with lice?

If you saw that great motion picture, The Covered Wagon, you will recall the scenes of terrible toil, of men and women and children pushing the wagons across rivers, and the trackless desert, and over the Continental Divide. Families on foot pushed hand carts from the Mississippi to Salt Lake.

Yet were those conditions due to greed and exploitation? No; they were working for themselves. What was wrong? Poor tools. The plow of the pioneer was a wooden plow, constantly breaking, constantly needing repairs. Yet in a newspaper recently I saw a picture of a wooden plow being used in Greece today.

Up in Vermont where I was raised, on land then worth two dollars an acre, a man back in my great-grandfather's time dug some iron ore out of a hill. He put a hundred pounds in a bag on his back and walked fifty miles through the wilderness to sell it to an iron foundry in Troy, New York, and then walked home — an infinite expenditure of human energy for an insignificant return.

What was wrong? Greed? Exploitation? The class struggle? No. He was working for himself. There was no relationship of employer and employee. No one was stealing the surplus produce of his labor. He got all of it and it was little indeed.

What was wrong? Why did he have to work so hard for so little? Poor tools. Today the engine, in the form of the modern locomotive, could move his hundred pounds of iron ore eighty miles for four cents; or a ton, one mile for one cent. Railroads, paved highways, motor trucks and automobiles have solved his problem, and will do it even better in the days to come if we stay American.

Let us say that James Watt, and the man who financed him, were not humanitarians. Let us say they put their brains and money together in a common enterprise for the profit motive. What of it? Was the result good or bad? Did they take women out of the coal mines or did Karl Marx with his gospel of hate and the class struggle?

What did the profit motive do? It made Watt and his partner and all who followed them, work to make still better engines and offer them at a lower price to get the market from their competitors.

Was the result good or bad? The profit motive is just as honorable and useful to mankind as the wage motive. Both can be pushed to excess. But, both do infinite good.

The wage motive prompts men to become skilled and efficient so they can produce more, and earn more, and because they do, all mankind benefits.

The profit motive prompts men to make better tools, to cut costs, to sell cheaper and again, all mankind benefits.

A radio that sold forty years ago for three hundred dollars, now sells for thirty dollars or less, and is a better radio.

Has the result of the competitive struggle in the world of radio and television been good or bad? The result has been mostly good — humanitarian, if you please.

It brings the news of the world, good music, and discussion of public affairs to the remotest farmhouse, to people on their sick beds.

It was not many centuries ago when starvation was a common occurrence, even where ninety percent of the people lived on the land, even in England.

Was the conquest of starvation a humanitarian thing? What conquered it? Who conquered it? Karl Marx? No.

It took thirty hours of human labor in 1830 to raise the same amount of wheat that can be grown today with one hour of labor. What did it? The steel plow, the tractor, the harvester, better seed, the conquest of insects and plant diseases, and cheap transportation. American wheat now feeds millions today in the Russia that adopted the philosophy of Karl Marx.

Aluminum was so expensive in 1870, that Napoleon III of France had an aluminum dinner set for state dinners, more valuable than gold. Today aluminum is found in all American kitchens, no matter how humble.

No, Karl Marx did not have the answer. He lifted no burdens from human backs. The answer is in free enterprise, kept competitive by anti-trust and other laws. The answer is not in the class struggle. The answer is in the co-operation of the inventor and investor, the manager and the worker with his "know how." The answer is substitute slaves of iron and steel for the strength of human backs. The answer is constitutional liberty which sets men free, and says that what any man honestly makes is his "to have and to hold!"

Wages can be paid only out of the product and the larger the production the higher the wage. The more money that is invested in horse-power and equipment; the more capital that is put to work, the less children and women and men have to work at killing toil.

Let's not divide mankind today in the struggle of classes. Let's unite men. In union there is strength. In harmony there is hope. Freedom is Uncle Sam's greatest asset.

As Woodrow Wilson said, the greatest progress comes from "the voluntary cooperation of a free society."

# A BOUNDLESS FIELD OF POWER

*Reprinted from* The Freeman, *April, 1962.*

"No political dreamer was ever wild enough to think of breaking down the lines which separate the states, and compounding the American people into one common mass."

These words were written by our greatest Chief Justice, John Marshall, more than one hundred years ago. He was wrong. Political dreamers are compounding the people into one common mass. Power is being concentrated at one point. Not only is the federal government encroaching upon governmental functions formerly reserved to states and communities, but it also is gathering to itself increasing control over financial (banking) and economic (prices, wages) affairs; and it is entering the field of education and the arts.

The Republic is being torn down and the Monolithic State is being erected. The business of city halls, county court houses, and state capitols, is being moved to Washington and put in other hands, far from the people.

This is being done in violation of the letter and spirit of the Constitution. It is true that in recent years the Supreme Court under political pressure has given its blessing to this consolidation of power in Washington, and the concurrent destruction of power in state capitols, court houses and city halls. But that does not settle the question. There is a judge above the Court, and to that judge we can appeal. The People who ordained and established the Constitution can enforce it, if they will, or change it if they choose. The Constitution does not belong to the lawyers.

As John Marshall said, "The enlightened patriots who framed our Constitution, and the people who adopted it, must be understood to have employed words in their natural sense, and to have intended what they said."

Since 1932 the People have amended the Constitution in the following respects only: changed the date for Congress to convene and for a President to be inaugurated; made provision in case of the death of a President or Vice-president elect before taking office; repealed the Eighteenth Amendment; declared against a President having a third term; and gave the citizens in the District of Columbia the right to vote for presidential electors.

Not one of these amendments delegated new or additional powers to the federal government to tax, appropriate, regulate or govern the states or the People.

Nevertheless these powers have been assumed or usurped. The federal government is taking over, in whole or in part, such matters as housing, water, sewers, urban renewal, depressed areas, the relocation of industries, health, hospitals, education, police, fire prevention, juvenile delinquency, and even snow removal.

Read and reread the plain words of the Constitution and ask yourself how these words were understood by the men who wrote them, and by great statesmen and jurists down to recent years.

First, George Washington, the president of the Constitutional Convention: "The Constitution which at any time exists, till changed by an explicit and authentic act of the whole people, is sacredly obligatory upon all. . . . The spirit of encroachment tends to consolidate the powers of all the departments in one, and thus to create, whatever the form of government, a real despotism. A just estimate of that love of power, and proneness to abuse it, which predominates in the human heart, is sufficient to satisfy us of the truth of this position. . . . Let there be no change by usurpation, for though this, in one instance, may be the instrument for good, it is the customary weapon by which free governments are destroyed."

James Madison, the "father" of the Constitution: "The accumulation of all powers, legislative, executive and judiciary, in the same hands, whether of one, a few, or many . . . may justly be pronounced the very definition of tyranny."

Alexander Hamilton: "It is the duty of courts of justice to declare all acts contrary to the manifest tenor of the Constitution, void."

Chief Justice Marshall: "To what purpose are powers limited and to what purpose is that power committed to writing, if those limits may at any time be passed by those intended to be restrained?"

Daniel Webster, the "great expounder" of the Constitution: "Good intentions will always be pleaded for every assumption of power. . . . It is hardly too strong to say that the Constitution was made to guard the people against the dangers of good intentions. . . . There are men in all ages who mean to govern well, but they mean to govern. They promise to be good masters, but they mean to be masters."

Thomas Jefferson, founder of the Democratic Party: "To take a single step beyond the boundaries thus specifically drawn around the powers of Congress is to take possession of *a boundless field of power*, no longer susceptible of any definition. . . . When all government shall be drawn to Washington as the center of all power, it will become venal and oppressive. I wish to see maintained that wholesome distribution of powers established by the Constitution for the limitation of both, and never see all offices transferred to Washington. In questions of power, let no more be heard of confidence in man, but bind him down from mischief by the chains of the Constitution."

Abraham Lincoln, founder of the Republican Party: "A majority held in restraint by constitutional checks and limitations . . . is the only true sovereign of a free people. Whoever rejects it does of necessity fly to anarchy or despotism."

Woodrow Wilson, father of the "New Freedom," would apparently have vetoed most of the laws passed by the New Deal and the New Frontier to concentrate power. Before his inauguration in 1913 he said: "If any part of our people want to be wards, if they want to have guardians over them, if they want to be taken care of, if they want to be children patronized by the Government, I am sorry, because it will sap the manhood of America. But I don't believe they do. I believe they want to stand on the firm foundation of law and right and take care of themselves."

Again he said, "The history of liberty is the history of the limitation of power, not the increase of it. . . . The concentration of power always precedes the destruction of liberty."

Franklin D. Roosevelt, when governor of New York: "Now to bring about government by oligarchy, the sovereignty of the States must be destroyed. We are safe from that danger as long as home rule in the States is scrupulously preserved and fought for whenever it is in danger."

This concentration of power so alien to our system has been brought about, not by the People, and in the manner prescribed by the Constitution, but by legislators and judges who have assigned new, strange meanings to such words in the Constitution as "interstate commerce," "general welfare," and so forth.

This has been done in the face of the fact that we have a written Constitution which delegates to the United States certain specified powers only, and it has been done in defiance of the tenth Amendment (put there by the People), which says in plain language that the powers not delegated to the United States "are reserved to the states, respectively, or to the people."

In the momentous case of Texas vs. White (1869), the U. S. Supreme Court said: "The preservation of the rights of the States, and the maintenance of their governments, are as much within the design and care of the Constitution as the preservation of the Union and the maintenance of the National government. The Constitution, in all its provisions, looks to an indestructible Union, composed of indestructible States."

In another great case, Gibbons vs. Ogden, Justice Marshall wrote: "Congress is not empowered to tax for those purposes which are within the exclusive power of the State." Apply this language to federal taxes for such matters as education, urban renewal, and the like.

In a veto message to Congress, President Franklin Pierce said: "I cannot find any authority in the Constitution for making the Federal Government the great almoner of public charity throughout the United States. . . . Such a conclusion the characters of the men who framed that sacred instrument will never permit us to form. Indeed, to suppose it susceptible of any other construction would be to consign all the rights of the States and of the people of the States to the mere discretion of Congress, and thus to clothe the Federal government with authority over the sovereign states, by which they would be dwarfed into provinces or departments, and all sovereignty vested in an absolute, consolidated central power against which the spirit of liberty has so often and in so many countries struggled in vain."

It is clear that the Constitution has been practically rewritten in vital parts, not by the People in the plain manner provided by the Constitution but by "usurpation," to borrow from Washington's Farewell Address. The crafty arguments of left-wing professors have been seized upon by ambitious politicians to increase their power and to appeal to the cupidity of voters.

States and their people who might have objected to these concentrations, if submitted as proposed amendments of the Constitution, have been denied their right to vote on them. During the "court packing" fight in 1937, *President* Roosevelt, forgetting what *Governor* Roosevelt had said, told the nation over the radio that "the Constitution is what the justices say it is rather than what *its framers* or you might hope it is." Therefore, change the Constitution by changing the judges! He rejected proposals to submit a constitutional amendment on the ground that it would take too long and that *the People might vote it down!*

There are at least three great reasons why the continuing concentration of governmental, financial and economic power in Washington, D.C. may be the "weapon by which free governments are destroyed."

One: If a state goes bankrupt its bondholders lose their investment, but it cannot destroy the value of money generally. A state cannot manufacture money to pay its debts. Nor can it continue to go into debt forever, because in time no one will buy its bonds. But the federal government can manufacture money, and as it goes deeper and deeper in debt, the value of all the money of all the people rots away.

If a state overtaxes its people, they can move out. But if the federal government does so, there is no escape except to invest in foreign lands.

Two: "A power over a man's subsistence is a power over his will," as Alexander Hamilton twice wrote in the Federalist Papers. The gathering of the people's wealth into Washington, and its disbursement by grants, gifts, loans, and "federal aid" creates a gigantic political machine, a super Tammany. Farmers, city dwellers, bankers, business men, even college presidents, begin to shut their mouths. So it happened under Hitler and Mussolini. "Whose bread I eat, his song I sing."

Three: The "white gold" of a nation is the character of its people. As ever larger numbers of people are urged by national political leaders to use their ballots to "vote themselves rich," what happens to the moral fiber of the people?

If the sprawling Colossus on the Potomac had made a shining success of balancing its budget, paying its debts, maintaining the value of money, "solving" the farm problem after forty years of effort, denying monopoly power to labor unions, reducing crime and juvenile delinquency and improving our world position by fighting three wars in one lifetime, we could, perhaps, view the future with some resignation.

But it has not succeeded in any one of these matters.

What the future holds, no one can say. The native common sense and love of country of the average American could cause him to see how he has been defrauded of his inheritance, and to recapture his right to pursue happiness within the framework of the Constitution that was written by the ablest and most disinterested patriots that history has known, and as it can be amended by the People.

We do know there is an ebb and flow in human affairs and periods of decadence and corruption are followed by the return of strength and honor.

We can begin with our children in school and college. A good start has already been made in this direction by several completely trustworthy organizations.

I conclude with the words of Supreme Court Justice Story addressed to the "ingenuous youth" of 1840. "The fate of other republics, their rise, their progress, their decline and their fall are written but too legibly on the pages of history. . . . Those republics have perished by their own hands. Prosperity has enervated them, and corruption has debased them. . . .

"They have disregarded the warning voices of their best statesmen and have driven from office their best friends. . . . Patronage and party, the triumph of an artful popular leader, and the discontents of the day, have outweighed in their view, all solid principles and institutions of government. . . .

"Let the American youth never forget that they possess a noble inheritance, bought by the toils and sufferings and blood of their ancestors. . . . The structure was erected by architects of consummate skill and fidelity. . . . It has been reared for immortality. . . . It may nevertheless perish in an hour by the folly or corruption or negligence of its only keepers, THE PEOPLE. . . .

"Republics fall, when the wise are banished from the public councils, because they dare to be honest, and the profligate are rewarded because they flatter the people in order to betray them."

# FALSE BALANCE SHEET

*Reprinted from* Life Lines, *November 9, 1966.*

*Wherein that mysterious bird*
*the Geeinpee*
*Is plucked feather by feather*
*and exposed*
*As a federal advocate of high-flying*
*fiscal foolishness.*

If a business company offered a stock issue based on a report of assets and liabilities as deceptive as that of the federal government, its promoters would go to jail. The U.S.A. has enormous assets which have accumulated since Benjamin Franklin caught lightning from the sky. It is the greatest nation in all history, its assets are printed in big type; but its enormous liabilities are printed in very small type, or not at all.

Let us begin with G.N.P., or Gross National Product, the value in current dollars of all goods and services produced in a given year. G.N.P. is the new shibboleth, battle cry and "hog call" of Keynesian economics and politicians of both parties.

"Look at our huge G.N.P.," they shout. "See how prosperous we have made you."

As we are now in the corn-husking time of year, let us strip some of the shucks off this G.N.P. and see what's underneath.

To begin with, G.N.P. is measured in current dollars which are constantly losing value. Abe Lincoln's remark about his law office, is appropriate when talking about G.N.P. "There's a rat hole over in that corner that's worth looking into."

For as dollars go down, G.N.P. goes up. Every time the price of ham and eggs goes up, G.N.P. also goes up. The more inflation, the bigger the G.N.P. Think of the G.N.P. in Germany when it took a million marks to buy a sandwich!

The high cost of funerals and the money paid to see Cassius Clay knock out somebody are all included in the G.N.P.

You have a bigger G.N.P. when the dollar is worth forty-three cents than when it is worth one hundred cents.

The federal government has not paid for its own contributions to the G.N.P. in real money since 1933. Its own spending in the market place has largely been charged "on the cuff" by issuing paper money. Its gross debt in June (1966) when Congress held its annual debate on raising the debt ceiling was approximately three hundred and nineteen billion.

That is billions, not millions.

What yardstick can measure this huge debt in figures all of us can understand? Aside from debt-free homes, our people chiefly depend on life insurance and annuities to soften the blows of death and old age. For more than a hundred years our life insurance companies have accumulated reserves against unforeseen hazards. In short, they have paid out less than the premiums they took in, plus earnings from their investments.

The federal government has done the reverse. It has paid out more than it has taken in by taxes for a total of three hundred and nineteen billion! This is more than twice the net assets of all our life insurance companies put together. In addition, it has guaranteed mortgages, losses from bank failures, etc. which could result in billions of dollars more. And it still increases the known debt. This year the federal government is spending more than in the highest spending year of World War II.

If you knew that your life insurance company was operating in the red, what would you do?

Despite the political hurrahs for the G.N.P., the startling fact is that the federal debt is going up at a faster rate than the G.N.P.

This is like a factory that is increasing its production, but is going into debt at a faster rate than its sales increase. Would you invest in it?

Gold has been taken from us, and silver, as money, is also disappearing. Do you take any pride in the new copper sandwich quarter dollars? Silver dollars have not been coined for several years and are becoming a collector's item. More and more of today's money consists of pieces of paper, or figures on a bank ledger.

The United States has experienced one total collapse of confidence in paper money. This was at the end of the Revolutionary War which was financed by paper money and bonds issued by the Continental Congress and the thirteen states. This paper became so worthless that foreign speculators bought as much as five thousand dollars of paper money for a single dollar of gold. "Not worth a Continental" was the way our forefathers spoke of worthless things. Troops had to be called out to control angry mobs.

It was because of this experience that when the Constitution was drawn up in 1787, our forefathers provided that "no State . . . shall emit Bills of Credit or make anything but gold and silver Coin a Tender in Payment of debts." ("Legal tender" means money which a creditor is required to accept in payment of debts owed to him.) What we have today is paper money somewhat similar to that issued by the Continental Congress because it is not redeemable in gold or silver. But foreign governments and their central banks can demand gold in exchange for U.S. dollars which they hold. Here, Uncle Sam is on thin ice; he doesn't have enough gold to pay them and still retain a small amount of the yellow metal to lend some degree of confidence in our paper money. Uncle is now in the humiliating position of the president of a bank that is close to going on the rocks and is begging its big depositors to hold off from presenting their bank books so as not to "start a run on the bank and ruin our town, yourselves included."

The late Franklin D. Roosevelt, before he had yielded to the hypnotic spell of John Maynard Keynes, the high priest of federal manipulation of the economy, said correctly that, "Any government, like any family, can for a year spend a little more than it earns, but you and I know that a continuation of that habit means the poor house." Was he right or wrong?

Theoretically, a case on paper can be made for Mr. Keynes, but his remedies could work successfully only in a dictatorship. They can't work for long in a republic such as ours with two party government, universal suffrage and non-postponable elections. The voters and pressure groups don't understand Mr. Keynes and would not follow him if they did.

The fact is that pressure groups can insulate themselves for a long time from worry about public debts and inflation, with escalator clauses in their contracts, providing automatic wage increases as prices rise. To enforce their demands, they can legally stop all airplanes from flying, all ships from sailing, all trucks and railroads from running.

When Congress has hesitated to increase the debt limit the bureaucrats leak the "news" that post offices, etc. must be closed half a day a week, and allocations for highway money and a hundred other purposes must be reduced. This frightens Congress which hasn't in recent memory refused to increase the debt limit when the demand was made.

The federal debt is now more than three hundred and nineteen billion. The total of all debts, federal, state, municipal and private, on January 1, 1966, was one trillion, two hundred and sixty-eight billion dollars. That's trillions, not billions. It is more today.

There are few states and cities that are not also increasing their debts. Governors and mayors of both parties, rarely tax their own voters enough to rebuild their own decayed cities, clean up their river sewers and ocean shores, purify the air they breathe, eliminate their slums and ghettos, get rid of their automobile junk yards and the huge scars of surface coal mining. So the officials of New York City, for example, petition Congress to tax the people of Philadelphia, Cleveland, St. Louis, etc. to solve the problems of New York. Governors and mayors demand their "fair share" of the federal gravy taken away from other cities and states.

Several big cities have opened offices in Washington to lobby for their "fair share" of federal aid. Foreign governments hire smart Washington lawyers to lobby for more "foreign aid." Meanwhile our own Congressmen and Senators have insulated themselves from inflation by twice increasing their salaries in recent years, plus huge sums for their staffs, and will keep on doing so.

The dollar today is losing value at the approximate rate of three and a half cents a year. If this continues the owners of savings bank accounts in banks and building and loan associations, and U.S. government bonds, will be getting an actual net return of nothing.

To keep the voters happy, Congress wants to increase the social security payments to the elderly and disabled, as the purchasing value of their checks decreases. This road actually leads to more taxes and an increasing debt. One U.S. Senator recently sponsored legislation to require the federal government to pay a monthly dole to everyone who is seventy-two years old, even though the recipients never contributed a dime to social security, and regardless of whether they are poor or rich. (NOTE: it passed and is now the law!) Is this fair to those who have been paying social security taxes all their working lives? If present trends continue, the minimum age of the recipients will grow less and less and the federal dole more and more.

The sad part is that most of the so-called intellectuals, teachers, professors, college presidents and business executives, are the beneficiaries of some form of "federal aid."

Do you know of even one college president whose college has received a gift or low interest loan of a million or so dollars from Washington, who has since opened his mouth to protest the growth of the Leviathan on the Potomac?

"Whose bread I eat, his song I sing."

Hitler went so far as to set up the "German Christian Church" and subsidize clergymen. Pastor Niemoeller was about the only minister who challenged him. He spent seven years in prison for doing so, but he won the admiration of mankind.

Thomas Jefferson said, "We are endeavoring to reduce the government to the practice of rigid economy to avoid burdening the people and arming the President with a patronage of money which might be used to corrupt the principles of our government."

# THE WORLD'S ILLUSION

*This was one of Samuel Pettengill's most famous columns.*

Did you ever hear the story of the old Boer farmer, his dog and the tax collector on the South African Veldt? The collector of taxes was telling the farmer why he had to tax him — to protect him from enemies, to care for him when sick, to feed him when hungry, to support him when out of work, to bury him when dead.

The farmer said, "Yes, I understand. My dog is hungry. He begs for food. I say to him, 'My dear faithful dog, I am sorry for you. I shall give you some meat.' I take my knife, cut off his tail and say, 'Here, faithful dog, be nourished on this nice piece of meat.'"

Such is the belief that the government can make people happy and rich. Some folks say we humans once had tails also. But that was before we had governments!

During my years in Washington it was a great education to learn what people, who were visiting the city for the first time, wanted to see. There was the Washington Monument, the Lincoln Memorial, Mount Vernon, the Declaration of Independence in the Library of Congress, the White House, Supreme Court and House or Senate deliberating upon the destinies of mankind. But there was something else they wanted to see. It was the Bureau of Printing and Engraving, where our paper money is made. It is a bewitching sight. You wish you could bring a bushel basket and that our dear, kind government would let you fill it with that magical, beautiful, crisp green paper.

But is it wealth? Isn't it just as easy for the government to print a one hundred thousand dollar bill as a one dollar bill? Does it take any more paper and ink? No. Why then, doesn't the government cease printing one dollar bills and print only one hundred thousand dollar bills and thus make everyone happy and rich?

Suppose that when you woke up this morning you found the whole countryside covered a foot deep with one dollar bills or one hundred thousand dollar bills. Your first impulse would be to get the snow shovel and all the baskets you could find before the neighbors woke up. But if it snowed bills a foot deep what would they be worth? Would they be worth any more than autumn leaves? But THIS is government wealth.

When you reason it out, it seems plain enough. I am convinced that the whole world is going through one of those mass hallucinations that sweep our nations from time to time. Centuries ago it was the Crusades. Then the world went crazy over the South Sea bubble, the Mississippi scheme and the tulip craze in Holland. More recently it has been the Wall Street "get-rich-without-work" insanity, the Florida land boom, Ponzi, Kreuger, and various other follies, furors, frenzies and frothings. A book, "Popular Delusions and the Madness of Crowds" shows the immense damage they have done.

The present delusion, created without benefit of mirrors, is the belief that the government can keep people happy by feeding them their amputated tails, or rich by taxing them with one hand and giving back doles with the other. It's the new way to make both ends meet!

Using radio and the silver screen, demagogues infect millions with belief in their supernatural powers more easily than ever before. It is the worship of the Medicine Man beating his tom-tom. And it is leading to dictatorship, the abandonment of personal and family responsibility, local self-government and free institutions generally. The State is the modern Baal.

Animals in herds, including men, do not think. They simply feel. A single steer lying down at night on a western plain, if frightened, may jump up and start to run. But before he has gone ten rods, he says to himself, "What's this all about?" and pretty soon he lies down again and starts chewing his cud. Five thousand steers however, if frightened, will stampede off into the night. They trample themselves to death or push each other over the edge of a canyon. Only physical exhaustion finally dissipates their delirium.

The world insanity that GOVERNMENT can make men rich, will probably have to run its tragic course. But here and there, a few of us might slip away from the herd and think of the old Boer farmer and the tail of his dog.

# THE FUTURE
# OF FREE ENTERPRISE

*This speech was considered by Samuel B. Pettengill to be one of his ablest. It was delivered at the Seventeenth Annual Meeting of the American Petroleum Institute in Chicago, Illinois, on November 11, 1936. Mr. Henry M. Dawes, President of the Pure Oil Company, said after the meeting, "I never heard business scolded so politely or so well." Although the speech was given over forty years ago, it is just as pertinent today as it was then.*

Let me say at once that I do not know the future of free enterprise, nor that it will have a future. This may well be the last generation of Americans to receive and cherish the legacy of liberty. This coming decade may bring the twilight of democracy right here in America. Another collapse such as we had in 1929, and who of you will give bond for the survival of freedom?

Before rejecting these forebodings as too pessimistic, let us make a brief but candid appraisal of the forces now loose in the world . . . In the United States you have federal infiltration on a wide scale into fields once exclusively occupied by free enterprise, the latter taxed to support its governmental competitor. Worshippers of the State (not the "states") grow in number. Bearing a banner with that strange device, "special privileges for all" they come to Washington seeking alms. Members of church, labor, youth, and women's organizations are sponsoring the surrender of human destiny to politicians idealized as demigods.

I am not at all certain that the swing toward the center has not gathered momentum that nothing can check until a disillusioned people have once more had their fill of Caesar. It may be that we are fighting a rear-guard action. But if we must yield, we do so reluctantly and with a presumption in favor of freedom.

There is a long flow and ebb in the tides of human destiny. Consider the following facts. The Constitution of the United States was written in 1787. When signed, Gouverneur Morris said, "The whole human race will be affected by the proceedings of this convention." Never was prophecy better justified by time. For down to 1917, when Russians established the "dictatorship of the proletariat" in place of the dictatorship of the Romanoffs, a period of one hundred and thirty years, there was scarcely a movement on this planet that was not toward democracy and freedom from concentrated authority. In the states of our Union, in the countries of Latin America, in the provinces of Canada, in New Zealand, in Australia, in South Africa and elsewhere, not less than four hundred constitutions were patterned by freedom-loving men upon the basic concepts of our own Magna Carta—1, the distribution rather than the concentration of power, and 2, that the individual, because created by God, and in His image, has dignities and rights as a human soul which are beyond the powers of princes or the might of majorities.

But in 1917 the tide turned. From that time to this hour, except for the short-lived German republic, there has scarcely been a movement on this planet that has not been away from democracy toward the concentration of power and in favor of the doctrine that the individual has no rights which the state is bound to respect. . . . Perhaps this swirling tide will break and turn before it overwhelms America. But if in the perhaps not distant future free enterprise, and with it free government, should vanish from American life, an inquest is certain to be held. On that day, one of the saddest in history, many witnesses will be called. Some will blame Moscow; others Roosevelt; others the failure to require the teacher's oath in the public schools; others the failure to deport the communists; still others the vain but reckless pretensions of pulpit politicians "most ignorant of what they are most assured."

All these may influence the verdict, but I believe the final judgment of the impartial historian will be that free enterprise died in the house of its friends, its death wound given by its beneficiaries, not by its foes. In my book, "Hot Oil" I said:

"Can business men run business in the interest of the whole people? Can profits be harmonized with the needs of the nation for today and for tomorrow? Must the states surrender their historic jurisdiction to the nation? In a word, can we secure social objectives without regimentation, prosperity without paternalism? Or turning the question around, will paternalism produce prosperity? How much of liberty can we afford to pay for the *promise* of security? Or will bureaucracy, in destroying liberty, also destroy the efficiency in the production and distribution of wealth which alone makes security possible?

"If democracy fails, as so many in these difficult days seem even anxious to predict, it will be because it fails to meet the new problems of a new industrial world in which economic structures transcend state lines.

"What, then, is the true boundary between business and government, the states and the nation, individual responsibility and public control, the line 'which shall combine that degree of liberty without which law is tyranny, with that degree of law without which liberty becomes license'?

"What are the proper limits of the functions and agencies of government? These limits will be extended only as the failures of industry make the extension seem imperative. If business proves incapable of self-discipline in the interest of the millions, government will occupy new ground. The millions will demand it, and they have the votes. They will fly 'to ills they know not of' rather than continue to embrace conditions that have become intolerable. No constitution, however revered and hallowed with the blood of the fathers, will long check their course.

"The fate of America is still in the hands of those who have the greatest stake in America — the leaders of enterprise and their shareholders. Will they, who have the most to lose, do most to serve?"

It is only because I know there are men in this audience who are keenly aware of the pressing need of industrial statesmanship of the highest order, it is only because I know that this and other trade organizations are hard at work to improve the standards of conduct of their numbers toward each other and the public, and thus to save free enterprise and free government to America, that I venture to speak today.

I am none the less your friend even though I am unable to accept the easy alibi, so commonly held in business circles, that the push of collectivism comes from without, rather than from within those circles. The thought I have principally to offer for your consideration is that business men are largely, if not chiefly, responsible for the very trends they fulminate against.

If we are to save free enterprise, I am convinced that it will be done chiefly by industrial self-discipline placing limits on greed, recognizing the trusteeship of management — not for stockholders only, but for labor and the consumer — thus eradicating the evils of capitalism by self-surgery and making it function in the interest of the masses, without whose support it cannot function at all.

I recognize the difficulty, as did Edmund Burke, of indicting a nation or a system; but I do not see how we can approach the problem effectively without pitiless self-appraisal. I take courage because I see so many business men who are willing to face the facts and take their share of the responsibility and the blame. But I sometimes lose heart when I see others "passing the buck," looking for a "goat" and blinded by partisanship and self-interest, charge the trend toward regimentation and collectivism to a "brain trust," and a "rubber-stamp" Congress.

Gentlemen, let us be honest with ourselves and with the truth. Without entering now upon the merits of N.R.A. or A.A.A., or the potato bill or other similar legislation, where did these bills find their origin? First, in the breakdown of capitalism, and second, at the urging of capitalists.

Take N.R.A. I was present at its birth. I was in the Ways and Means Committee room when a representative, not of Karl Marx, but of American business, the president of the United States Chamber of Commerce, urged that legislation upon the Congress of the United States in behalf of the business interests of the country — a fact eloquently corroborated by Mr. W. T. Holliday in his testimony before the Cole Committee.

Take A.A.A. Whence came the demand for and ready acquiescence in "regimentation" by the most individualistic and sturdy of all members of the capitalist class — the American farmer? What apparent necessity induced him to reverse the habits of centuries, to kill pigs before they matured and to plow under cotton and wheat before it was ripe for the harvest? It was because the loss of foreign markets had caused unsalable surpluses to accumulate. And why did farm markets disappear? It was, in part at least, due to tariffs lobbied for by American capitalists which in turn provoked reprisals abroad, and thus farm surpluses and crop control and "regimentation" at home. For a decade American industry, in power at Washington, saw the free enterprise of farming slowly starve to the point of desperation.

If in the future there shall be a struggle for power in this country between the classes, industry would do well to have on its side the thirty million Americans who live on the farms and in the county-seat towns and villages of America. The "farm problem" is your problem.

When it is said that free enterprise has failed, my answer is that we have not permitted it to work. We have impeded it with a tanglefoot of our own making.

Despite all this sudden talk of a "planned economy" the fact is that we have never had a wholly free economy in this country. A policy of protective tariffs, for example, is in itself a repeal of the law of supply and demand.

Everywhere we see business men seeking to sustain themselves and their prices by controlling the market by monopoly, by subsidies, by franchises, by licenses, by certificates of public interest and necessity, by patents, by trademarks, by "pegging the dollar" to sustain credits, by devaluation to obtain advantages in international trade, by cheapening the dollar to pay debts through rising prices, by shifting the tax load to their competitors, by statutory price fixing, by retail sales control; in other words, by "regimentation" — for the other fellow.

In a notable paper two years ago Gustav Cassel of Sweden pointed out that the pressure of business interests upon government for special privileges for themselves or legislative handcuffs for their competitors leads inevitably to "planned economy" and hence, to dictatorship.

No government can write tariffs, license importers and exporters, pay subsidies, impose quotas, increase production, restrict production, regulate rates of foreign exchange, secretly manipulate huge stabilization funds, enter upon competitive under-valuation of national currencies, extend or restrict credit, raise and lower interest rates, fix prices, issue embargoes, regulate division of earnings between spending and investment, etc., without making mistakes which require corrections leading to more mistakes, without calling forth claims for compensating measures, in the same way that tariffs for manufacturers led to a demand for a "farmer's tariff" or its equivalent; or more recently, when the control of cotton production led to tobacco control, and from tobacco to peanuts to potatoes. Similarly government-financed hydroelectric power plants, which compete with coal, increase the demand for subsidies for coal mines and for restriction of production.

Because government grants favors to capitalists, it is appealed to to grant equalizing favors to workmen.

Because it creates agencies to benefit producers, it perforce must create other agencies to protect consumers — the consumers' bureau and the producers' bureau, each begging Congress for more money to checkmate the other!

And so government goes about grasping for more and more power to cope with the abuse of the privileges it has itself created.

If it be said, "upon what meat doth this, our Caesar, feed that he hath grown so great," the answer must be that the pressure of business interests forced the meat down the great man's throat.

Meantime the invisible government is constantly at work behind the scenes to hog the cake and distribute the crusts of governmental favor. And all of this, let me repeat, is initiated not by pink young professors, but by business interests seeking statutory refuges from the competitive struggle they praise so highly — on paper.

And meantime, members of legislative bodies are overworked with problems beyond their time, strength and experience, and outside their proper jurisdiction. The inevitable tendency is to delegate their powers to a vast bureaucracy. What they themselves do is done poorly, and the resulting loss of confidence in the ability as well as the disinterestedness of parliamentary government calls for louder cries for stronger men, and hence for the Strong Man himself, who in turn makes his mistakes — of which Napoleon and the former Kaiser are only two of many that sent whole nations to disaster.

Out of this tanglefoot that is throttling and discrediting free enterprise, there is an opportunity for an economic Abraham Lincoln who will free business men from the shackles wrought by themselves.

Whatever may be said in justification of any one of these governmental favors to a particular group, considered by itself, yet in their total aspect it is almost certain that the pocket of some American is impoverished by the exact amount by which another pocket is legislatively enriched; that the total wealth and purchasing power of the nation as a whole is not increased a nickel. On the contrary, it is almost equally certain that our people have been denied the almost limitless potentialities of our science and technology by these policies which hold the umbrella of paternalism over inefficiency and senility. In proof of this, is it not true that the enterprises which are in the van of recovery today — notably automobiles and petroleum — are those which are farthest from bureaucratic control, the freest of the favors and subsidies and protection of government, and the most subject to the competitive stresses of free enterprise?

I would listen long and attentively to an argument that the future of free enterprise requires the abandonment, step by step, of all these immunities and privileges and the gradual restoration of competition in all things save theft, fraud and the exploitation of human beings.

It cannot be denied that the same government that fixes prices for commodities, rents, and interests can with equal logic fix wages, either up or down, and shorten or lengthen hours of work. It all depends on who controls the government. Is this to be the reward of the American workman for rushing to Washington for the solution of his troubles? If so, planned economy will have a sour taste for his children.

In their international aspect this Chinese maze of trade restrictions might as well be recognized for what it is — the economic and monetary equivalent of war, with Armageddon only a step away.

The future of free enterprise goes far deeper than "is dreamed of in our philosophy." It not only involves the future of free government, but the future of civilization — any kind of civilization.

It is one thing when business competes on its own hook for international markets. But when government itself becomes the active partner of business men in throttling their international competitors, the latter rush to their governments to make political and military answers to economic arguments.

Thus the struggle is broadened and intensified. Is not the whole effort for national security rapidly increasing national insecurity? And is not every supposed trade gain offset a thousand times by the weight of armament and the cost of war — actual and potential? The world, it seems, can have trade and peace — or trade stoppage and war.

Coming nearer home, what bill in recent years had more of the essence of collectivism, the destruction of states' rights, the regimentation of enterprise, than the Thomas-Disney bill which would, if enacted, give an official at Washington the power to fix the daily production of petroleum from every well in America and therefore, indirectly, the income of the owner and the price paid by the buyer.

Again, without discussing the merits or necessity of the bill, it is the simple truth that it was the representatives of the industry itself who rushed to Washington, crying, "O beneficent bureaucrats, uncontaminated as you are with any knowledge of the problem of petroleum, and with that high detachment and objective viewpoint — resulting from never having seen an oil well — save us ere we perish, save us from ourselves!"

From my conning tower at Washington I saw another great industry, not rushing to the Capitol, but dragged there to stand trial for its own misdeeds. I heard the astonishing story of a dark jungle of holding companies pyramided ten stories high upon each other, the hiding place of financial freebooters. I saw the leaders of that industry, with ashen faces, unable to defend themselves. Some were personally vulnerable, and those who were not, felt forced by a spurious fraternalism to keep the door shut upon the skeletons in the closets of their industry rather than clean house. I said to some of these men that it passed my understanding how they could do such a marvelous job on their physical plants and equipment, a miracle of science, and be so utterly dumb and deaf and blind on their public relations. I said to them, "What you need is a Kenesaw Mountain Landis, a czar of your own choosing, whose sole function shall be to call foul balls, and whose contract shall expire the instant he ever says 'strike one.'"

Industrial self-discipline. I saw the stock exchanges and banks finance the bubble of speculation until it finally burst in ruin in 1929 with a shrinkage in values of stocks and bonds alone — to say nothing of commodities and real estate, rural and urban — of almost ninety-two billions of dollars, or three times the amount of the World War debt. And then, with little help and much opposition, my committee wrote the stock exchange act of 1934.

I heard the story of stock split-ups, the watering of capital structures, the sale in interstate commerce of worthless Peruvian and European bonds and domestic stocks in which twenty-five billions of the savings of thrift and toil were lost beyond recall, and my committee wrote the securities act of 1933.

Industrial self-discipline. In times called prosperous I saw eleven thousand banks, nearly a third of the nation's total, close their doors with five billion dollars of hard-won savings dissipated to the four winds of heaven, and under the very dome of the nation's capitol I heard an old man say. "To hell with the Constitution. It did not save my savings."

Industrial self-discipline. A few years earlier I saw the legitimate wine, beer and liquor industry — through illegitimate practices winked at by themselves, write their own ticket to exile and heard them pronounce the death sentence on their own hundreds of millions of investment.

I pick up the Statistical Abstract of the United States and read that, in 1928, five hundred and eleven men had net taxable realized incomes of a million dollars or more, averaging over two million dollars each or seven thousand dollars a day apiece, and totalling altogether over a billion dollars, only two percent of which, let it be noted, represented compensation for services actually rendered — a total *net* income to five hundred and eleven men greater than the *gross* income of all the wheat and cotton farmers of the nation, aggregating, with wives and children, some ten million Americans.

> "Ill fares the land, to hastening ills a prey
> Where wealth accumulates, and men decay."

And then, a little later, I saw this capitalistic system collapse, stabbed in the house of its friends, its blood sucked by its beneficiaries, and fifteen million idle men dependent upon private charity or public dole — an army which, placed in single column two feet apart, would reach across the continent and back — America's question mark to free enterprise.

In 1933 I spent a year as a member of a committee on government competition with private enterprise. We developed the facts. We showed socialism coming through the back door, but except their own ox was gored we got practically no support from either business men or political leaders.

This year I saw members of Congress — so often referred to as cowards or rubber stamps, risk their political lives to defeat a bill that would have opened the floodgates of inflation to the destruction of one hundred and eight billion dollars worth of life insurance and then in the election this fall go up against the radio guns of opponents, all without a word of thanks or an ounce of support from the presidents of the great life insurance companies, who are, if they are anything, the trustees of the helpless aged, the future widows and orphans on sixty-four million policies.

Gentlemen, I ask one intensely serious question: If the leaders and owners of the American system are too lazy to wash their dirty dishes, too selfish to be intelligent and too timid to stick their necks out in defense of free enterprise and constitutional government, *who will defend it?*

I see business men economize down to the last two inches of the lead pencils of their clerks, and themselves sweat and slave for twenty or thirty years to achieve a competency for the evening of life, and then, when the periodic crash comes, but with youth behind them, and the old push and drive no longer theirs, I see them with sublime courage start to weave anew the pattern of their hopes, but apparently with no thought whatever to softening the downward curve of the next collapse, or to the survival of the system itself to which they have given all their strength.

I have no thought to be unjust. The average business man is so engrossed with the daily task, so harassed with making out reports to government bureaucrats, that he has to keep his nose to the grindstone from dawn to dark. As an individual he is practically helpless. But it does seem to me that trade associations generally, as well as many of the larger companies, could well afford to have on their boards a man whose sole responsibility is public relations in the broadest sense, a man of unimpeachable integrity, to act as a tribune for the people, whose constant care it shall be that the priceless ingredient of character and fair dealing with worker and customer and people and government shall be woven into the fabric of free enterprise. Such a man would not only sell his industry to the public, but would be equally diligent to sell the public to his industry. And then, to pursue the idea further, suppose the public relations members of each of the five hundred and more existing trade associations were to organize informally, a Supreme Council of American Enterprise, endowed with sufficient funds to conduct inquiries and report from time to time on "the state of the Union." Let me italicize the word *"Union."*

Certainly it is becoming plain that the profession of public relations requires experience and training as specialized as that of sales manager or of laboratory technician.

Perhaps this suggestion is wholly impracticable, but as I reconnoiter the field it seems desirable, if not imperative, that some means be found to mobilize the conscience and enlightened self-interest, not of one division alone, but of the entire army of American industry, business, agriculture and finance. Such a mobilization would be for both offense and defense. It would be the sharp critic and ruthless surgeon of evil practices on the one hand, and on the other the stout champion of the American system, minus its crooks and its hogs.

I know there are those who will sneer at what they would call my naive assumption that there is a conscience in American business, and will use against me the articles of indictment which I myself drew a few minutes ago.

Gentlemen, I know better. I know the average business man is just as anxious to deal justly with his men and with the public as the average politician. I would rather have the judgment and conscience of the man who is close to his men and the public than the ipse dixit of the intelligentsia who would rule the universe from their garrets or their thrones.

The fault, or rather the failure, of business executives, as I see it, is not that they are soulless and selfish, but rather that they are, or have been, too preoccupied with the daily problems of their business. It may be due also, in part, to the fact that so many of the top men and members of executive committees have spent their previous years as specialists in a single branch of their industries and have never been under the necessity "to see life steadily and to see it whole."

But all this only explains, yet does not refute, my contention that industry's greatest weakness today is public relations.

Let me return to what I was saying about conscience in business.

On Constitution Day in September I addressed the Daughters of the American Revolution. I told them this story and it is a true story. The editor of a fine little newspaper in Indiana told me how he went through the depression. When advertising and subscribers fell off, he called in his men, sixty in number, from the oldest pressman to the youngest cub reporter. He said to them: "Boys, we have got to retrench to keep this paper alive. But we will all go up or down together. This paper is in the red, but I do not intend any one of you to see red. I will show my good faith by taking the biggest cut, both in dollars and percent." They faced the music together. Not a man deserted the paper and the paper did not desert a man. The editor said to me: "If St. Peter ever pins any medals on my bosom, it will be because all through the depression every man in my employ found something in his pay envelope every Saturday."

And I said to the D.A.R.'s: "That man did more to save the Constitution than all the editorials he might have written in its honor and glory after he had fired half his men."

There are thousands of such men who made similar sacrifices to keep their men employed, and who equally "deserve well of the Republic." Others had the desire to do so, but were forced to shut down by circumstances beyond their control. I am ready to go to bat for that kind of business man.

But unfortunately there are many others who retrenched only in payrolls, dumping their workers out on the streets to be taken care of by relief agencies, and now beef about the public debt incurred in keeping their former workers from starving.

It is a harsh thing to say, as harsh and as kind and as kindly meant as the surgeon who tells you an operation is imperative, but is it not the cold fact that business men generally have lost the confidence of their own workers? Is it not the fact that the business man and the politician have been competing for the good will of the worker and the business man has lost? Maybe it is not his fault. Maybe it is due to forces beyond his control — the war, the depression — but I think we would be more sure of the survival of free enterprise if we stopped looking for alibis and said, "Well, *some* of it is my fault, and *all* of it is my job."

Where did business men get within the past month with their attack on the social security act? They got the Bronx cheer! That attack was the supreme blunder of the Republican campaign. The workers refused to believe that their employers wanted to improve an admittedly imperfect law. They were convinced that the attack was on the principle of the law itself.

How wrong were they? No answer, perhaps, can be given. But certainly the principle of avoiding the appearance of evil was so clearly indicated that I am surprised that persons who call themselves astute began throwing boomerangs so viciously — at themselves.

To wait until the law has been on the statute books for fourteen months before suddenly notifying workers how terrible it is, was in itself an open advertisement that shoddy goods were being sold.

An objective viewpoint would have avoided a blunder like that. That is why free enterprise needs a lot of Judge Landises of public relations. Many sincere business men, busy as they are in the squirrel cage where losses constantly chase profits, had never even heard of the social security act until a few weeks ago. But that again proves the very point I am trying to make — the need for a division of enterprise marked "industrial statesmanship."

Consider, as one among many, the problem of old age in this machine civilization of modern city life. The most amazing change in population trends is going on before our very eyes. There were thirty-four percent more people over sixty-five in 1930 than in 1910 — only twenty years earlier. That proportion in the upper age levels is almost certain to increase. In fact, actuaries for great life-insurance companies predict that by 1970, only thirty-four years from now, there will be more people over fifty than under twenty; in other words, that the problem of the average man only a few years hence will be to take care of his parents rather than his children — the greatest shift in age groupings, probably, since the world began. It is due of course, to two main factors, fewer babies born per one thousand of population, but of those who are born, because of the marvelous conquests of medicine, principally in the diseases of childhood, youth and young manhood, more live into the upper age levels.

But as your average age line moves up, the industrial deadline moves down. The two lines cross, and the point of their crossing marks one of the battlefields where free enterprise and free government is to be saved — if it is to be saved. For when the age line passes the industrial deadline, there is little point left in the old slogans of rugged individualism, or initiative, or courage. These old virtues have then lost their meaning. The door to the land of opportunity in which these virtues can alone live and thrive has then been closed.

Combine all this with the passing of the free land of the West, the recurrence of "boom and bust," of depressions which wipe out banks and other institutions where the savings of thrift and toil are invested, and last, that other great shift to city life from rural life where, as in the "good old days" there were always useful chores for grandma and grandpa to do, and you have a challenge that cannot be laughed off.

When I speak of industrial statesmanship it is problems like this I have in mind. What are the leaders of our enterprise going to do about them?

If they do nothing — or little that is effective — free enterprise in the years just ahead, is going to be subjected to a constantly increasing and irresistible pressure from these opportunity-less groups to have the politicians take over the management, if not the ownership, of your business — for their benefit.

Take unemployment. In terms of social ethics, where does the dollar derive a claim to being paid dividends during periods of depression, superior to the claims of the laid-off worker to being paid unemployment reserves? Why are reserves justified for depreciation, depletion and amortization of machinery and plant, and reserves not justified for human obsolescence?

These are not the questions of a long-haired radical or soap-box orator. I quote the exact language of Charles Evans Hughes, Chief Justice of the United States Supreme Court, who wrote the minority opinion in the recent railroad pension case:

"What sound distinction, from a constitutional viewpoint, is there between compelling reasonable compensation for those injured without any fault of the employer (as in workmen's compensation acts) and requiring a fair allowance for those who practically gave their lives to the service and are incapacitated by the wear and tear of time, the attrition of the years? I can perceive no constitutional ground upon which the one can be upheld and the other condemned. The fundamental consideration which supports this type of legislation is that industry should take care of its human wastage, whether that is due to accident or age."

If the social security act is declared unconstitutional or is generally overhauled, I should like to see, first, permission to employers to set up their own retirement systems under the auspices of government so that the fund for workers will not be lost to creditors in event of bankruptcy; and second, actual encouragement to set up these reserves by granting them special tax treatment such as we grant to contributions to charities under existing income and estate-tax law. I hate desperately to see the moral sense of responsibility between management and men diluted by transferring all functions to Washington.

On some other occasion I should like to discuss ways and means for securing social objectives without regimentation, prosperity without paternalism. Some of the indicated avenues for explorations are: 1, further strengthening of trade organizations to conduct a constant warfare on those practices, like price fixing, which are the very negation of free enterprise; 2, developing departments of public relations as already discussed; 3, interstate compacts; 4, uniform state legislation; 5, further powers to the Federal Trade Commission to approve voluntary arrangements in industry; 6, the application of the principle stated in a recent opinion of the United States Supreme Court which took the protection of the interstate commerce clause from prison-made goods offered for sale in violation of state law; 7, a similar principle as set forth in Section 2 of the 21st amendment to the Constitution with reference to intoxicating liquors. All of these points could be widely extended to the strengthening of social legislation by the *states* and by informal rules self-imposed on industry, without the necessity of transferring all power to Washington, where it is bound to be an immense prize to be striven for by pressure groups led by demagogues who compete in auctioning off the treasury for votes, and in despoiling the worker to enrich the drones.

There is no need for destroying the states and erecting a bureaucratic empire in America. Elihu Root pointed the way, as far back as 1908, when he said at a conference on the conservation of natural resources:

> "The nation cannot perform the functions of the state sovereignties. If it were to undertake to perform these functions, it would break down. The machinery would not be able to perform the duty. The pressure is already very heavy upon national machinery to do its present work.
>
> "I feel deeply impressed, however, with the idea that the forty-six sovereign states, in the performance of their duties of government, are lagging behind the stage of development which the other sovereignties of the earth have reached. As the population of our states increases, as the relations between the people of each state and other states grow more frequent, more complicated, more important, more intricate, what every state does becomes more important to the people of every other state . . . .
>
> "Now the states in the exercise of their sovereignty, in the exercise of the powers reserved to them, rest under the same kind of duty, a duty that forbids any state to live unto itself alone.
>
> "The Constitution of the United States prohibits the states from making any agreements with each other without the consent of Congress, but you can make any number of agreements with the consent of Congress. Why should not the powers that are reserved to the state sovereignties be exercised by those sovereignties with wise regard for the common interest, under a firm resolve to make it wholly unnecessary that this continued pressure to force the national government into the performance of the duties that the states ought to perform should continue? It is high time that the sovereign states of the Union should begin to perform their duties with reference not only to their own local individual interests, but with reference to the common good."

And then, above all, we must recognize that our "need is not to emphasize our differences but, rather, to understand our interdependence," to quote Louis Taber, master of the National Grange. What is desperately needed in America right now is an era of good feeling and fair dealing between capital and labor, industry and government. With that, plus our technology, invention and power, nothing is impossible. Without it, anything is possible.

355

American industry has been built on the struggle for the consumer's dollar by offering most and best for least. That is competitive capitalism at its best. It becomes destructive when it is a competition of who will pay the least wages. The responsibility of industrial management to build a floor below which wages are not to go is tremendous. American industries must cooperate with each other, and with government, to find ways and means by which the masses who wish to work may live in decent comfort and security. The choice, as I see it, is between wages and taxes; between self-disciplined capitalism and state socialism; between free government based on the consent of the governed and ancient tyrannies under modern masks.

Although I cannot demonstrate it on a blackboard, I have a feeling — as compelling as a religious conviction — that if industry will constantly pass on to the worker and the customer the savings of labor-saving machinery and invention, rather than siphon them off into the pools of watered securities, it will by that process keep distribution and production in balance, and go as far toward Utopia as our poor human natures will go or be driven.

Gentlemen, what is this legacy of free enterprise which we received from our fathers? Even with its failures and shortcomings, it is the best in the world. We have six percent of the world's land area and seven percent of its people. But that seven percent has thirty-two percent of the world's railway mileage, fifty-eight percent of its telephones, thirty-six percent of its developed water power, seventy-six percent of the world's automobiles — enough so that every man, woman and child under the flag, one hundred and thirty million Americans, could climb into these cars and all ride on rubber at the same instant of time, a nation on wheels, a miracle of achievement in which bureaucrats played no part. The rubber that goes into the annual production of tires would make a tire that would go around the world and six thousand miles to spare — a rubber tired planet, if you please. When Stalin, or Hitler or Mussolini do half so much, it will be twice as much as they have done!

This little seven percent of the world's population has forty-four percent of its radios; produces sixty percent of the world's petroleum, forty-eight percent of its copper, forty-three percent of its pig iron, forty-seven percent of its steel, fifty-eight percent of its corn, fifty-six percent of its cotton, twenty-five percent of its sugar, thirty-three percent of its coal. Of the commodities it does not produce, this little seven percent of the world's population goes out into the world's markets and buys fifty percent of its rubber, fifty percent of its coffee, seventy-five percent of its silk. This seven percent of the world's population has forty-five percent of the world's total wealth; and far more than half of all the wheels that turn on this planet, from locomotive drivers to the wheels in milady's wrist watch, turn on American soil. In the worst year of the worst depression in our history, thirty million out of thirty-two million American boys and girls of school age stayed in public schools. And on the point of security for old age this little seven percent has one hundred and eight billion dollars of protection on the lives of sixty-four million Americans, more security than all the rest of the world put together.

Gentlemen, I am a friend of the system which has done these things. With all its faults, follies and crimes, it has produced and distributed more of the goods and comforts of living to more people over a greater territory and for a longer period of time than any other system in any other country since Adam walked out of the Garden of Eden. Neither the princes of Babylon, the Pharoahs of Egypt, the emperors of Rome, the lords of feudalism, or the dictators of today ever served the common man half so well.

It is worth saving, gentlemen! But praise of its virtues alone will not save it. We must cure its defects, remedy its abuses. If we resolutely set our hands to this great task, we can be confident of the prophecy of Robert Burns that:

> "A virtuous populace will rise the while,
> And stand, a wall of fire, around their much loved isle."

# THE GRAND STRATEGY OF FREEDOM

*Address given at the Henry George School of Social Science, October, 1949.*

Many people are fighting different phases of Socialism. The efforts have been brave, but what are they accomplishing? We sweep back the sea, but the tide rolls in. If the tide of Socialism is to be turned, it is necessary to understand its secret weapon and to plan a grand strategy to meet it.

Socialism's secret weapon is money. Governments formerly gained power by the sword and swelled their coffers by conquest and tribute. That method is still used, but chiefly against foreigners. Modern governments obtain power over their own people in a more subtle fashion. They tax away the earnings of their people, and then dole some of it back to them in subsidies, gifts, grants-in-aid, and the award of huge government contracts. By this process they become the masters of men, and cease to be their servants. The historic relationship is reversed. Instead of government coming to the people for its support, the people come to the government for *their* support. Hitler put all groups in Germany in pawn to him via the money route. In the face of the granting or withholding of public money, opposition died away. People began to keep their mouths shut — business men first, — but finally editors, educators and ministers.

In this country, governors of states, mayors of cities and members of business organizations — Chambers of Commerce — including those most opposed to socialism in the abstract, became beggars at Washington for a return of some of the money collected from them in their own communities — less the political brokerage. As beggars, they fawn and smirk. The great "power of the purse" — with which the representatives of the taxpayers once held the executive branch in check, is rapidly passing into the hands of a Santa Claus.

Not one of the extensions of Socialism could be put into effect without money. Cut off the money supply — and the power to borrow — and you stop them in their tracks.

Harry Hopkins gave the formula for Socialism — tax, spend and elect. Yet because they fail to grasp the grand strategy of freedom, various groups exhaust themselves on scattered tactical skirmishes — good in themselves, but futile in the face of this overpowering flood of money.

Justice Holmes used to say, "We must strike for the jugular and let the rest go." I would urge no one to abandon the fight for his own group, but the number one plank in all patforms must be the exact reverse of the Hopkins formula — "Reduce taxes and spending, especially at the federal level. Keep government poor and remain free."

Make that the number one plank in *all* platforms for freedom. The doctors can then fight socialized medicine; owners of real estate can fight public housing; others can fight federal control of education, — others can fight to relieve privately created wealth of some of the tax burden, and shift some of the *necessary* taxes to socially created wealth. With that as the number one plank of all groups, all can then fight with some chance of success. As it is, with each group fighting some single phase of Socialism in which the others are not particularly interested, you are picked off like sitting ducks.

The Socialists, who always deny they are Socialists, — but believers in a "planned economy" instead, lull the unthinking with the trick question, "What freedom have you lost?" That's easy to answer. It is my freedom to keep what I earn and spend it as I please. That's the vital distinction between European Socialism and American individualism. "To have and to hold" — written into millions of title deeds, tells the story of the individual incentives and rewards that have produced America's magnificent achievement.

Other freedoms, of course, are being lost — including the right of the citizen to not have his vote cancelled by the bought vote of millions on the public payroll, and many other historic freedoms. But their keeping or losing all depends on one question: Who controls the purse strings? Who dispenses the income of the people?

The federal money route to Socialism is destroying the Republic in another way few understand. Money strengthens the federal government and weakens the state and local governments. This is so because states and cities are forbidden to print or coin money to pay their debts. They cannot make the money markets their creatures nor drive down interest rates at their caprice. When states, counties, cities and towns undertake to borrow money, they have to pay interest rates established in a free market, and have to satisfy the lender that the loan is sound and secure. To pay interest and principal of their debts, states and municipalities have to get the cash the hard way — by taxing the people. This puts some brake on their borrowings, some resistance to socializing the business of their tax payers. You see this force at work in every municipal ownership election.

The federal government, however, is under none of those restrictions. It can force interest rates down, borrow huge funds cheaply, pay its obligations of interest and principal by converting more of its promises into federal reserve notes, by devaluing its gold and silver hoardings — or by outright greenbacks.

The federal government has a printing press; the states do not. This easy money route promotes the extension of federal power and subtracts from state and local self-government, which we thought for centuries to be necessary to prevent the return of Caesar.

Many state and local governments have constitutional limitations on their power to tax or incur debt. The federal government has none. The adoption of the 16th Amendment with no limitation whatever on the power of the federal government to tax away the earnings of the people opened the gates to Socialism. It is a strange thing that the Constitution places limits on the power of the federal government over the life and liberty of the people, but no limit on the power to tax away their incomes or their property itself, as the estate tax does. As taxes go up, liberty goes down. In Socialist Britain, the tax on income goes up to 97½ per cent. It is not necessary for the Socialists to confiscate paper titles. Many think that "can't happen here" due to voter resistance by the owners. All the Socialists need to do is to socialize income. Then it can call the tune for all pipers to pay.

> "For this is the law and the law shall run,
> Till the earth in its course is still,
> That whoso eateth another's bread
> Shall do that other's will."

That Socialism is already far advanced is plain from a $44 billion federal budget (for 1949). With that vast revenue, what is it now doing? The federal government now operates light and power plants, builds and rents houses, buys potatoes that rot and butter that turns rancid. It is in the banking business, financing even such things as race tracks, beauty parlors and soda fountains. It is heavily in the insurance business for war veterans and their dependents. It is in the peanut, wheat, cotton, beans, eggs, turpentine, turkey and wool business. It owns at least two railroads, barge lines, merchant shipping. It smelts metals, refines sugar, proposes to build steel plants. It operates scores of hospitals and hires doctors, dentists, oculists, and surgeons. It is in the business of fixing wages, pensions, prices, profits, interest rates and dividends. It proposes to finance public education from the kindergarten through college and look after everybody from the cradle to the grave. All this and much more in the name of "security." But outside of the actual businesses that it enters into competing with its own taxpayers, it is socializing the incomes of *all* the American people, taking from Peter to pay the Pauls of vast pressure groups who are told that they will be ungrateful if they do not vote for the administration in power.

To direct your attention to how far one-man government has gone, it is to be noted that in 24 countries which have recently devalued their currencies it was all done without the prior approval of any legislative body. Yet if these devaluations are to be effective in stimulating export trade and restricting imports they can succeed only in reducing the real wages of millions of people through more rigid controls. This vast power over their earnings; over their money; over their savings is now exercised by a few men in the different capitals of the world who issue a decree to that effect without submitting the merits of the case either to the people or any legislative body anywhere for prior approval.

As excessive debt and devaluation takes away the value of all savings through cheapening money, the thrifty people of the world have become the helpless pawns of government. We have not seen the last of this. We devalued the dollar ourselves. We have set the precedent, and the pressure is on to do so again. Stealing the savings of the people by the government is as old as history. The British pound was once an actual pound's weight of silver. The French franc and Italian lira, once worth 20 cents in our money, are now worth miserable fractions of one cent. Every devaluation has plundered the savings of the industrious. Greek, Hungarian and Chinese money is now as worthless as autumn leaves. Yet the demagogues ask "What freedom have you lost?"

The money flood sweeps on submerging the valleys where free men once lived. Debt ridden politicians are always quick to conceal their bankruptcies by cheapening money. We spent more than we took in in seventeen years of the last nineteen and are now again going into debt at the rate of at least $6 billion a year.

The danger to the future of every American is concealed from them by three devices. One is the propaganda trick that public debt is of no importance, because "we owe us." Second, by artificially supporting the market for government bonds, and preventing their true worth from becoming known in a free market, just as England tried to conceal the value of the pound. Third, having made it a crime for the citizen to have gold coins, he can no longer put a brake on public spending by demanding gold for paper money.

Taxes leave the citizen less, and increasing the public debt by what is, in effect, printing money, dilutes the value of all savings. It is as dishonest as pouring water into milk. A government that promises social security when it is continuously diluting money, is not only a hypocrite but morally a thief. Nothing is safe unless the dollar is secure. Promising welfare programs to be paid in rotting money is Ponzi finance. The federal government is taking in taxes now three times as much each year as the twelve year Roosevelt average. Every tax dollar not absolutely necessary simply furnishes ammunition to the Socialists.

Since the shooting stopped, the federal government has spent more than the total spent from 1789 to July 1, 1941. The federal government is taking the entire income of 42,000,000 people over and above the cost of keeping them alive.

If every one who holds life insurance cashed his policies, the amount would not run the federal government one year.

If every urban home owner sold his home, the total would finance the politicians on the Potomac for eight months.

If every farmer sold his farm, equipment and live stock, the total would run the government for only seven months.

If every industry converted its net working capital into cash, it would last the federal politicians less than a year.

Yet, spending these gigantic sums, the politicians continue to issue their fraudulent promises of the more abundant life.

This makes a grand strategy for freedom imperative. We must unite on one point, easily understood, which touches the pocketbook nerve of millions of voters. We must find the common denominator of mass resistance to socialism. On that concept and that only can we mobilize an army sufficient in numbers to wage successful war.

We must show millions of voters how they are being hurt — how their security for old age is melting away.

There are 78,000,000 life insurance policy holders. As money becomes cheap, their security vanishes. A $10,000 policy paid up in 1940 has lost $4,000 or more in terms of what it will buy today.

A life insurance president has just told of the disastrous effect of the cheap money policies of the past twenty years on life insurance security. The insurance companies are forced to earn less on their investments. Therefore, they must charge higher premiums for the same protection. Then when the policy is paid, the money received is taxed more, and buys less. To cover all these losses, a typical life insurance holder needs to take out seventy per cent more insurance to provide the same purchasing power as in 1929.

Most of the beneficiaries of life insurance are women. Tell them what taxes and debt and rotting money are doing to the security their husbands have worked so hard to provide.

The school teacher who formerly earned four per cent on her savings bank book now gets on the average of one and one-half per cent. Cheap money has reduced her chance to live out her old age on the earnings of her bank deposit by sixty-two per cent. There are millions of voters in this group.

Then there are other millions who own government bonds. A bond bought ten years ago for $75 can be cashed today for $100. But the

$100 will buy you less than the $75 did when you turned it over to the government. And you are ten years older.

Also you have forty or fifty million people who have been compelled to buy what are called "social security" cards. Their hoped for security melts away as dollars become cheap. To make up the loss, bills are in Congress to pay them more of these cheap dollars, adding to the tax burden to be carried by all industry, forcing prices still higher, and the music goes round and round.

The guarantees of a government that constantly pays out more than it takes in are writ on water and carved in sand. Something for nothing is the moral cancer of a free society. Once begun, there is no stopping its deadly course except to find the lowest common denominator of the mass resistance of millions of voters. This is the grand strategy of freedom.

# NOT THE SUPREME LAW OF THE LAND

*Reprinted from* Human Events, *1963.*

The general acceptance of today's slogan that nine or even five men, neither elected nor removable by the people, can rewrite the Constitution as they see fit, and that it then becomes everyone's duty to accept their views as "law" is a long stride towards Bonapartism in this country.

The saying that "The Constitution is what the Supreme Court says it is," is attributed to Charles Evans Hughes. But I have a letter from a former justice of the Supreme Court who says that Hughes told him that he was speaking in a jocular mood and had always regretted the remark.

A decision by the United States Supreme Court on a constitutional question is not *any kind of law*.

This is because no court has authority to make law, or amend the Constitution. Its judgment, whether right or wrong, is of course, binding on the litigants in the case, unless reversed on appeal. But it is not binding on other persons. As Chief Justice Harlan F. Stone said in 1942, a court's judgment "is binding only on the parties to the particular proceedings." This statement by the chief justice should dispose of the question, especially as there was no dissent to it.

It is true, of course, that other persons may agree that the reasons given by a court for its decisions are sound and right, and decide to follow them in similar decisions. But they may not agree, and that is their right. Why? Because a court judgment is not law. No court has the authority to make law.

Law can be laid down only by those who have the authority to make law. In our country, that authority is given only to legislators, elected by the people, and removable by the people. Or it is in the people themselves in adopting, or amending their Constitution, federal or state. There *let it remain!*

The Constitution says how it can be amended — only by the people, in the manner prescribed. No court is mentioned.

Second, the Constitution says that *all* legislative or lawmaking powers of the federal government are vested in Congress. It does not make the Supreme Court a constitutional convention. As *all* federal legislative power is vested in Congress, *none* is vested in the Supreme Court.

Third, the Constitution says that "this Constitution and the laws of the United States (by Congress) in pursuance thereof (plus treaties) shall be the supreme law of the land," and "all judicial officers, both of the United States and of the several States, shall be bound by oath or affirmation to support this Constitution."

All judges take this oath. It is a contradiction in terms to argue that a judge can lawfully change what he has taken an oath to support. This was universally accepted until recently.

As Chief Justice Marshall said in 1824, "Judicial power, as contradistinguished from the power of the law, has no existence. Courts are the mere instruments of the law and can will nothing." They can decide cases, rightly or wrongly, and the parties to the case are bound by their judgments, but no one else. If their decisions were to bind other persons, then such persons would be ruled against without being heard, without their day in court. This would violate all concepts of justice and law.

Judges can say what they *think* the Constitution means, and apply that to the decision of the case before them. They can overrule, or refuse to follow what they or other judges have previously *thought* was the law. But they cannot *make law*, or rewrite the Constitution. A court decision is an *opinion!*

On the other hand, Congress, in which is vested all legislative powers of the federal government, can decide what it *thinks* should be the law; by a majority vote what it *thinks* becomes *law*, assuming that it is constitutional. But what a court thinks should be the law, does not become law because it thinks it should.

If that were not true, the Supreme Court could never overrule its own previous interpretation of the Constitution, as it has done time and again. But if these previous decisions were "the supreme law of the land" which the judges had sworn to uphold, how could they reverse such decisions without violating their oath?

That the Supreme Court has at times acted as a super-legislature has been many times stated by Supreme Court judges themselves in dissenting opinions. Conferences of the chief justices and attorneys general of the states have also charged the Supreme Court with violating the Constitution.

Those who are making a fetish of the segregation decision should remember that the opponents of slavery were once shouted down by the same political ballyhoo. The Fugitive Slave Act of 1850, which was held constitutional by the Supreme Court, was not considered "the supreme law of the land" by men and women of the highest character in the North who kept right on helping fugitive slaves to freedom via the "underground railroad." The shoe was then on the other foot.

The same thing can be said of the Dred Scott decision of 1857. Did the people of the North bow down to this decision as the supreme law of the land, binding on them? They did not. In fact, the man who did more to abolish slavery than any other, Abraham Lincoln, said that if he were a member of Congress, and the same question arose, he would not be bound by the Dred Scott decision. And so, on other occasions, Thomas Jefferson and Andrew Jackson said that while a court decision bound the litigants, it did not bind *them!*

In the interest of stability and uniformity of the law, it is generally desirable that lower federal and state courts should abide by a decision of the U.S. Supreme Court, even if they think it is wrong. But they do so, not because the Constitution says they must — for it does not — but for the practical reason that if they do not abide by it, they will be reversed on appeal.

It is also true that a court may participate in the lawmaking process by giving reasons for its decision which seem so convincing that they are gradually accepted by the people *as good law*. This is how the common law of England developed.

For example, the reasons of Chief Justice Marshall for deciding that an act of Congress is unconstitutional when clearly repugnant to the Constitution, were so powerful and convincing that other judges, Congress and the people gradually accepted his decision as sound law under which they wished to live. The process is like that of a principal ratifying the act of his agent. But Marshall did not *make law* by his own say-so. *He had no such power.*

The political shibboleth that "the Constitution is what the judges say it is," no matter what, is so destructive of constitutional principles, that every patriotic American should condemn it. For there is a rapidly growing concentration of governmental, economic and financial power in Washington, and particularly in the chief executive, who appoints all federal judges.

If this trend is not soon reversed, then the statement by a high official that "the Constitution was written for an entirely different period in our nation's history" may become the epitaph of American liberty.

# POETRY AND THE POET'S MISSION

*Considered by Sam Pettengill to be one of the best things he ever wrote.*

The Round Table may not, possibly, be the finest organization in the world, but it has as its motto as noble a sentiment as ever caused men to break bread together. "I am a man and nothing human is alien to me." The same thought was once beautifully expressed by Emerson to some eager college boys when he said, "The secret of the true scholar is to recognize his teacher in every man." And it was Lord Bacon's fine saying that "he would light his torch at every man's candle."

Our candle tonight is one form of Art. What is Art? Art is man's most relentless self-criticism. By it he measures himself, not by what he is doing, but by the best he *has* done, by the impossible he *would* do. "Whom the impossible allures, I love" was Goethe's fine dictum. Art creates ever new standards of excellence. It teaches men to know what is good. It is the one thing that makes the ideal real. It is the Ark of the Covenant in which man bears before him in his long wandering his Holy of Holies. It is man's *own* contribution to the infinite processes by which he has evolved. No one can weigh its influence in human development. In the special fields of sculpture and painting, it is likely, by the standards of strength and beauty which it has created, that it has profoundly influenced even the biological evolution of the race itself through ideals of mate selection. "Discobolus" and the "Venus de Milo" may have become a part of human protoplasm.

But how hard it is to get men to light their torches at every man's candle. We erect barriers of prejudice; barbed wire entanglements against the intrusion of a new idea. The dislike for the unlike has been man's highest hurdle.

The spiritual walls which in ancient times separated Greek from "barbaros" still stand. The go-getter of today, as in all days past, looks on the artist as a weakling; the artist returns this scorn with compound interest. Imperfect sympathies on both sides! The practical man, caught in the squirrel cage of affairs, finds himself extremely busy getting nowhere — but old. He should have imagination enough to realize that the dreamer alone may have sufficient detachment to envision a cageless world. Practically all the labor saving machinery on earth which has to some extent freed man from the treadmill of grinding toil, and given him time to live, has been the work of men whom their practical contemporaries sneered at as dreamers. The young James Watt, who was scolded by the busybodies of his day for wasting his time over a teakettle's lid, was in fact the most practical man of his century, if not of the last three centuries. The artist, on the other hand, should be humble in the presence of a steam hammer, a chemist's test tube, or a hog butcher's slaughterhouse. He should realize that the "world is opening to the poet with every question the crucible asks of the elements, with every spectrum the prism steals from the star." Artist and artisan should work together. Life, and its countless satisfactions, depend on every phase of doing and dreaming. The whole is the sum total of its parts.

> "*All* are architects of fate
> Working in these walls of time,
> Some with massive deeds and great,
> And some with ornaments of rhyme."

It was a very modest thing for Mr. Longfellow to speak of rhyme or poetry as an ornament, and therefore by implication of lesser rank and worth than the pilasters and concrete that go into the building of this materialistic civilization. But poetry, while it is an ornament, is far more than an ornament. Poetry is food. The complete man is a triune being. His physical self will die of starvation for want of physical food. And the fact that so many people go through life, satisfactorily to themselves, without anything that appeals to the imaginative, the emotional or spiritual self, does not prove to us that these things of the spirit can be dispensed with. It proves only that *their* spiritual selves have died. As Ibsen said, "There is a corpse on board." One might as well argue that bread and butter, beets and potatoes are worthless because a dead man has no use for them. If he is alive physically he will need beets and potatoes, and the man who grows them performs a vital, an indispensable service. If there is one kind of snob who is more offensive to me than another, it is he or she who elevates his or her delicate and well-groomed eyebrows at the man with the hoe, the horny handed rustic, the kind of human beings who are immortalized forever by the poetry of Robert Burns, by Millet's "Angelus," by the life of Abraham Lincoln. But man lives not by bread alone. If he is alive spiritually as well as physically he will need things to feed his spirit, and the man who produces *them* plays a part fully as important as he who grows beets and beans or erects factory buildings or skyscrapers. If his part is not fully as important it is for the sole reason that man's spiritual self is of lesser dignity than his physical self, and this we are not yet willing to concede.

The man who affects to sneer at aesthetic values not only confesses his own ignorance which is obvious but his incompleteness which is profound. He admits without proof that he is but a half or a third or the tenth part of a man. "I am a man and nothing human is alien to me."

I have this justification for my choice of subject — that it is so seldom presented to an audience. Here is a great art — perhaps the greatest of all — but how little do we ever hear of it, how seldom are we given an opportunity to reflect upon it? In high school and college and university — in schools of fine and plastic arts — in women's clubs and organizations there are courses in music and its appreciation, in painting and its interpretation, in sculpture and its meaning. But where is there a course in poetry and its appreciation made available? In such a course as English literature, one may get glimpses of the subject, but mere glimpses, mixed up with the Essay, and the Novel and History, and Biography and dates, and who his grandfather was, and how long he served as 'prentice in a law office, and whether he stole deer as a youth. We have Shakespeare clubs and Heaven knows how many editions of the Bard's works, but never a preface to a single volume that treats of the drama as poetry — magnificent poetry — immensely difficult poetry — with its complex and protean structure. All you find are the facts of Shakespeare's life, the chronology of his plays, and from what source he is supposed to have gotten his plots. When I come across such a line as:

> "Out, out, brief candle
> Life's but a walking shadow, a poor player
> Who struts and frets his hour upon the stage,
> And then is heard no more. It is the voice
> Of an idiot, full of sound and fury,
> Signifying — nothing."

When I come upon such a line do you suppose I care whether it first appeared in the Folio of 1623, or where its plot was taken from?

Is it any wonder that boys and girls, with their fine imagination, are chilled by such pedantry, and never again perhaps, pull Macbeth from the shelf? But as Robert Louis Stevenson when once asked the date of his birth truthfully replied by giving the date of his marriage, so I can fix the birth or at least the budding of my appreciation of poetry as one warm June afternoon twenty odd years ago when I heard a man who loved poetry and could read it aloud, read with perfect understanding and poetic accent — Wordsworth's "Beggar on the Cumberland Road."

Many do not like poetry or poets. It is not to be wondered at. The reasons are too obvious. It was Charles Lamb who said to a friend who did not like someone — "Then why not make his acquaintance?" And even if you have tried in good faith to like poetry, but cannot, you are not thus proved to be a son of Anak. This is a large world and has many interests. The only fair argument which can be addressed to those who care to be cultured is that they do in fact pursue some phase of culture. What phase — what does it matter? A bird in the forest can perch but upon one bough. Pursue one and still recognize that there is charm and beauty in all the rest. It is foolish and fruitless for those who follow one phase to look down upon those who follow another. What can be fairly said of poetry as against other arts is that it is the more accessible. Architecture, painting, sculpture, music, sandwich glass, old lace, chinaware, period furniture, can be studied and appreciated only where are the visible and audible symbols of these arts. But

> "The most magnificent literature in the world is the birthright of every man and woman who can read. In every hour that can be won from toil here is a House Beautiful with its open ivory gate. Nay, at any time and anywhere, if you can but remember the lines you love, the fadeless pictures rise and Pan's pipes are once more playing."

Poetry enjoys with literature this great advantage. It is the only one of the fine arts in which a copy is as good as the original. A cheaper paper bound duodecimo has all the limited edition contains. A newspaper clipping pinned over a washerwoman's tub is the equal of the original manuscript. Poetry also performs, it seems to me, a wider service than the other arts — due to these two qualities — accessibility and power of perfect duplication of the original. For example, Tennyson did more for Arthur Henry Hallam than the praise of Gladstone; Whitman and Markham and Lindsay and Mackay have done more for Lincoln and his spirit than St. Gaudens. Emerson has done more for "Concord Bridge" than all the historians, and no memorial of Paul Revere or the heroes of Balaklava even though made of triple bronze could secure for its subject as wide or as enduring a fame as have the great poems written on them. Poetry is therefore, it may be, more worth while studying than the other arts, and is presented for study the least.

A discussion of poetry is hard to carry on without something being said about its structure and technique. I do not believe that one can or should entirely avoid the mechanics of poetry.

One phase of this matter that I have thought a good deal about is the physical and psychic basis for poetry. I am satisfied that here is a wide field which has never been thoroughly explored. Why is poetry so universal? Wherein lies its charm? Why does it appeal to the feelings and emotion more than prose? Why do hard headed business men write advertisements in rhyme, as "A car of beauty that does its duty?" Why do great orators conclude their perorations with a quotation from the poets? Poetry has certain rules and standards.

But what makes the rules? Something "offends the ear." But why does it offend the ear? Why does a verse seldom have more than six or seven feet? Why does blank verse produce a certain kind of effect and rhymed verse another? Why is a rhyme ending with the last syllable accented, like all iambic pentameters in which most of our verse is written, suitable for a certain kind of thought or emotion, and another kind of thought finds better expression in a trochaic line, such as Evangeline or Hiawatha? And of these two why does the hexameter suit the one, and the tetrameter the other? Could Evangeline have been written in the measure of Hiawatha, or the reverse? The Greeks, it is said, could feel the joy of the iambic, ta-dum, ta-dum, ta-dum — "I come from haunts of coot and hern," and the sorrow of the trochaic meter, dum-ta, dum-ta, dum-ta, — "Tell me not in mournful numbers." Is it possible that every thought has its own peculiar meter and cannot be perfectly expressed in any other?

I have long sought an answer to these questions. I have found none. There are, however, certain hypotheses for their explanation. First as to the effect of rhyme and rhythm. Strike a tuning fork on the table and a chord in a silent piano will pick it up. In fact it is powerless to resist it. That particular chord will be shaken as helplessly as a tree in a tempest. Play a violin and what is there in nature that can deny its power? Not a sounding board certainly. But how about even less sensitive things such as brick and stone? It is said that with a violin, if the right note and pitch is used, that you will set in motion the molecules in the masonry of a bridge and if the playing could be made intelligent enough in its timing so as constantly to add force and length to the swing of the wave, that the bridge would go down from the ineluctable compulsion of a fiddle, just as a little child can send her two-hundred pound father six feet into the air when seated in a swing. Why are infantry troops on march ordered to break step when crossing a bridge? Did Joshua work a miracle when he and his thousands shouted down the walls of Jericho or did he use a well known law of physics? If such an inert and soulless thing as a piano chord or a sounding board pays tribute to rhythm, if light and sound and heat and the X-ray, and the ultra-violet and the infra-red, and the radio sending messages through thousands of miles of space, yes, perhaps through the great ball of earth itself — if these are mere matters of regular recurrence of wave lengths, then is it any wonder that man with his infinitely delicate nervous system is affected in like but a greater manner? Is there any mystery then in the greater power of poetry over prose, which also has a metre, but a less regular and noticeable one?

So I venture as a hypothesis that the regular recurrence of rhythmical beats (which is the distinguishing feature of poetry as against all other kinds of literature) has objective force on the human brain and nervous system. One man is more delicately sensitized than another and therefore more greatly likes or dislikes what he hears or reads.

But it does have a physical effect and a physical foundation for its potency. "Music hath power to soothe the savage breast" and when played by Orpheus even the trees and rocks on high Olympus moved from their places to follow the song of his golden harp. This is not a fable. You have all seen this happen in the familiar experiment in physics when sand is sprinkled on a glass and then forms in various wavy lines as different sounds are made with a musical instrument. Another remarkable experiment is that the pulse beat of a human being is proved to accelerate or retard as different music is played, or different poetry is read aloud. And still more remarkable is the fact that this is also proved to be true in the case of the rhythm of a chant *heard internally*, that is, simply gone over in silent memory, or as Keats said, "Pipe to the spirit, ditties of no tune."

There is indeed more in this matter "than is dreamed of in our philosophy." You have all, no doubt, seen negroes working on the railroad, or stevedores unloading ship, making the movements of their physical bodies synchronize with the melody of their song. In a book called "Labor and Rhythm" it is demonstrated that rhythm has been an essential force in building civilization, that men toil by it, that armies march to it, that soldiers fight by it, that the great stones of the Pyramids could have been carried and raised only by a rhythmical step, yes, and that savages are frenzied by it, — that the incessant and monotonous clamor of their gongs and tom-toms, and the wail of their war songs makes them insensible to prudence, to danger, to reason.

For example, the Botocudos, a primitive South American tribe, have the same word for both song and dance. The only song they sing on great occasions is Calani-a-a, Calani-a-a, over and over and over again. No white knows what the word means, nor probably does the savage. But to them it is a satisfying expression of their emotion. The beat of their dancing feet marks the accent of the song. Even civilized men feel this magic, the poetic hypnosis. A favorite line keeps running through our heads long after we have ceased to think of the significance of the language. It goes on singing to the inward ear exquisite little songs and fairy symphonies quite apart from the meaning of the words. I knew an old country doctor who used to repeat over and over the resonant words, "Not a drum was heard, nor a funeral note, as his corse to the rampart we hurried" when his conscious mind was entirely concentrated on a problem of saving life.

So we approach the mysterious glory of poetry and its nearest ally, music, two of the most powerful forces in the world, powerful because they act upon the most hidden and deepest elements of human personality. Where is there not rhythm? The systole and diastole of the heart, the intake and exhaling of breath, hunger and satisfaction, activity and rest, joy and sorrow, work and play, ebb and flow, morning and evening, day and night, new moon and full moon, springtime and harvest, youth and age, growth and decay, or as the poet Spencer said,

> "Sleep after toyle, port after stormie seas,
> Ease after warre, death after life, doth greatly please."

We have then some grasp of the significance of poetry and the reason for some of its rules. "A well constructed phrase" says Flaubert, the great French novelist, "adapts itself to the rhythm of breathing." All poetry is influenced by the fact that men and women breathe about eighteen times a minute. This accounts for the pause, or caesura,

> "Arma virumque cano
> Troiae qui primus ab oris."

It also accounts for the length of the line, depending on whether the thought is spirited or quiet, and seldom exceeding seven or eight feet. If we were made to breathe three times a minute instead of eighteen, all our books of poetry would at once go on the scrap heap, and we would have to reconstruct our newly congealed emotions in a metre we cannot now imagine. It would be beyond the violet or below the red of our experience.

So the poetry of different nations varies in accordance with national characteristics, among which must be mentioned the shape of the larynx, the length of the vocal chords, the ability to handle gutterals, etc. The poetry of the American Indian with its short, staccato phrases, characteristic of the race, is very different from the poetry of Goethe, Schiller and Lessing, or of Dante or Petrarch. You can translate prose from one language to another but not poetry. It is for this reason that Dr. Johnson said that poetry perpetuates a language, because to read it you have to learn the original tongue in which it was written. That poetry perpetuates a language is illustrated by the fact that in the time of Chaucer there were very many dialects in use. But the Canterbury Tales established for all time the rich Midland dialect as the literary language of England.

Now for some reason which I cannot explain, but which I imagine is connected with what we have already discussed, poetry is the language of the emotions. And because the emotions are the most powerful factors in human conduct, fear, anger, love, hate, not being creatures of reason, but often flying in the face of reason, so poetry is the most perfect language of the complete man, "that in which he comes nearest to being able to utter the truth," as Matthew Arnold says. The poet conveys not so much the external fact as what he sees behind the fact. What is water? Why, water is $H_2O$. But the chemical formula leaves out the coolness and sparkle of the old oaken bucket; it leaves out the roar of Niagara, and the song of the surf, and the beneficence of rain. What is a skylark? A skylark is "a small oscine, passerine bird of the family Alaudidae, insectivorous and migratory." So says the scientist in precise prose. We turn from him to Shelley for a better definition. To the poet the skylark is an "unbodied joy."

> "In the golden lightning
> Of the sunken sun
> O'er which clouds are brightening,
> Thou dost float and run
> Like an unbodied joy whose race is just begun.
>
> What thou art we know not;
> What is more like thee?
> From rainbow clouds there flow not
> Drops so bright to see
> As from thy presence showers a rain of melody."

What are daffodils? Ask Wordsworth. They are a "jocund company." What is a nautilus? Ask Holmes. It is a guide to human conduct, and

> "Thanks for the heavenly message brought by thee
> Child of the wandering sea."

What was the Roman Colosseum? Read every prose description in the world, and then go with Manfred when he

> "Stood within the Colosseum's wall
> Midst the chief relics of almighty Rome.
> The trees which grew along the broken arches
> Waved dark in the blue midnight, and the stars
> Shone through the rents of ruin; from afar
> The watch dog bayed beyond the Tiber, and
> More near from out the Caesar's palace came
> The owl's long cry. . . .
>
> And thou didst shine, thou rolling moon, upon
> All this, and cast a wide and tender light
> Which softened down the hoar austerity
> Of rugged desolation, and filled up
> As 'twere anew, the gaps of centuries,
> Leaving that beautiful which still was so
> And making that which was not, till the place
> Became religion, and the heart ran o'er
> With silent worship of the great of old —
> The dead but sceptred sovereigns, who still rule
> Our spirits from their urns."

The prose writer speaks in terms of thought, the poet in terms of feeling. One gives logical truth; the other emotional truth.

In the long debates in the United States Senate men talked for days on why the Union should be preserved and why slavery should be abolished. And then two poets came along, one with the "Battle Hymn of the Republic" and the other with "John Brown's Body," and under the spell of the emotions which they called up the Union was preserved and slavery was abolished.

And when the fighting was done reason dictated that we should bind up the nation's wounds and care for him who had borne the battle and again be brothers. But men did not feel like responding to reason. Lincoln had been murdered and Ben Wade and Stevens were insisting that the South should be treated like a conquered province; that Lee and Davis be hanged as traitors. Then an event occurred such as those upon which the gods themselves throw incense. In the obscure town of Columbus, Mississippi, in 1867, only two years after Lincoln's death, a group of Confederate women went to the cemetery to lay wreaths on the graves of their fallen dead. As it happened there were two or three Union soldiers buried in the same God's Acre. With a divine inspiration one of the women suggested that they lay some flowers on these graves also. And so it was done. Just a few Rebel women, touched with that quality of mercy and tenderness for which their sex is honored. But it happened also, that the crop of murders and divorces had been small that day, and so the press, for want of something better, devoted a tiny inch of space to what they had done. This carried the news farther but it would have been soon forgotten if it had not fallen under the eyes of a poet, not one of the authentic poets, you understand, like Lowell, or Longfellow or Whittier or Holmes, but an amateur poet. His name was Francis Miles Finch, a distinguished New York lawyer, judge and dean of the law school of Cornell University. He took the meagre prose item and transfigured it with a haunting rhyme and a magic melody. His lines have been recited hundreds of thousands of times.

> "Sadly, but not with upbraiding,
>     The generous deed was done;
> In the storm of the years that are fading
>     No braver battle was won;
> Under the sod and the dew,
>     Waiting the judgment day;
> Under the blossoms the Blue;
>     Under the garlands, the Gray.
>
> No more shall the war cry sever,
>     Or the winding rivers be red;
> They banish our anger forever
>     Who laurel the graves of our dead.
> Under the sod and dew,
>     Waiting the judgment day;
> Tears and love for the Blue,
>     Love and tears for the Gray."

It seems therefore, that Jules Lemaitre was wrong when he wrote "soon the last poet will offer to the muse the last dove." If he were right he would prophecy an event in history more to be marked than the downfall of Rome. But he is wrong. It may be that the old themes have been worn threadbare, — spring, autumn, daffodils, dead roses, unrequited love, death and other "old, happy, far-off things and battles long ago." But the garment that is weaving on the roaring loom of time is constantly changing in color and texture, and it is the function and the mission of the poet to explain its meaning to his less sensitive and articulate fellows in words and symbols which they can understand. As life and its problems become more and more difficult, it becomes increasingly necessary for the sanity of the race that its problems be solved, and correlated, and made one with the experience and comprehension of the average man. Who shall solve them save the poet who sees through appearances to the reality beneath and "grasps this sorry scheme of things entire." The mystery of the atom, the theory of relativity, fourth-dimensional space, the doctrine of evolution — all these things may yield their solution in the lightning flash of genius in a poet. In fact, with respect to evolution, Watson, in his beautiful poem, "The Dream of Man" pictures him, undaunted by his humble origin, as saying:

> "This is my loftiest greatness
> To have been born so low,
> Greater than Thou, the un-growing,
> Am I, that forever grow.
>
> From glory to rise unto glory
> Is mine, who have risen from slime.
> I doubt if Thou knewst at my making
> How near to Thy throne I should climb,
> O'er the mountainous slopes of the ages
> And the conquered peaks of time."

Watson's idea of evolution is apparently not that of the Tennessee law-makers.

What is the stuff of which poems are made? It is too often said to be spring violets, and star dust and moon shine (if you know what I mean) and asphodel and milady's handkerchief. Well, this universe is not small and I for one would not omit either the star dust or the handkerchiefs. And yet poetry is not decorative merely. It concerns itself with love, and war, and a parent's dream for his child, and the march of empire, and home and passion and struggle and despair. It deals with the deepest feelings and feeds the keenest hungers of the human heart. If it did not, it would not survive. May I cite a few examples? Here is one from Sappho. It is about Hesperus, the evening star.

> "Hesperus, thou bringest all good things —
> Home to the weary, to the hungry, cheer;
> To the young bird the parent's brooding wings,
> The welcome stall to the o'erlabored steer.
> Whate'er of peace about our hearthstone clings,
> Whate'er our household gods protect so dear,
> Are gathered round us by thy look of rest,
> Thou bringest the child, too, to its mother's breast."

Is it any wonder that this exquisite gem of home and motherhood has outlived the centuries? It is as fresh and lovely now as it was in the morning of the world when it was written twenty-five hundred years ago. And in honor of the sex of its author, and that of our guests tonight I will add that Swinburne considered Sappho by all odds and past all comparison, the very greatest poet this planet has ever seen.

Here is a fragment from Aeschylus:

> "O Death, the Healer, scorn thou not I pray,
> To come to me. Of cureless ills thou art
> The one physician."

Here is a story about a man and his dog. Ulyssus, gone to the wars for twenty years, finally returns. His faithful dog which has been kept at home has grown so old and feeble that he can no longer rise from the floor. But when he hears at last the warrior's footfall and sees the gigantic form in the doorway, he struggles with his entire body to demonstrate that his love for his master has not grown dim.

> "He, not unconscious of the voice and tread,
> Lifts to the sound his ear, and rears his head.
> He knew his lord, he knew, and strove to meet;
> In vain he strove to crawl and kiss his feet;
> Yet (all he could) his tail, his ears, his eyes
> Salute his master and confess his joys.
>
> Soft pity touched the mighty master's soul;
> Adown his cheek a tear unbidden stole —
> Stole unperceived; he turned his head and dried
> The drop humane. . . .
> The musing monarch pauses at the door;
> The dog, whom Fate had granted to behold
> His master, when twenty tedious years had rolled,
> Takes a last look, and having seen him, dies;
> Now closed forever, faithful Argus' eyes."

Many years have intervened between that incident and the adoption of a certain trademark by the Victor Talking Machine Company, and the passage will be read for unnumbered years to come. It will last as long as men love dogs and as long as dogs love men. It is one of those priceless things which the winnowing centuries have been unwilling to discard.

No, it is not the mission of the Poet to be a dilettante.

> "To get at the eternal strength of things
> And fearlessly to make strong songs of it
> Is to my mind, the mission of that man
> The world would call a poet. He may sing
> But roughly, and withal ungraciously,
> But if he touch to life the one right chord
> Wherein God's music slumbers, and awake
> To truth one drowned ambition, he sings well."

A good deal of fun is had with the poet over his daemon, his frenzy, his divine inspiration. There is nothing unusual about it. Except possibly for a difference in the degree of its intensity you have all experienced it. How many times have you sat down, shall we say, to write a letter to a friend. As you begin you do not know what to say. But the subject is close to your heart. It may be that you are writing a note of condolence over the loss of some one loved. The inhibitions of every day drop off. You lay aside the mask. You begin to be genuine — to say what you really feel. And under the warm spell of that generous emotion words flow to your pen point that you scarcely ever use; your thought clothes itself in felicitous phrasing. Beauty creeps into your diction. Ideas "come" to you, from you know not where. As Socrates said, "Do I appear to you, my dear Phaedrus, as I do to myself, to have been speaking under some influence divine?" To which Phaedrus replied, "There certainly can be no doubt, Socrates, that an unusual kind of fluency has come upon you." You read the letter over at the end with a feeling of pleased surprise and if you see it months or years later you wonder how you ever did so well. You feel that you had, like Joan d'Arc, been listening to voices in the air — that for the moment you had been a delicately attuned radio instrument receiving messages from unseen sources, unheard by the normal ear. It is a sense of possession. And it is easy to understand how the prophets and seers and poets of old did believe that Holy Writ was inspired — that the Tablets of Stone were carved by God's hand, not man's. It may be that the inspiration of the major prophets will be proved to be but the psychology of the subconscious. If so it will be another of those explanations which do not explain. The mystery will remain. Only we will then have a greater comprehension of what the subconscious is, and if it be true, as the psychologists assert, that the conscious mind is only one-twentieth of our latent powers, we will be more humble in the presence of those gifted ones who can call these silent genii to their service.

Well, that is all there is to a poet's frenzy except a difference in degree. And if the illustration of letter writing which I have given does not convince, I will add that every man in this room has been a poet at least once in his life, unless he is a bachelor.

Another animadversion to which I must allude is one made by the go-getters and "happy well-fed drummers" to use Walt Whitman's phrase. These gentlemen presume to "tell the world" — a modest phrase — that not only has the practical no connection with the aesthetic, but further, that a sense for the beautiful unfits a man for the necessary employments of our common day. Suppose it to be true — what then? Is it to be supposed that a great artist can win his fame by a desultory pursuit? Is it so in any other branch of human endeavor? The Law, also is a jealous mistress; too jealous, I sometimes think. So is banking, brokerage, manufacturing. These on their side too often unfit their votaries, or shall I say slaves, for the enjoyment of beauty. And yet I deny the general implication. A great artist is sure to be a great man, a man, possibly, with different viewpoints from those of Mr. Babbitt, but a great man nevertheless. Art, it cannot be said too often, is an integral part of the life-process. It is experience revealed. It draws its sap from the same rich soil of reality that sustains all men. To quote Emerson once more, "The scholar" (and he might as well have said "the artist") "loses no hour that the man lives." And so, while the artist must often withdraw from the hurly-burly for his hours and days of intense concentration, he is but recording his own experience. And how often even supreme artists have played a great part in this bread and butter world! Our drummer friends may have heard that a recent vice-president noted for his fire and brimstone, plays the fiddle, composes music even, but they have surely forgotten, or more accurately, have never known, that the painter of "The Last Supper" dug the canals of Lombardy; that the "hand that rounded Peter's dome" rebuilt the forts of San Miniato; that the dreamer of Genoa discovered two continents; that the architect of Monticello added an empire to a seaboard; that he whose chief wish it was that he could have written the "Elegy" was the gallant soldier who took Quebec. Among the modern poets I think of Joyce Kilmer, and Alan Seeger, and James McCabe and Rupert Brooke whose silent dust is now a place "that is forever England." I think also of another warrior poet, Sir Philip Sydney, dead with an undying fame, at thirty-two. He wrote lyrics and sonnets that have outlived the merchants and money changers of his day; he wrote "Arcadia" and the noble "Defence of Poesy" wherein he speaks of the poet "who cometh unto you with a tale which holdeth children from play, and old men from the chimney corner." Yet this did not prevent him from receiving his death wound very gallantly on the field of Lutphen, and as he was dying, handing a cup of water to a common soldier with the simple word, "His need is greater than mine."

Aeschylus, whom I quoted earlier, was another of those supreme artists who played a great part in the external world. In a time of tumult and turmoil he probed the human heart to its very depths and achieved realizations so final that two and one-half milleniums have not gainsaid them. Yet he became a national hero in the campaign of defense against the Persians, and in the battles of Salamis and Marathon. And when he died he had carved on his proud tomb only this boast, "The grove of Marathon could bear witness to his good soldierhood, and the longhaired Mede who felt it." Parlor poets would do well to remember Aeschylus. Intellectual and spiritual lounge lizards have never written any poetry and never will. Poetry is the way — one way — by which those who have loved beauty and lived greatly and suffered deeply have transcribed their experience. It is that. It is nothing else. Intensity of living is preliminary to all great art. Idealism, if it is worth its salt to this pragmatic world, has passed through realism and come out on the far side. It has become tempered by the flame of life.

When I think of those men who have been both idealist and realist my mind turns to Jefferson whom I alluded to a moment ago. Jefferson was an excellent violinist, an inventor, the leading architect of his day, a linguist who could speak German, French, Italian, Spanish and read ancient Gaelic. He was, beside, a master of his own mother tongue, and tremendously interested in natural science. Yet these artistic traits did not prevent him from writing two notable law books, one of which remained standard for fifty years; from having perhaps the finest and most remunerative law practice during the few years he was at the bar of any young lawyer in the colonies; from being a consummate politician, a long-visioned statesman, a shrewd handler of men, and the founder of the oldest — and best — political party in these United States. Other practical men have found relaxation and growth in a similar way. John Hay, Secretary of State, wrote verse; so did Abraham Lincoln; so did Blackstone, the author of the great Commentaries; Edward Everett, Benjamin Franklin, many others. I have taken so much time with this phase because it seems to be part of the "Mucker Pose" which Harpers Magazine so recently dwelt upon, to pretend an indifference to spiritual values. It is, on the other hand, a favorite thesis of mine that one *must* take an interest in some subject which appeals to his imaginative or creative self. It is imperative that he do so if he wishes, at whatever age death overtakes him, to die *young*. If the business man or housewife would not be old at thirty-five he must have an avocation in which he can express his own creative urge. President Coolidge said he might go back to Vermont and whittle. He would not stop growing if he did. I recall an old Vermont whittler who turned out beautiful wood carvings with a rude jack knife. He was a young man at eighty and died with the last of his dreams unborn.

I have promised that this paper would not be technical. Nevertheless, a word or two on technique. It is an old adage that "familiarity breeds contempt" but this is true of such things as derive their beauty only from veneer. It is not true of mahogany nor sterling nor Delft, nor Brussels lace nor Venetian point, nor friendship, nor art. In cases of genuine worth the deeper the familiarity, the greater the appreciation.

Technique of course never makes art and Emerson was quite right in condemning those who

> "Love not the flowers they pluck and know them not,
> And all their botany is Latin names."

And so while I agree that neither poetry nor botany should be a matter of Latin names, I do feel that the average man would enjoy poetry more if he had some small knowledge of its structure. In the first place he would be more apt not to overlook supreme craftsmanship when it is before his eyes. He would appreciate how difficult it is. For consider what the poet has to work with — just a few scratches on paper — that is all; nothing to see, nothing to hear, nor to smell, nor to feel, nor to taste — nothing for the five senses. It is indeed difficult — as is all art. People think a poet just dashes off something on an old envelope. They are like the lady who approached a sculptor and said, "How easy that is." He replied, "Yes, Ma'am, all you do is to take a chunk of marble and with your hammer and chisel knock off all you don't want." So all a poet does is to string words together — but he may search for days for the right word — a word with just the right number of syllables — with the requisite length of vowel sound — one that will read easily and alliteratively with its comparisons, and rhyme demurely with another that has gone before, one that is not obsolete nor technical but a part of daily speech, yet not trite and threadbare — and withal with a symbolic suggestive value beyond the dictionary's definition. You remember such a supreme craftsman as Edgar Allen Poe, how he struggled with the mediocre lines

> "To the beauty of fair Greece
> And the grandeur of old Rome"

until finally he transfigured them

> "To the glory that was Greece
> And the grandeur that was Rome."

two mighty lines that compress in six words the magnificence of centuries.

That same poem has a line that illustrates the magic of carefully chosen consonants, four "W's":

> "Helen, thy beauty is to me
> Like those Nicean barks of yore,
> That gently, o'er a perfumed sea,
> The *weary, way-worn wanderer* bore
> To his own native shore."

But let us not in counting the rose's petals, forget the rose.

The power of concentration and economy of material is one of the most remarkable things in poetry. Multum in parvo. For example, a single quatrain many contain a whole philosophy,

> "Hark at the lips of this pink whorl of shell
> And you shall hear the ocean's surge and roar;
> So in a quatrain's measure, written well,
> A thousand lines shall all be sung in four."

I suppose a word should be said about *vers libre*. This verse is not new. Walt Whitman who died the year of the Chicago World's Fair wrote it. And he wrote some wonderful lines. You can go back still further and find it in the Psalms and the Prophets of the Old Testament. To the extent that it is characterized by irregular rhythms it is not necessarily objectionable, although, to the measure of such irregularity it seems to violate some of those deep laws of man's being and the universe which we have been discussing and therefore is not poetry in its highest form. But the free verse we have mostly in mind is this modern stuff which is distinguished by something besides irregular rhythms and that is what is called "realism." Actually, it is no more *real* than is mushy sentimentality. It is not life. It is only the bizarre and grotesque and raw and ugly part of life. Its creators "dance to a madder music and thirst for a stronger wine." I confess to a personal antipathy. Like Titania in Midsummer's Night Dream, they seem to me to have fallen in love with an ass, a pretty dirty and unkempt ass at that. They desire their images to be *"hard, clear and concentrated,"* their work is objective rather than subjective, materialistic rather than idealistic. Now and then they achieve a rather arresting picture. Take for example Carl Sandburg's "Fog"

> "The fog comes
> On little cat feet
> It sits looking
> Over harbor and city
> On silent haunches
> And then moves on."

That may be a poetic thought, but it is not, in my judgment, in poetic form. I personally agree with Mencken in the opinion that much if not all *vers libre* is written by those who are either incompetent or unwilling to master the pentameter.

This new free verse is probably the result of the immense psychic dislocations of the World War. It is characterized by the modern revolt against old forms and traditions. It is allied to cubism in art, to jazz in music, to Bolshevism in government, and possibly to bobs in coiffures. It will perhaps last as long as the revolt lasts. As an example of this falling-in-love-with-an-ass poetry, take this sample from a recent anthology (think of using this beautiful word, anthology, meaning a collection of flowers, in the present connection):

Here is the flower. It is called "The Barber."

"I wield the razor, sling hot towels and talk.
My daily newspaper is the racing chart and my
    pastime making bets on fleet-footed horses.
Whatever is left from betting I divide with
    my wife and a yellow woman who lives in an
    apartment on Wabash Avenue. (Poor Wife. She
    gets very little.)
I love gay clothes, a good supply of Fatimas
    and the fire in gin and whiskey.
I love life. Who doesn't?"

Grant that this is a picture of life. Grant that the thing pictured exists and that it is real. Well, garbage is real, too, but most of us have cans to put it in, and most of us prefer to put it in the cans. It is, I suppose, after all a matter of personal taste and de gustibus non disputandum!

I am not a descendant of a prognosticator but I venture to predict that when we have caught a few more whiffs from this literary sewage we will return for light and leading to the old poets or the new poets dressed in the "singing robes" of their spiritual forebears — men who do not flinch from the reiterated assertion that "It was my duty to have loved the highest"; men who in the teeth of doubt insist that "a man's reach should exceed his grasp, or what's a heaven for;" men who in the philosophy of failure and decadence assert that "God flings back to man his failures," men who like poor Malvolio in the play "thought very nobly of the soul" and who say to us with Goethe,

"Whether day my spirit's yearning
Unto far blue hills has led
Or the night lit all the burning
Constellations at my head —
Hours of light or hours nocturnal
Do I praise our mortal fate —
If man thinks the thought eternal
He is ever fair and great."

We may trust time, which is the coldest and cruelest of anthologists to render the final judgment upon this so-called "realism."

In making their images "hard, clear and concentrated" the writers of free verse offend against the law of symbolism. By symbolism we mean shadowed intimations that the thing contains more than itself.

What is the cardinal principle in the technique of poetry? Regular recurrence of rhythmical stress. But beyond that is restraint, symmetry, balance, sanity, conformity to established standards which are inherent and find their birth in man's highest nature. Poetry is beautiful, *is* poetry because it speaks in symbolic terms. It never uses the last descriptive word, the last splash of color. Art that leaves nothing unsaid is not art. Art *suggests*. It leaves the completion of the thought to the imagination of the reader. The result is that every poem is a different poem to every man. It is the reader who completes the picture. It thus permits him to enter into, become a participant, a co-worker with the artist in the creative process which brought it into being. Hence the joy that comes to the reader. It is the joy of creating. Poetry, art, therefore, is never obtrusive, blatant, "hard," self-assertive. For while a too rigid formalism kills the flower, anarchy grows weeds. To the extent, therefore, that vers libre is free from symbolism and a reasonable restraint, to that extent it is not art. Amy Lowell herself has said, "verse is verse just *because* it has more pattern than prose; free verse" she says, "is a misnomer; verse can never be free." She might have added that art is never free; that man, and his life on this planet, is never free.

If symmetry, restraint, balance, sanity are the keys to art, art teaches us to live. For the greatest of all arts is art of living, and the gentleman or gentlewoman is the ultimate artist in the galleries of the world. As Plato said, "What matters is not the life of art, but the art of life." Here are some phenomena of ultra-modernism. As Exhibit A, let us take the flaunting of sex. It came because two or three centuries of puritanism and prudery were finally destroyed by the stark realism and disillusionment of the World War. The inevitable reaction is now on. In time the pendulum will again swing towards its center. The momentary excess is an inevitable, a passing, a not-too-serious phenomenon. Yet while it lasts I cannot persuade myself that it is lovely, any more than that the French or Russian revolutions were lovely, however inevitable and justified they may have been by a thousand years of tyranny. Why is it not lovely? Because it violates this cardinal principle of art — restraint, symmetry. The commercialized flaunting of sex in the movies, novels, magazines, theatres, elsewhere and everywhere as if it were the *only important* fact in the cosmos, is the negation of beautiful living. I am speaking, of course, not of this sex phenomenon only, but of many other anarchic and centrifugal social attitudes such as the precious doctrine entertained by sob-sisters of both sexes that the vicious ought not to be restrained, that criminals should not be convicted, and the frowzy theory that children should do or study only what they desire to do or study, or as epitomized by Dr. Mitchell of the University of Virginia the other day, "Education without effort. Information painlessly imparted. How to know the birds from the flowers." And that other theory which has crept into college curricula that callow youth should be denied, at their own election, the priceless discipline of doing hard work which made Lincoln and Garfield, and Henry Ford and Edison and Madame Curie and Jane Adams and Herbert Hoover and Alfred Smith, the men and women they became. Beautiful living has, must have, standards, rules for social conduct which set apart the gentleman and the gentlewoman from all mankind. The rules may change, will change from generation to generation, but if in each generation there are no standards by which to judge excellence, there is no excellence. All sinks into the mediocrity of a Byzantine night.

Just now the process is to flee from repression neuroses to expression neuroses. (I have distinguished authority for that statement.) Modernism follows the cult of *anarchy* in the sacred name of *liberty*, and justifies itself with the philosophy of individuality and self expression. *Self expression should ever be accompanied by self criticism.* This is always true of the artist for, as we said in another paragraph, *art is man's most relentless self criticism.* Self expression, even in social relationships, is a good word. I endorse it without flinching. But it also is an unstable word. Self expression turns into selfishness as easily as cider turns to vinegar. Ibsen, the most profound of modern dramatists, understood the paradox of the age when he said, "suppress individuality and you have no life; assert it and you have war and chaos." In other words, individual and social life together require the most delicate balance and sanity. As the old Greeks said, "Nothing to excess" — "the golden mean" — a phrase which puts into three words more wisdom for every relationship of life than any five foot shelf of books I have ever read.

Freud solved, perhaps, the problem of the psychoses which make men too moral. We need a greater than Freud to solve the problem of being too unmoral, too antinomian. Freedom from prudery, from inferiority complexes, from defense mechanisms, and subconscious inhibitions is, or will be, a great step in the emancipation of the race, perhaps as great as the abolition of chattel slavery. I have that hope for it. But standards must remain. When all restraint is removed, the creative energy wastes itself to emptiness. Of what avail is the fire and fuel in the locomotive if the steam is not restrained and directed to the piston head? And the final worth while standards are those erected by each man, with all experience as a teacher, for the conduct of his own life.

I said that ultra modernism follows the cult of anarchy in the sacred name of liberty and self expression. Except possibly in rare instances, I cannot believe, although I know nothing of psycho-pathology, that conscious, self-imposed restraints such as those which guide the hand of the artist in his quest for excellence are anything but beneficial. Such restraints lead to self-mastery. It was the Romans in the brave days of old who said, "Steadiness is the foundation of all the virtues." And before the Romans it was Plato who compared the human soul to a charioteer driving two horses, one mild and tractable, and the other wild and unruly. As Havelock Ellis writes, "I believe in Freedom but only because I believe at the same time in Discipline." And as was said by a greater than Ellis, Goethe, "Everything that frees our spirit without giving us command over ourselves is ruinous." So in this age of jazz, noise, sex, blatancy and instability; in this age which repudiates tradition and scoffs at history, art with its symbolism which transfigures and transmutes the real into the ideal; art with its respect for the past, its reverence for great traditions and the men and women who gave them life, and its still unsatisfied hunger for a yet nobler future; art with its symmetry, its standard and restraints, its good taste and ancient landmarks to beauty and excellence, is the saving salt in the bread of modern life. A double duty is in fact imposed upon Art, now that the voice of authoritarianism in religion is sinking into a whisper.

Our country has produced many poets, a few really good ones, possibly one or two who deserve the word great, but none, I am sure, of the first rank. Indeed, in my opinion none who rate with even John Keats or Robert Browning, and these, of course, gifted as they are, are not the supreme masters. Our teeming millions have produced many lyrists, but not one dramatist, not a single epic poet. It is, indeed, a thing to pause upon. For there has been a great drama played on this continent, and a great epic has passed before our eyes. If you say, we are too young, I reply that the great epics have been written when nations were young. We have not been young enough. We have conquered a continent, become the greatest and richest of the nations and have not been able to commemorate it in verse, not adequately in any form of art. Consider, for example, the mighty migration across the Alleghenies from 1750 to 1850, "Westward the course of empire took its way." Consider the second great trek to the farther west beginning with the gold rush of '49 and (with the Klondike) continuing to our own day. Has there ever been such an adventure of human spirit in all the tide of time? But when the pioneers of '49 had surmounted the Sierras their material success was balanced by as complete a spiritual failure as the world has ever witnessed. After two thousand miles the covered wagons ceased their creaking and the slouch hatted men and hatchet faced women emerged from the hoopstretched canvas. The final and greatest of the world's migrations had come to an end. But neither the Golden Gate nor the Willamette Valley nor the Puget Sound saw even the prologue of an American Iliad. There rose no Parthenon. The only types of architecture for which we are noted are the skyscrapers and the railroad station, both of which are linked with material success. We have produced no new shrines for the human spirit alone.

These pioneers who were engaged in the winning of the West were too practical minded, too intent on the gleam of gold. They had imagination but they suffered from over-weaning self assertion in the face of a blind destiny which should have been manifest on every hand. They were too Puritanical. Their religous inhibitions blinded them to the Wood-Spirit, the Rain-God, the Thunder-Bird. They did not hear the appealing voices of the Rockies nor the whispers of the desert. A little relaxation of their grim religion, a few sacrifices on a pagan altar, and they might have seen Proteus coming from the sea, or reflected that the god of the New England pulpit had preceded them in their great migration and that it was his own hand which had sprinkled the Sierras with the gold they sought when the world itself was young. But they were too blind to see this. They have remained so. In a short lyric, written under the fleeting influence of a transitory emotion, our poets have been able to free themselves from the mental and spiritual impedimenta of their ancestors. But they have not been capable of a sustained effort such as a drama or epic where at all times, in order to achieve a vast unity and a perfect perspective, the creating mind must be able to "command the elementals of his legend and the pure essence of his muse."

The ancient British bards called themselves "Those who are *free* throughout the world." The really great poets, unhindered by civilization and untrammelled by a too tribal consciousness or a too dogmatic creed, have stripped through the husks to the kernels of Truth and so have written not for a day nor a decade, not for a town nor a country, but for all time and for all men. The poet therefore, if he would write lines that the years will not fade must be free from prejudice, from intolerance, from ego, from self assertion, from selfishness, from mental inhibitions and spiritual boundaries, or as Sir Walter Raleigh said a long, long time ago, "He must not fear that some of the great light of Heaven will slip through an unstopped chink in his creed." Hand in hand with "Nature, the dear old nurse," he must wander wherever she leads, yielding himself utterly to her gentle teachings and thus through all the "vast driftings of the cosmic weather," keep the clear gaze of a little child; retain as the years slip by the simple and primitive faith that he and God are at one, and so reveal to his less clear visioned fellows the underlying Truth and the half hid Beauty which they themselves have sometimes glimpsed.

Few can be poets in the strict sense. But there is another kind of poet without whom the others would live and die in vain. They are not the anointed ones with the divine gift of expression but their heart-strings also vibrate to great cadences. They read poetry and love it and memorize it and make it a part of themselves. I have met many of this latter kind — an old farmer who loved the Scottish Bard, a child enamored with Riley and Stevenson, a girl who loves Longfellow, a boy wrapped up in "Danny Deever" and "The Recessional," a woman who finds peace in "Omar Khayyam," a man who finds refuge in Shakespeare. These are the poets the world needs most. If the world had more of them there would be less of righteousness, more of goodness; more of justice, less of judging; fewer prisons, more Parthenons; more bridges, fewer fences; more brushes daubing canvas; more chisels chipping stone; more parks and public squares that "students from afar would choose to starve in rather than go home."

And now, as Lady Godiva said near the end of her ride, "I am approaching my close!" The final service of the poet, as of every artist, is not alone to interpret the world for us, but to give us beauty. Beauty is earth's one absolute. The only other comes from another world. Marble and triple bronze may pass; beauty endures. Political systems, schools of philosophy, moral codes, come and go. The scientist of today is he who throws on the scrap heap the science of yesterday.

> "All passes; art alone endures to stay with us;
> The bust outlasts the throne; the coin, Tiberius."

And so in this world of flux how worth while it is to spend an occasional evening with Beauty. If not poetry, then beauty in some other form; it does not matter. Beauty gives us the long view. The frustrations and conflicts of life sink into insignificance. Under its mild persuasion we become tolerant of life, tolerant of our fellows. Like the old Greeks, "we see life steadily and see it *whole*." We join a great company — Praxiteles, Homer, da Vinci, Shakespeare, Beethoven, Goethe. We march with them on the long pilgrimage. Toward transient things we adopt an attitude of suspended judgment. We become less sure that the Almighty has signed the temperance pledge; less sure that political preachers can be trusted to write textbooks on biology; less sure, on the other hand, that trial marriage is the final solution to one of civilization's greatest problems. But as we become less sure of transient things, we become more sure of the worth and dignity of life, of the integrity of the universe. We adopt the mood of the stars.

> "Give us thy mood, O patient stars,
> Which climb each night the ancient sky,
> Yet leave on space no tears, no scars,
> No trace of age, no fear to die."

We see unity in diversity and realize that all discord is harmony not understood.

And so we come at last to know that poetry, music, sculpture, painting, architecture is beauty, and that beauty alone

> "Gives grace and truth to Life's unquiet dream."

ABIGAIL E. WEEKS MEMORIAL LIBRARY
UNION COLLEGE
BARBOURVILLE, KENTUCKY

328.73
P499    Pettengill
            My story

328.73
P499

Pettengill

    My story